Orphan No More

Orphan No More is a gut-wrenching, unembellished story of a woman who, through Christ, has found freedom and victory. Jen's vulnerability in sharing the details of her life, including the deeply private and painful points, will inspire readers to know that their story also matters, and their voice needs to be heard. I believe this book will inspire, encourage, and open eyes to the reality of both broken humanity and the love and power of Jesus. Jen paints a beautiful picture of redemption through her words and lets the world know that there truly is a God who gives beauty for ashes, joy for mourning, and a garment of praise for the spirit of heaviness.
—**Janice Rigel**, Co-Founder of *Stirred Up Ministries*, Podcast host of *Just Janice*

***

Orphan No More is the real, raw, heart-wrenching testimony of an abused young girl who attempts to navigate life into adulthood. The twists and turns of brokenness, betrayal, and heartache are outlined in painstaking detail, truly allowing you to feel the heart of the author. BUT that's not the end of this story. This book is a beautiful representation of the transformative power and loving mercy of Jesus Christ. God's Word promises to trade us beauty for our ashes, and this testimony is absolutely illustrative of that. I highly recommend *Orphan No More*. It will encourage your heart no matter what season of life you may find yourself in.
—**Brooke Greskowiak**

***

This book takes you on a deep quest of finding God's nature amongst the pain. Through this powerful story from victim to victor, you will not only answer the question of who God is, but you will experience the power of what Jesus' victory has done for you. As you read Jen's raw and rugged journey within these pages, you will cry with her and rejoice with her as God's sovereignty is displayed through forgiveness. May you truly find God through the good, the bad, and the ugly, and I pray after reading these words that you will never be the same.
—**Anna Pranger**, Speaker, Podcaster, Author, *Loved*

***

A brave and authentic account of one woman's journey through childhood trauma into young adulthood and into mid-life. Jen Koning walks us through the stages of her life to date and helps us see how trauma impacts our bodies, minds, and spirits. This book offers a valuable understanding to child welfare professionals and foster, adoptive or kinship parents as they care for kids who have endured horrific abuse. Jen also offers hope toward healing to readers who may relate to the suffering she endured as a child and the self-doubt that plagued her for years.
—**Jennifer R. Patrick**, M.A., Certified Family Life Educator

***

Orphan No More is a powerful story of hope, healing, wholeness, and freedom. Jen allows herself to be vulnerable, real, and honest, as she discloses the deepest, darkest, and most broken pieces of her being. She gives witness to the transforming, healing power of Christ's love and amazing grace in her own life. No matter where you are in your spiritual walk, this book will challenge you to go deeper and draw closer to a trusting God with your own brokenness to find freedom and victory. This book is a must-read for anyone who asks themselves, "Who am I?"
—**Lauree Quada** MA, LPC, Licensed Professional Counselor, Founder and Owner of *Embracing Hope Counseling*

***

Some stories require great courage to write, and this is one of them! Jen's story of abuse and transformation is powerful and inspiring. Those who have walked similar paths will find opportunities for growth and healing in these pages. Foster/adoptive parents and others who work to establish healthy, supportive relationships with kids from hard places, will gain insight and understanding as they consider the experience of trauma, foster care, adoption, and healing from a child's perspective. Anyone who reads *Orphan No More* will be amazed by the God who captivated Jen's heart and led her out of brokenness toward wholeness and healing!
—**Kristin Porter**, Foster/Adoptive Parent

Orphan No More

By Jen Koning

Published by KHARIS PUBLISHING, imprint of KHARIS MEDIA LLC.

Copyright © 2021 Jen Koning

ISBN-13: 978-1-63746-107-5

ISBN-10: 1-63746-107-0

Library of Congress Control Number: 2021952708

Artwork by Dawn Leno, *Wings of Freedom and Stages of a Butterfly*. Used by permission. August 20, 2021. E Dawn Leno. dawnescapes18@yahoo.com

All KHARIS PUBLISHING products are available at special quantity discounts for bulk purchase for sales promotions, premiums, fund-raising, and educational needs. For details, contact:

Kharis Media LLC

Tel: 1-479-599-8657

support@kharispublishing.com

www.kharispublishing.com

ACKNOWLEDGEMENTS

My thanks to Janice Rigel for permission to use her poem "My Mat for Your Mercy."

My thanks to Dawn Leno for the artwork on the front cover of my book and within my book.

Please note: There are parts of this book which may be triggering to survivors of sexual abuse.

Contents

FOREWORD

Jen Koning is not only a survivor but a *thriver*. Having the privilege to know her and her story has been a journey of friendship, partnership and a joy to behold. It has been an honor to help her navigate her healing journey and be there to watch her excel and pursue her destiny in Christ.

You want to read this book. You need to get this book in the hands of those who have been in the foster care system, anyone who has been abused in any way, and those who work with the abused.

You will find Jen's story is difficult to comprehend, but the redemption, healing and hope that is found here will inspire and lead those lost in their pain to realize healing is possible, and there is an answer. They will discover that Jesus Christ is the Redeemer, Healer, and Purpose Giver and as He helped Jen, He will also help you.

I have watched Jen fight for her healing and fight for her purpose, despite the pain and radical blows of the enemy assaulting her in her fractured childhood. Her determined tenacity to grasp the hem of Jesus' garment is a beacon to those lost in the memories and agony of their childhood wounds. There is hope. There is joy in the morning. There is beauty for ashes. In the pages of this book, you will find the light to lead you to the glory of God, and the healing balm of His love. Take this book and allow God to do what only He can do, through the anointed writing of someone who has been in the dark terror of childhood abuse and loss but embraced the healing available to her. He waits with open arms to do the same for you, and those you yearn to see set free and healed.

Valerie Norton

Director of Operations, Break the Grey, INC
Certified Christian Counselor
Facilitator of "Into the Wildflowers"
Ordained Minister of the Gospel

PART I – THE BIOLOGICAL FAMILY

CHAPTER 1

For the majority of my life, January 14, 1980 is the day in which my memory starts. I was six years old. It is the day in which I lost my mom and, in the simplest of terms, I became an orphan. My mommy and I were cooking dinner together while my daddy and brother were in other parts of the house. I was very excited to be Mommy's big helper. Laughter flowed freely between us while we cooked. While we were preparing dinner, Mommy suddenly grabbed her chest, walked over to the table and leaned on it for support. Confusion was written all over my face. The sound of a chair being dragged across the floor echoed in my ears as Mommy pulled out a chair to sit down. I was very worried about her, but she kept reassuring me that she was going to be okay. Before I could process what was happening, she had abruptly fallen face first on the floor with a deafening thud. I screamed, "MOMMY!!" as I fell to my knees. Screaming and crying, I shook her in an attempt to wake her up. "Mommy, what's wrong? Wake up, Mommy! I don't understand! Talk to me Mommy, please? Please? Just tell me what to do and I'll do it. I'm your big helper, remember? Mommy!" She laid there unresponsive to my screams or tears. I called to Daddy to come help, but Daddy started into another one of his "episodes." "Daddy, not now! I need you! Mommy needs you!"

We never knew what caused these episodes with Daddy, but I learned long ago to stay away from him during those few minutes or I'd be on the receiving end of his swinging fists. During these episodes, he would pass out on the floor. It was scary to see your Daddy fall to the ground like a rag doll and wonder if he would be okay or not. When he woke up, it was almost as if my daddy had been replaced with a raging monster. He wasn't my daddy but some stranger in my daddy's body; his eyes were not Daddy's--they were almost vacant. He would then swing his arms wildly, completely out of control, hitting people, cupboards, whatever was in his path. He destroyed many things and hurt me a few times over the years. After a few minutes of his ranting and raging, he would pass out once again. The anxiety would rise wondering if my daddy would be back or not. He then awoke and got up off the ground and, as was typical with these "spells," he wouldn't remember anything he had done or said. We learned to hide and stay out of his way when he was in a mood like this.

After this particular episode was over, Daddy came into the room and impatiently shoved me aside so he could get to Mommy. I sat there hurting and broken trying to understand why Daddy had just shoved me aside. *Had I done something wrong? I must have done something wrong.* Self-blame and self-loathing covered my grieving heart like a heavy, smothering blanket as I sat there hugging my knees and rocking back and forth. *It was my fault that Mommy was laying there! I knew she wasn't supposed to sit when she had pains, but I let her do it anyway. She's not responding because it's my fault. It's all my fault!*

The ambulance was called. When the EMTs arrived, they immediately went straight to my mommy's side and tried to help her. They quickly transferred her to a stretcher and rushed her into the back of the ambulance where they continued working on her. Daddy climbed into the back of the ambulance. As the doors closed and the EMT ran around to the front, my heart was confused and terrified of what was going to happen. So much I just didn't understand. *Where's Mommy going? Is Mommy going to be okay?* My brother and I were standing with neighbors almost like an afterthought as our daddy rode away in the ambulance with mommy to the hospital. Cold fear and a rush of abandonment descended upon me like a tidal wave as they rushed off with the sirens blaring.

As the ambulance drove further away, the sound of the sirens faded into the distance as tears rolled down my face. Our neighbors gently guided us over to their house. My brother and I were shuffled from one place to another that night until we ended up at Grandpa's house. The looks on the faces of all the adults we ran into that night were mixed with compassion and pity. They tried to distract us and offered comforting words such as, "It's going to be alright," or "Your Mom will be okay." Yet, the expressions on their faces didn't match the words that came out of their mouths. It was such a long, scary night. In my child's heart, panic and fear mingled with confusion as I lay in bed unable to sleep. *Would Mommy really be okay? Why did Daddy shove me aside? Why do these adults keep telling me that it's going to be okay, when their body language says something completely different? Was Mommy gone forever? No, she can't be gone forever! I need my mommy! Why doesn't anyone seem to understand that?* I finally fell asleep as sheer exhaustion overtook my small body.

I don't remember who delivered the news, but I was told that Mommy had died of a heart attack on the way to the hospital. I didn't understand what that meant. She was only thirty-six years old, and I was one month away from turning seven. As a child, I had no comprehension of what had just taken place. *I just wanted to finish making dinner. When was Mommy coming home? What do you mean that she's never coming back? I don't understand! I want my Mommy!! Mommy!! Where are you? She's gone. Lost forever. It was my fault she's gone, because I was her big helper. I was supposed to help. I didn't help her. If I would have helped, then Mommy would still be here. So, it's my fault that Mommy died. I am all alone.*

CHAPTER 2

The next couple of days were a complete blur. The day arrived where I got to see mommy for one last time. I couldn't understand why all these people were crying when they looked at me or why no one was waking Mommy up, especially since they were here because of her. Wasn't she just asleep in that box? I so desperately wanted to go and shake her awake, but instead I was told to be quiet and place a flower in her hands. I slowly approached the box in the front of the room with a rose in my hand, dressed in my prettiest dress. I gazed with confusion and longing at Mommy lying there cold and lifeless. She was so still; it looked like she was just sleeping. I wanted to shake her and wake her up, but I was told I had to be a big girl. Since I was Mommy's big helper, I did what I was told to do. I gently placed a single red rose next to Mommy's hands. The rest of the funeral was a blur to me. I remember being sheltered a lot by my extended family in their efforts to protect me from death; but their efforts were in vain. Death had left its marks deep in my heart like a knife slashing unmercifully over and over again.

Family came from all around to say hello and how sorry they were. *Didn't they know that it was my fault that she was dead? I don't understand why they are saying sorry, when it is me who should be saying sorry to all of them. Daddy is drinking that bad stuff again. It makes him walk and talk funny. A lot of people are drinking it. I'm just trying to figure out what I could have done to save Mommy. I was disposable and unimportant. I was so scared of what was going to take place next. Where would we stay? Who would take care of us? Would anyone try to protect me like Mommy did? Did I have to stay with JUST Daddy? All I knew was that my life was turned upside down that day. I had just lost the person who had loved me and tried to protect me with all her heart. I was abandoned by my own mommy.*

CHAPTER 3

The years that followed Mommy's death left me truly alone for the first time in my life. I was an orphan in every sense of the word. I was in and out of many schools and homes, never really having a chance to get settled in any one place. We stayed at Grandpa's place for a while following Mommy's funeral. Then, just when it felt like I was going to be staying put, we were moving on to another house or apartment. Those years were filled with countless rapes and abuse, and yet there was an unspoken expectation to never speak of those things. My mommy was the comfort amidst the cycles of abuse, and when she died a part of me died as well.

After a while, we found a new place downtown, but it was only a two-bedroom apartment. My brother got his own room since he was the oldest, and my bed was placed in my daddy's room. Long after my brother was asleep, the abuse would start. I was touched, molested, and raped by my father. I was so confused. I didn't understand why he was doing these things, but every time I questioned him I was told that it was because he had lost Mommy and needed comfort or because he loved me. If I questioned too much, I was beaten. After he had taken his pleasure from my small body, I was sent away to go sleep in my own bed. It was the ultimate rejection - isolation. It impressed a hurtful message upon me: *I was a toy to be used by others for their entertainment.*

Over time, I learned to do things that pleased him just so I could earn his love and attention. I so wanted to make Daddy proud of me; what little girl doesn't? In trying to make him proud, I allowed things to happen and kept my mouth shut. But it wasn't as if I would have a choice at the age of seven anyway. At one point he decided to try something different. I remember thinking: *This is wrong and it shouldn't be happening. Why is he doing that?* I felt the stubble from his beard on the inside of my thighs. It was a bit scratchy, but that feeling was overpowered by what Daddy was doing. It felt pleasurable, and I wanted him to continue, but in my head I knew it was wrong. It left me with a difficult time hugging, let alone kissing, any man with a beard even to this day. It became a trigger for those memories. Daddy would periodically stop. I begged him to continue, because I didn't want those feelings of pleasure to stop. Daddy seemed to enjoy having me ask him for more. It brought him pleasure in a very weird way. He continued to do this over and over for a couple of days to get me used to those feelings and asking for him to do those things to me.

After a while, he changed things up a bit. He wanted me to return the favor as he wanted me to do the same thing to him. He wanted me to put his "thing" in my mouth. I told him that it was too big, that I didn't want to do that. At this point, I was hooked on those feelings, and I knew that I had no choice but to do as he wished. I was so torn on the inside. He was going to get his way because I was addicted to those strange feelings that he had created and which I had never experienced before he started. The first time was awful. I gagged and almost threw up because it was too big for my little mouth. Yet, he forced me to continue until he had his pleasure. Every once in a while, he would "pee" in my mouth. It tasted so horrible! Daddy would laugh at my response. He took a sick sense of pleasure at my reaction; thus, he would do it here and there just to see my reaction.

These games continued for months. Daddy never seemed to tire of them. Many times, I would still gag, but I very clearly knew that under no circumstances was I to throw up. I would be severely punished. So, Daddy and I would exchange oral sex almost every night. Sometimes there would be other things that I would be forced to do. Sometimes he would rape me instead. I never knew what would happen from one night to the next. Yet, as time went on, I grew accustomed to the abuse and it became my new normal. I enjoyed some of the abuse that I endured, thus my daddy told me that I was the cause of the abuse and that it was all my fault, that I had asked for the things that he did to me. There were times in which I did ask for it, because I enjoyed the feelings that it created within my body. Despite whether I asked for it or not, when he finished raping me, he would toss me aside like I was a toy to be played with or a tool to be used. Then he'd tell me that someday I would make a wonderful wife. My young mind was so confused, broken, and disillusioned. *I had become a substitute for my mommy. Was this what mommies and daddies did with each other? I was very confused and had so many conflicting emotions. I didn't want Daddy to do these things to me, but at the same time I did. Mommy, what is going on? I wish you were still here. Why is Daddy doing these things? Is it really my fault? Am I to blame for the things that he is doing to me?*

CHAPTER 4

We found a new house on the outskirts of a smaller town. Our house was up on the top of a hill. I finally had my own room just off the kitchen on the main floor. Daddy had his room on the other side of the house. Brother had his room near my room. I would walk to school each morning singing as I went along. Our backyard had a swing set off to one side as well as a big tree in the middle of it. I spent many hours outside playing with my friends, trying to be normal. One day I was climbing on the side of the swing set trying to get on the top bar so I could swing from it. Suddenly, a myriad of bees was buzzing around me. While frightened and screaming from pain, I attempted to get away from the bees. I ended up with several huge welts from those stings. At least it was from something innocent this time. However, it did make me question whether the fun was worth it? *Maybe I was being punished for having fun.*

At night, I sucked my thumb in order to fall asleep. It was a self-soothing act that brought me temporary comfort and peace. Daddy tried many times to break me of the habit because he thought I was too old to be doing that. He tried to put my thumb in hot pepper juice and other things, but all his attempts failed. *If only he knew the real reason behind why I sucked my thumb; but Daddy was too caught up in his own needs to ever pause to look at mine.* One night I was so tired that I fell asleep before taking the gum out of my mouth. When I woke up, I had gum stuck in my hair. I talked to my brother and he decided to help me out. He cut the gum out of my hair so that I wouldn't get in trouble. We thought that we had outsmarted Daddy; we were wrong as he noticed that my hair had been cut. *Someone was about to get a spanking with Daddy's belt.*

CHAPTER 5

After a time, Daddy got a girlfriend who became our sitter when Daddy was at work. Her name was Millie, and she stayed in our house in Daddy's room. She was nice sometimes and allowed us to simply play with our friends. Most of the time she was very controlling and would tell Daddy the littlest of things that we did wrong.

Daddy taught me many things over the years that he should not have but neglected to teach me things that I needed to know. He never taught me how to take care of myself, or even basic hygiene. He would allow me to take bubble baths, but he would always touch me underneath the bubbles under the guise of "washing" me. I learned to dislike baths; feelings of panic and repulsion would arise every time he insisted that I take one. I equated baths with the things he did to me and these feelings persisted into my later years as well.

At school, before the day would start, my teachers would comb my hair and put pretty barrettes in my hair. It was nice to get the extra attention from my teachers. They felt sorry for me because I had no mommy, but I didn't care. It was nice to have someone help me with my hair. It was like I had a mommy at school. I often wondered if they knew what was going on at home. *Did they know? What would happen if they found out? I was too afraid of Daddy to say anything. I couldn't even tell my big brother. I knew that he would try to protect me from Daddy, but that in the process he would get beaten.* So, the secrets sat like concrete blocks in the pit of my stomach, crying out to be told, yet terror would flood over me at the thought of ever breaking the secrecy code my daddy had programmed into me.

Things were not always horrible with Daddy. I loved his work picnics! There were fun games to play, lots of food, lots of others to play with, and cool prizes for the kids. It was always a day in which my daddy was like the other daddies, and we left stuffed, tired out, and had tons of candy and prizes. We had participated in bubble blowing contests, 3-legged races, potato sack races, and lots of other games. The lady who organized this was Jackie. She drove a funny looking car! The front end was like a station wagon with a truck bed for the back end. It was loaded with game supplies and all the prizes. My brother said that it was an El Camino. That was about the only "fun" memory I have of my daddy.

CHAPTER 6

During these years, my young, immature mind just couldn't handle the confusion and torment that my father dished out faster than I could deal with it. My mind shattered in order to cope with the abuse. I wouldn't truly understand the depths of what that meant until I was almost 40 years old. I was an orphan left to be raised by my abusive father who had very strange rules and even harsher punishments for breaking them. One of those rules was that no one was allowed to touch me--unless it was him or he gave someone else permission. One evening we had a bunch of people over and they stayed upstairs, which was a place we didn't go very often. I asked Daddy if I could sleep upstairs that night; he agreed but his eyes told me that I had better behave or I'd pay the price later.

During the night, one of Daddy's "friends" began touching me in areas that were off limits within our home, though in other places it was permissible. I pretended to be asleep in the hopes that he would understand that he shouldn't be doing this here, but it only made him want me even more. The next thing I knew he was trying to rape me. I didn't want to be the one to pay the consequences of breaking Daddy's strange rules, so I slapped him. It was enough to startle him and I ran downstairs to inform my daddy what he had done. My daddy was furious that he would break the established rules and called the police. I remember my daddy speaking with his friend. I could only imagine the things that were whispered between them, but it was clear that he was afraid of my daddy.

The next day, I sat on the top step of the porch at the back of our house between Daddy and the police officer. The police officer was very patient as I slowly told him what happened. My head was hung in fear of looking directly at the officer while Daddy placed his hand on my back. I knew that if I looked at him directly, I might break the secrecy code, or the police officer might see the terror that was in my eyes. *What would happen if I told him that my daddy was also doing those things, plus more?* Then I remembered the unspoken rule and chose to not say anything about my dad. As a result of my statement to the police, my daddy's friend was arrested and sentenced to jail. Deep down, I wished that my daddy was the one being sent away. The way that Daddy supported me that day left many unanswered questions in my heart. *Why didn't he support me for other things like he was supporting me now? Was he even truly supporting me? Or, was that hand on my back just a subtle reminder to not break the code? IF I told, would they arrest me for the things that I've done?*

CHAPTER 7

There were many times in which Daddy would have me sleep with him and Millie in their bed, though I was never permitted to leave in the middle of the night. My daddy would always abuse me with his girlfriend sound asleep next to him. *Why? Why would she be okay with me sleeping in their bed? Why couldn't I leave after everyone was asleep?* There were so many unanswered questions swirling around in my head. I had endured so much abuse from a man that was supposed to protect me. *Was I the one who was wrong? Maybe the things that were happening were normal and happened in everyone's home. Maybe I was the one who needed to get help.*

One day my daddy decided it was time to "teach" me about the birds and the bees. He told me to stand in one spot and not to move. As he walked into his bedroom, I noticed that Millie was lying on the bed naked. The sight of her made me wonder what she was doing. *Why was I being asked to stand here and look at her naked?* Out of the corner of my eye, I saw Daddy getting undressed and climb on top of Millie. Then he proceeded to have sex with Millie. Millie seemed to simply ignore me and enjoyed what Daddy was doing. I stood there knowing that I couldn't turn away or I'd be punished, but also wondering what I had done wrong that I needed to be replaced. My body was beginning to react like it did when Daddy touched me like that. *Why was my body doing that? My young mind couldn't comprehend why he was doing these things with her and not with me? Maybe, I wasn't doing it correctly, so he felt he needed to show me what it was supposed to look like. Was I supposed to watch and learn how it was done correctly so I could be better the next time?* All I knew was that I hated Millie even more as she participated in this torture. Daddy must have seen the confusion on my face, because the look on his face was one of pure enjoyment. He took pleasure in watching my reaction to what he was doing.

CHAPTER 8

Oftentimes in the summer, we would play outside with our friends, frequently by the river. My brother often went swimming there with his friends. On one occasion I wanted to go swimming with him, so I jumped in. That day I lost one of my shoes in the river, as I had forgotten to take them off before I jumped in. Brother protected me from Daddy's wrath by telling a story about how I lost my shoe. Thankfully Daddy believed him, and we went shopping for a new pair of shoes. My brother protected me once again from the inevitable punishment I would have received if Daddy knew the truth.

One evening I was outside playing, although I was told to be inside by dusk. I thought I came in on time, but it was beyond dusk according to my dad, and so I was late coming home. Since I had broken the rules, I was punished. As I headed to the bathroom to get a wet washcloth, I got a glance of my daddy smiling as if he thoroughly enjoyed what would happen next. I had to drop my pants and use the wet washcloth to get my bare butt damp. After it was sufficiently damp, he would pull his belt off and spank me with it. The sound of a belt flying though belt loops and coming to a snap is one I will never forget. A belt smacking onto wet skin stung so badly and the sound echoed in my ears! The tears silently fell down my cheeks, as I received one blow after another. I can't recall how many times he actually hit me that night, but I knew that no matter how bad it hurt, I could never let him hear me cry out. He seemed to take pleasure in knowing that he was causing pain, so I refused to give him that satisfaction. Needless to say, I never came close to missing a curfew again!

Ever since Mommy died, Daddy had turned to beer for comfort when he wasn't abusing me. He spent many hours at the bar, and we always had beer in the fridge. I will never forget the smell of it, or the look of all those Pabst Blue Ribbon cans, or the Old Milwaukee cans, or how the beer affected my daddy. He was not a pleasant drunk, unless you did exactly what he said the very first time he said it. During those years, we never knew what mood he would be in when he came home from work or how much he had already been drinking. Daddy had many of his "passing out spells" throughout the years, similar to the one he had the day Mommy died.

CHAPTER 9

Three years after my mom died, my daddy made his first "public" mistake: he abused a friend of mine who had spent the night. It was nearing the end of Christmas vacation and Daddy said I could have a friend spend the night. I was SO excited! I had never had a friend spend the night before. It was going to be a fantastic night! I thought that since my friend was staying I would be left alone for one night and could sleep in peace. As my friend and I were getting ready for bed, my daddy told us to get in his bed instead of our own. My friend had a puzzled look upon her face not really understanding what he meant. My heart sunk at his request, and the panic I felt suffocated me like a wet blanket that fell over my heart. I could barely breathe! I stared at Daddy pleading with my eyes for him to change his mind, but the look on his face told me that I dare not disobey. So, as deadly fear crept into my heart, we climbed into his bed. After a few minutes, Daddy and Millie joined us. I was SO embarrassed by Daddy! *What if my friend found out what Daddy was doing to me? Would he hurt my friend if she told the truth like he hurt me?* Shortly after Daddy and Millie went to bed, my daddy said, "Sweetie, come here." Without hesitating, I started to come to my daddy, but he said, "No, your friend." *Just as I had feared, he had plans to hurt my friend! I was petrified beyond words! Why does he want my friend? Why doesn't he want me? What was he going to do to her? I pleaded to the heavens that he wouldn't embarrass me or hurt my friend.* After a while, I fell asleep oblivious to those around me.

Sometime during the night my friend woke me up to ask me where the bathroom was. I was very confused because she had used it earlier that afternoon, but I got up and showed her where it was. Once in the bathroom, I shut the door behind us only to see tears falling down her face. As she began to tell me what my daddy had done to her, an unspeakable dread crept into my frail body like an impenetrable darkness. She was so upset and uncomfortable being in my house any longer. She wanted to go home immediately and tell her mom what had happened, but I pleaded with her as tears streamed down my face to not only stay until morning, but also to not say anything to anyone. I told her how much trouble I would be in if she told anyone, that Daddy would severely hurt me if she said a single word to anyone. Seeing the terror in my eyes, she promised that she wouldn't say anything, that it would be our secret. She agreed to stay until morning as long as we didn't return to his bed. We embraced in a tight hug trying to comfort each other as the tears flowed freely between the two of us. After a while, we silently creeped into my own room and fell asleep. The next morning, she went home and I thought everything would go back to normal, as I hoped beyond hope that she would keep her promise to me. What I didn't know was that my friend, with the loving support of her family, had gone to the police and told them what my father had done to her.

CHAPTER 10

The following Monday we returned to school. While in the middle of grammar class, I went up to the teacher's desk to staple some papers together and mistakenly stapled my thumb instead. Doing so, I accidently broke the stapler. My stomach instantly filled with butterflies as fear arose with each passing moment of my feeble attempts to repair the stapler so I wouldn't get into trouble. *If my dad found out, I would be whipped!* My attempts became more frantic as each second ticked away without success. When I realized that I had truly broken the stapler, I sheepishly approached my teacher to tell her what I had done. My head hung in shame as my heart had prepared for the upcoming punishment. My teacher shocked me! She was more concerned about whether or not my thumb was okay, which made me very confused. She asked me to take my seat and continue working. I headed back to my seat truly baffled!

A few minutes after I had returned to my desk, the secretary came onto the speaker in our classroom and asked me to come to the office. *I didn't understand! When I told my teacher about the stapler, she genuinely seemed to care more about me than the stapler, so why was I going to the office?* I pleaded with her, telling her that I was sorry I broke the stapler and that I didn't do it on purpose. Despite my objections, she still made me go to the office. When I arrived at the office, the secretary told me to go straight into the principal's office. The look on her face confused me as it was a mixture of compassion and regret. I kept thinking to myself: *I really didn't mean to break the stapler. My dad is going to be SO mad at me for getting into trouble at school!*

When I opened the door to the principal's office, I saw two police officers standing there. As the memories of the past weekend came flooding into my recollection, I knew that the reason I was called to the principal's office was no longer about the stapler but about what Daddy had done to my friend. As instructed by the principal, I sat in one of the chairs as the police began to ask me question after question about this past weekend and even more specifically about my daddy. *I knew I shouldn't lie to the police, but my heart was torn! Do I tell the truth and get severely punished by Daddy? Or do I lie and get in trouble with the police?* Those two questions fought for supremacy within my mind as the police kept asking questions. I knew that I couldn't lie about what happened this past weekend, since it was obvious that my friend had broken her promise or they wouldn't be here.

The police informed me that they would be taking me to a foster home that day while they investigated the allegations that were made against my dad. What was a foster home? I was clueless. They asked me to go gather my things from my locker and to return to the office once I finished. As I left the office to go to my locker, the final bell rung and excitement filled the air as kids poured into the hallways to head home for the day. As I stood at my locker placing my things into my backpack, thoughts of sneaking out the door along with the other kids raced through my mind. I thought of hiding from the police, but in the end I knew that I could do no such thing, as the reality of right and wrong crashed into my heart like a tidal wave. On some deep level within my heart, I knew that what my daddy was doing was so wrong; however, my devotion and loyalty to him was unwavering as was my dedication to the unspoken code between us. I slowly returned to the office and the waiting police officers.

They escorted me their car as all the kids stared and talked quietly amongst themselves. They were wondering what was going on and why I was being escorted away with the police. It was almost impossible to not feel the layers upon layers of guilt and blame being thrown upon my tiny shoulders with each agonizing step. Yet, could anyone blame them? I was the guilty one, wasn't I? It was my fault that all of this was happening in the first place! I was the one to ask to have a friend over. I was the one who couldn't stand up to her daddy. I was the one who caused my friend to experience a pain that she never should have had to endure. I should be punished! As I got into the back of that police car, I took one last look at the countless faces around me and at my school, trying desperately to find the face of my friend amongst all of them. The door closed and, unbeknownst to me, that was the last time that I would ever see any of them again. I never saw my classmates, friends, or my teachers again. I didn't even get a chance to tell my friend how sorry I truly was that my daddy had hurt her, that I had failed her by being a horrible example of what a friend should be, or that the things that happened to her were all my fault. Even to this day, I wonder how she's doing, if what my daddy did to her affected her like it has affected me.

As the car drove away from the school, I wanted to cry but knew that it wouldn't change anything. Plus, it might make these policemen start asking even more questions. Instead, I stared out the window as questions bombarded my brain like a firing machine gun, all the while being so, so scared of what my daddy would do when I didn't arrive home from school.

My thoughts ran wild: *Where was this home at? Would I ever see Daddy again? What was going to happen next? Would I be attending school tomorrow? What was this foster home going to be like? How long would I be staying here? What was Daddy's reaction going to be? Would he hurt someone or break something when I didn't show up? Would he drink more and more beer? What would this family think of me? Would they treat me the same way as Daddy did? How many kids were there? Was it a prison of sorts? Would this family know the things that I was guilty of?* The drive seemed to last forever! Finally, we pulled into a really nice subdivision and stopped in front of a beautiful house with a huge front porch. I couldn't believe that this was where I would be staying! It was the most gorgeous home I'd ever seen.

PART II –THE FOSTER CARE SYSTEM

CHAPTER 11

I walked into the Johnsons' home scared of what was going to happen next. The first thing I saw among the unarranged furniture was the smiling face of Dianne Johnson, my new foster mom. Dianne was doing something that I had never seen done before (or even knew that it existed in the first place): she was spring cleaning even though it was the middle of winter. Dianne seemed to already know that I was coming, as she greeted me by name and a smile. That smile melted away the fear and put me instantly at ease. She and the police officer exchanged a few words, as I stood like a statue absorbing the new surroundings and the kids that were helping her clean. I was shown to my room in the basement; it was a divided off section of her sewing room, but I didn't mind as it was mine! I had my own room, something that I never had the privilege of having before.

Dianne was an amazing foster mother. For the first time in my entire life I felt safe and loved for being me (though I didn't realize this for quite a while). I didn't have to earn Dianne's love as it was given freely. This was a foreign concept to me! Life was very busy and chaotic for me during the next couple of months. I was in and out of so many appointments. Throughout them all, I kept the secrets that Daddy swore me to keep tucked in the depths of my mind and heart, though I felt compelled to say something in response to all the questions that I was being asked. So, in my attempts to "tell the truth," I spoke lies to the counselors and social workers, but it was also my attempt to test the waters of whether I would be believed or not. The courts made me actually sit in a room with my daddy, the police, and my advocate and tell everyone what I had said that he had done to me. The look in my daddy's eyes made it very clear to me that I would never be able to tell the actual truth, EVER!

Even though I felt safe without my daddy around day in and day out, my allegiance and loyalty to Daddy was strong and deeply rooted. I felt as if I needed to protect him in some way, though the longer I was away from him, the less I wanted to protect him. I saw doctors, counselors, social workers, lawyers, etc. I had appointments at the court house, at the hospital, at school, and supervised visitations with Daddy. The courts assessed Daddy as well as his girlfriend, Millie. The courts said that both Daddy and Millie had speech disabilities which made it difficult for others to always understand what they were saying. Daddy was even harder to understand when he started drinking, but I had learned to understand him and it had become second nature to me. The courts also said that both of them were somewhat limited in intelligence and education. I don't know about Millie, but Daddy dropped out of school to work on the farm with Grandpa, so that made sense to me. He wasn't "book smart," but we managed okay.

One of the things that Dianne did shortly after I arrived was to cut my hair short. She said that I was old enough to know how to take care of it and, until I learned how to do so, I didn't need to have long hair. My daddy was FURIOUS!! He didn't think anyone had the right to cut my hair without his permission, but I liked the shorter hair as it was really easy to manage. I was slowly adapting to a new school and a new environment. Life was going better for me, and I found myself more and more at ease. However, I still had my secrets that I held close and didn't share with others. Soon I was thinking of maybe sharing them with Dianne because she was really nice. It seemed as if she could be trusted. However, just when I was getting up the courage to tell her the truth, I had a huge setback. My brother told me something that would echo in my head for a long time to come: "Things may not be the best, but Mom is dead and Dad is all we have left." It was like he was trying to tell me to keep my mouth shut about the things that were going on at home. That moment made me remember Daddy and his unspoken rules. *I will not tell anyone my secrets.* Instead, I buried them even deeper so they wouldn't try to pop out like they almost had done with Dianne.

Even though I felt safer with each passing day away from Daddy, it was also agonizingly hard being away from him. I had grown accustomed to the abuse, and now to not have it occur every day was culture shock for me and my body. I craved the feelings that my daddy had prematurely aroused. I knew now that what he did was wrong, but it didn't change the fact that I enjoyed it and thought that I willingly participated in it. *So, if it was wrong for Daddy to do those things, then I was just as wrong. Wasn't I?* So many confusing, conflicting thoughts ran rampant in my head. These interior conversations went on as I weighed the pros and cons. I couldn't tell anyone what was REALLY going on or I would get into trouble, so I had to have the conversations with myself. All I knew was that I missed those feelings that Daddy had created, so I found creative ways for my body to feel that way once again. I took extra special care to make sure that no one was around, so I wouldn't get caught. I didn't want to go to jail.

CHAPTER 12

A fter about 6 months in foster care, the courts said it was not safe for me to return home. So, I remained in the care of the Johnsons. Secretly, this made me extremely happy! I didn't want to go back to living with Daddy. I was safe here. I had friends here. I was allowed to simply be a kid here. I could actually play and not get into trouble. I enjoyed the freedom from the random and unexpected punishments. I kept these thoughts to myself and tried not to reveal anything on the outside.

As fate would have it, I was there for two and half additional years while my case was in and out of the court system. During that time, Dianne taught me so many things that Mommy didn't have a chance to do and things my daddy didn't think of. She taught me how to shower and wash my own hair, how to make a bed, how to wash dishes, how to vacuum and dust. Dianne told the social worker that I "was so good it scared her." No one understood that I HAD to be good. She didn't understand that my daddy had programmed me to be good and to do as I was told. I could not do anything less than that.

While I was at the Johnsons, there were many other children that came in and out of their home. Dianne's husband, Bill, worked nights and slept during the day. I had very little contact with him, which was very safe for me. He was a very gentle man and we got along well on the weekends and on vacations. Dianne and Bill had a couple of natural children and one other that they had adopted. Their oldest was out of the home and I didn't have much contact with them. The other children and I got along pretty well with each other.

While at the Johnsons, I learned how to play. It may sound strange, but my childhood was taken from me, and I was never able to just have fun like most normal children. So, for the first time, I learned how to simply play and have fun. I rode my bike around the neighborhood; I played on the swing set in the back yard; I built snow forts and snow tunnels in the yard; I played soccer and softball on local teams. It was as if I had been given another chance to be a kid once again. I was thoroughly enjoying the opportunities that were given to me at the Johnsons. I even went on family vacations with them! Dianne loved me the best she knew how, even though I struggled to reciprocate those feelings. The only way in which I knew how to display love was to follow instructions and do as I was told. I was made a part of the family and treated as such, never as an outsider.

Dianne took me to church with her family and introduced me to Jesus for the first time. I really enjoyed going to church and Sunday school. It was something that I looked forward to every week. It was as if I was starving and the lessons that I was taught there were feeding my soul in a way that I couldn't explain. One day we woke up to a blizzard outside. My foster parents decided that they were not going to go to church that day and thought that it would be cancelled anyway due to the weather. I was upset and they told me that if I wanted to go that badly, then I could always walk there. So, I did just that! I walked to Sunday school in the middle of a blizzard because I didn't want to miss out on the lesson that was being taught.

CHAPTER 13

E very year, Dianne always made my birthday something special by baking and decorating a cake just for me (a tradition that I now keep with my own children). To actually be celebrated was something that had been challenging to process. All my life I hadn't been celebrated in a healthy way. I could only recall one birthday party while in my daddy's care and that was at Grandpa George's house with my aunt and my cousin. The way that those specially decorated cakes made me feel caused a conflict inside of me. Here I was in limbo with the court system, Daddy wasn't visiting me as often as he hated the supervised visitations, and Dianne had made a cake especially for me! It was always decorated with something that I liked, and each one held a special place in my heart. *Why would she voluntarily choose to spend time on decorating a cake for me? Was I really that important? Didn't she know what kind of person I actually was, deep down on the inside? Wasn't she aware of the things that I had done wrong?* In the midst of the chaos that my life had become, there was a momentary feeling of normalcy but always interrupted by these conflicting thoughts.

Dianne also taught me that a child can be disciplined in a healthy way when they make poor choices. While in her care, I had two incidents that resulted in consequences. The first time, I got caught stealing money from my foster dad. I had asked for some money to participate in an activity and I was told no. I really wanted to participate and Dianne's response had disappointed me. One afternoon I was using the bathroom and saw my foster dad's wallet on the counter in the bathroom. I decided that he wouldn't notice and took the money so I could participate regardless of Dianne's decision. My foster dad noticed the money missing, and Dianne asked me if I had taken the money. With my head hung in shame and fear in my heart, I admitted to taking the money. I was consequently grounded, but the look of disappointment in Dianne's eyes would not be forgotten. I wasn't beaten or whipped with a belt as I had been in my daddy's care. I was lovingly disciplined to teach me the difference between right and wrong.

There was another time in which I was disciplined in a healthy manner. I had been at school cleaning out lockers in small groups. A classmate thought it would be funny to dump my color pencils on the floor. I was so angry that I literally called him a bad word but, instead of saying the word, I just spelled it out.

"You b-a-s-t-a-r-d!"

At that moment, a teacher flew out into the hallway.

"Who just said that?"

I was triggered and immediately went into fear mode. *What kind of punishment would I receive? How would Daddy respond when he found out? I am in so much trouble.* The teacher repeated the question, but fear had a tight grip on my tongue and I was speechless.

Finally, a classmate said, "She did."

Then the teacher asked which one of the girls said that. I finally seemed to snap out of the fear mode and admitted that it was me. She sternly instructed me to go to the office. I was concerned about my things that were sprawled all over the hallway.

"What should I do with my things?"

Ignoring my question, she replied, "Down to the office!"

Since she didn't answer my question, I asked her again.

"Down to the office!"

I didn't want to ignore her request, but I thought it was inconsiderate for a teacher to not answer a simple question, so I asked a third time. Her reply didn't change though the tone of her voice did, so I slowly started heading to the office. *What would happen to my things? Would I ever see them again? Would I get in trouble for leaving my things all over the place?* I had never been in trouble at school before, and I was fearful of what would happen next.

As I approached the principal's office, fear overtook me. The last time I was in the principal's office, I had been questioned by police. *Were there police in the office this time as well?* As I walked into the office, I was slightly relieved to see no police. The principal and I talked about the situation. I received an hour detention that day: thirty minutes for saying what I did and another thirty minutes for disobeying a teacher. *I didn't understand why I was being punished for asking a simple question! What about that teacher, would she be in trouble for not answering my question? Would she be held responsible if I had things missing?* The words of the principal brought me back to reality.

"I will be calling your foster mom to let her know what happened today."

The fear rose instantly similarly to how bile rises just before you throw up. I was dismissed and instructed to go back to class. As I walked up the stairs to my classroom, I could see that somehow my things were placed back into the locker, and I proceeded to my desk. I no longer wanted to go home. *What would Dianne do? I know what my daddy would have done; I would have been whipped with his belt.* Dread filled my heart as I walked home that day with a heaviness that increased with each step I took. Instead of being beaten, I was grounded for an entire month! I went to my room trying to process what had just happened. *I had gotten into major trouble at school, and my only punishment was to be grounded? That just didn't make sense. I had expected to be severely beaten and instead I was physically untouched.* Dianne kept surprising me at every turn. This new "normal" was so challenging to adjust to.

I learned how to interact with children my own age and with those who were physically different from me. Dianne had adopted a son who had no left arm; his right arm was about three inches in length with two or three fingers at the end of it. I remember him sitting on the floor playing with GI Joe action figures with his feet. He could manipulate the arms and legs of those action figures with his toes as well as I could with my fingers. He was (and still is) an amazing young man. He flourished in the love and acceptance of his family. For the first time in my life, I was beginning to do the same thing.

CHAPTER 14

At some point during my time at the Johnsons, I began to feel that this home was MY home. I felt truly safe for the first time. At times, it felt that Dianne was more of a mom to me than my own mommy had been. Dianne had taught me more things than Mommy had, simply because Mommy died before she had the chance to do so. I really wanted to call Dianne, "Mom," but I fought that desire in the depths of my being. *What would Mommy think? Would she be upset if I called her Mom?* Though Mommy might be upset or even angry, I had to be true to my heart. I finally made the determination that I would begin to call Dianne "Mom." It flowed so easily off my tongue. She fulfilled the very definition of what a mom is. She was my mom, so I began to call her such.

During the first nine years of my life, I was taught that love had to be earned. It was never free. It always came at a cost. Many years later, Dianne would describe me as a funnel: no matter how much love she poured into me, I was just incapable of accepting it--though I desperately needed it. The years in the Johnsons' home were some happy years, and I was beginning to forget about Daddy and all the abuse that he had inflicted on me. The visitations with Daddy had become few and far between. After a couple of years in the courts, my daddy's parental rights were ultimately terminated. I found out later that the courts didn't terminate his rights, but rather he voluntarily gave them up. *Once again, I was abandoned by my daddy. He found yet another way to hurt me even though he couldn't physically touch me. He had officially made me an orphan of the state of Iowa. He did so VOLUNTARILY!!* I ultimately know that it was in my best interests. Yet the fact that he did so of his own choosing was like the ultimate revenge that my daddy had on me. He made that choice before it was made for him, and it hurt deep down in my heart and left wounds that began to fester like an infection years later. *I was now an orphan.*

CHAPTER 15

A t the age of 12, I had to make a decision that would affect my life
from this point forward: to either be placed up for adoption or to
simply remain a foster child until I aged out of the system. *Would I
be a foster child forever? Or would I come to have a family like the Johnson, who loved
me unconditionally? I chose to be adopted, to try to find a family that would make me a
part of theirs. I didn't want to be an orphan forever.* I wanted a family to call my
own, one that would love me and treat me with respect, just like the
Johnsons had for the last three years. The news that I had been placed on
the adoption list made me so excited, but the realization that it wouldn't be
with the Johnsons was a very hard concept to grasp. Secretly, I hoped that I
could stay with the Johnsons and become a permanent part of their family,
but for reasons that I couldn't understand, that wasn't a possibility. I was
just beginning to feel at ease, just beginning to feel that maybe my daddy
was wrong and I really was worth the love and time of others. Now all I
heard in my head was: *I am unlovable; I am unwanted; I am an orphan. All my
hope was shattered.*

If I couldn't be a part of this family, then I needed to get used to the
idea that Dianne wasn't going to be my mom. I had to stop calling her
"Mom" --she would be Dianne moving forward. Even though it tore my
heart apart to make that switch, I had to make that separation before a new
family was found. Not calling Dianne "Mom" had really affected her but,
on some level, she seemed to understand what it was that I was doing. I had
to prepare for my new family. However, deep in my heart, I had just lost a
mom for the second time in my life. My heart was devastated and broken in
many pieces. Still, I had no choice if I was to prepare for a new family. If I
wanted this new family to actually adopt me, then they could never see how
much I loved Dianne and this family; how much I wanted to be called their
daughter/sister. Therefore, I shoved these feelings way down deep behind
the barriers, hoping that they would stay put. They had to stay put! These
feelings had to have many layers of protection, I had to be perfect once
again. I was looking for a forever family, and they needed to know that I
wanted them. My case worker warned me that it might take some time to
find a family, as my age put me in a category that classified my adoption as

a special case. Despite my desire to be adopted, it might never happen due to my age. *Who wanted to adopt a twelve-year-old? I was an orphan. I would always be an orphan.* The next month was very hard as I started to retreat from those who had shown nothing but kindness to me. *I was alone, and I just needed to get used to the idea that I would always be alone.* I would need to figure out how to negotiate life without needing anyone else.

After just a couple of weeks, Dianne told me that there was a family who showed interest in adopting me, and that I actually knew the mom. She proceeded to tell me that one of the substitute teachers in my school had heard that I was being placed up for adoption and wanted to adopt me. I actually remembered this woman, and she was always a nice substitute. I was so excited! I wouldn't have to switch schools or lose the friends that I had made over the last three years. I slowly packed my things and, with great sadness, I said goodbye to the Johnsons. I really didn't want to leave, but I had found a family that was interested in adopting a twelve-year-old and was lucky it had happened as quickly as it did. So, I buried the sadness and grief behind the barriers of my heart. I didn't have time to grieve, I was moving in with my new family! My new home was only about fifteen minutes from the Johnsons. *Maybe, I would still run into the Johnsons around town? I must stop! I couldn't let them know how hard this move was going to be!*

CHAPTER 16

As I entered my new home in the country, it reminded me a lot of my grandparents' farm, which made me very nervous. There were tanks to fill the machinery with gas, lots of equipment around the grounds, and the two-story farmhouse looked like it needed a good paint job. This was nothing like the home I had just left, but that didn't mean that it would be a bad thing. *I needed to give this family a chance.* I walked into the house very nervous and leery, but a little spark of hope had been ignited: *maybe I wouldn't have to do life on my own.* I had a two-year-old sister named Kate who had been adopted as well. It would be enjoyable to have a little sister around to play with. My room was smaller than my room at the Johnsons, but it was mine. My parents' room was on the main floor and mine (as well as Kate's) was upstairs.

We went to church every week, and my new family were devout Catholics. It was a bit different than what I was used to, but I didn't mind. My new family wanted to change my name, but since I was so old, they settled with just changing my middle name. My new name would be Jennifer Vencentia Roberts (the last name has been changed for privacy reasons). The middle name was the female version of Saint Vincent, who was known for his charity and compassion for the poor. Things started out pretty good with this family. Summer had arrived and my new dad played in a local band. We often went to music festivals that were local and supported him. At one of those festivals I actually saw the Johnsons! It was really cool to see them, but my heart sank when I saw Dianne. Just a reminder of what I had lost. *Must shove that down! It can't be allowed to surface!* I had to do everything that I could to survive in this home and comparisons would not be my advantage.

Mom, Kate, and I went on a trip to Detroit, Michigan for doctor's appointments; Dad had to stay home to work. After all of the doctor's appointments were over, we drove further north to see Mackinaw Island and to visit some extended family. As we started across the Mackinaw Bridge, I was truly enjoying looking out the window at the beautiful scenery and the Great Lakes. Shortly after we crossed onto the bridge, Kate threw up all over me! YUCK!! The smell was atrocious! I kept begging Mom to pull over, but she told me that it was illegal to stop on Mackinaw Bridge. It was only a mile long and she would find a place to stop as soon as she could on the other side. I sat there covered in puke totally grossed out, while my mom was asking me to comfort Kate who had gotten car sick. *Are you serious?* I couldn't believe that I was being asked to comfort my baby sister who had just thrown up all over me! That was the LONGEST mile car ride in my life!!! We pulled in on the other side at a rest stop. Mom cleaned up Kate while I went to the bathroom to change clothes. After we were changed, Mom allowed us to play for a little while to give Kate a break from being in the car. Kate and I enjoyed feeding the seagulls some breadcrumbs.

Once we arrived at our relatives' house, we had some other adventures. Some extended family took me fishing on Lake Michigan, and I caught my first king salmon (I think that was what it was called). It was really exciting to hold that fish. It was almost as big as me! After a great week with extended family, we made the long trip back home. Thankfully, Kate didn't get car sick again! Later on in the summer, my new parents sent me to camp for an entire week. It was a lot of fun to get away for a week, to hang out with kids my own age, and to try different things. I made some new friends and didn't really want to return home, but I had no choice.

CHAPTER 17

School began in the fall and things were starting to get a bit more hectic at home. The arguments between Mom and I became more frequent. We would argue over the chores, but mostly the arguments were all about how I treated Kate. Mom didn't like the fact that I was bossy towards Kate. She was her precious baby girl, and how dare I boss her around! She was the favorite and there was no questioning that! Seriously though, what twelve-year-old wants a two-year-old in their room, going through their things, constantly asking "Why?" and destroying the little possessions that you own? *Why couldn't Mom understand that I didn't have very much to call my own and that those things were very precious to me? Was it really that hard to understand?* Mom no longer trusted me. She often used Kate's baby monitor to spy on me and my conversations with Kate. Soon all Mom and I did was fight. Nothing was going right. There were many times that I had to take my dinner upstairs and eat in my room as punishment and wasn't allowed to eat with the family. Forced isolation. This was the absolute worst punishment that one could dish out to me. Once again, I was simply discarded and tossed aside when it was inconvenient for them. Would things ever change? It was beginning to appear that this was my life's destiny, to be abandoned and isolated from others. *Was I really that unlovable? Was I really that disobedient? Would this family ever love me the way that Dianne had? Maybe I wasn't worthy to be loved. What had I done to be discarded like I no longer matter?*

We had a ton of snow that winter. The snowplows had created huge piles of it at the end of our long driveway. One morning, while waiting for the bus to arrive, I thought it would be fun to try walking on top of the snow. There was a crunchy, almost hard surface on the top. I started at the lower end of the pile and things were going really well. I was walking on snow like Jesus had walked on water. I was super excited about my accomplishment! I kept walking towards the top. Out of the corner of my eye, I saw the bus coming down the road. I moved too quickly and, the next thing I knew, I was chest deep in the snow pile. Panic began to rise in me as I struggled to get out before the bus arrived. The bus came to a stop at the end of the driveway and with one final struggle I finally managed to get out.

I quickly grabbed my backpack and jumped onto the bus. After a little scolding by the bus driver about not being ready immediately, I quickly found my seat as the other kids began to snicker and laugh at me. Apparently, they saw me struggling to get out of the snow pile. I greatly disliked being the subject of their conversations and laughter. I vowed to never put myself in that position again. In the back of my mind, I wondered if the bus driver would call my mom to inform her of my indiscretion or if the warning, she gave me would be the end of it. I knew that if Mom was called, that it would only serve as yet another issue that would end in an argument.

CHAPTER 18

O n the last day of school before Christmas vacation, Mom and I had gotten into a pretty heavy argument. I had to leave in the middle of it in order to catch the bus. I was never so relieved to get out of the house and walk to the bus stop. I was not looking forward to Christmas vacation! Later that day, I received a message from the office saying that my mom had called. The message said that I was not to take the bus home because she would be picking me up after school. I spent the rest of the day fit-to-be-tied. I was SO angry with my mom. I told my friends that she doesn't even trust me to take the bus home anymore.

The final bell rang and, as I walked out to the pick-up area, I spotted my mom's brown car. As I opened the back door, I was left speechless. I got in the car, buckled up, and stared out the window in complete silence. In the backseat next to me was a basket of my clothes with a single wrapped present on the top. My mom said, "I didn't think you wanted to spend Christmas with us, so I am taking you to a foster home and you are going to spend it with them. I will pack up your things and you will be able to get them after Christmas."

The tears fell silently down my cheeks as I stared out the window in total disbelief. *What was going on? Was this really happening? This family was finished and wanted nothing else to do with me. Without discussion or even trying to work out our differences, this family simply gave up on me.* As we drove in silence, I came to the realization that I would never see my friends again. The last thing that I ever said to them was an angry rant about my parents. No goodbyes. No warnings. *Why would anyone give up on a child after only five and a half months? I was an orphan once again.* The spirit of rejection and abandonment rooted even deeper as the pain of yet another rejection fractured my already crushed and wounded heart and mind.

CHAPTER 19

My name was changed back to my birth name of Jennifer Denice since the adoption was never finalized. *I was officially a foster child once again. I was an orphan. I didn't understand what I did that was so wrong. Don't siblings argue? Don't older siblings tell younger siblings what to do?* I was placed in an emergency foster home for about two weeks until a more permanent placement could be found. I tried to enjoy the holidays, but it was difficult to be joyous. *I had been abandoned once again. Then to add insult to injury, it had to happen over the holidays? They didn't want me to ruin their holidays, so they simply discarded me like an old toy who had outgrown its usefulness. What had I done that would have made the Roberts turn away from me in such a permanent way?* I searched for answers to questions that couldn't be answered.

In my temporary home, Mr. Paul tried to get me to smile by including me in the football games on New Year's Day. He took the time to explain the rules of the game and my love for footfall was developed in that home. It was a great distraction from the internal pain that life was dishing out faster than I could figure it out. *Would the crashing waves of grief and pain ever stop? Was I destined to be an orphan forever?*

CHAPTER 20

J ust after the beginning of the year, my case worker informed me that she had found another adoptive placement, and I moved in with the Smiths (the last name has been changed for privacy reasons) on January third. My heart was once again so confused and disoriented. I was told that it would not be easy to find an adoptive placement because of my age, yet here was a second family willing to adopt me in less than six months. Was this a good thing? Did I even have a choice? Things seemed to move so quickly, but who was I to question? I was just a child. I was very hesitant to get attached to my new parents. They only wanted to change my last name, so I was permitted to keep my middle name. I didn't want my name to change as Mommy had given me that name. It was the only thing that I had of hers. *Mommy, I wish you were still here! So much confusion and I wish you were here to help explain to me what was going on. I was so alone. I didn't want to be an orphan! If you were still here, then I wouldn't be an orphan!*

The Smiths seemed like a nice family. I was almost thirteen at this point. I had two brothers, one sixteen and one eight. Josh had a paper route and, from the very beginning, it was obvious that he was given certain privileges and allowances because he was the first-born child. Trevor was definitely the baby of the family and was treated as such with no chores and no expectations. My room was upstairs along with all the bedrooms and a bathroom. The main floor had two different dining rooms, the kitchen, a formal family room, and a bathroom. In the basement there was a family room, a weight room, a storage room, and the laundry room. Pretty much right from the beginning, I was expected to do chores (which I had no issue with).

My new mom caught me "stuffing" the dishwasher and, as a punishment, I was no longer allowed to use it. From that point forward, I had to wash all dishes by hand. *I was so confused. Why didn't she just show me how to load it properly? Isn't that what a parent is supposed to do-- teach their children?* In the Johnsons' home, Dianne explained and taught me whenever there was something that I didn't know how to do. Weren't all moms supposed to do that? I was so confused.

Mom had very high expectations from the beginning. I didn't think that it would be a problem, because I had such high expectations for myself. *I demanded perfection from myself. I had no choice, if I was to ever be adopted.* She expected me to get my chores done before I started any homework or practiced my clarinet. This expectation was very much a contradiction, as my brothers had no chores to do. And *before* school work? That put me at such a crossroads. For my entire life, school was my only safe place. Her expectations were putting my safe place in jeopardy. Was I really expected to complete chores before learning? School was my only way out of the hell that I had endured throughout my childhood. Even though I disagreed with Mom, I decided to try to meet her expectations. Mom worked hard all day. Dad was a full-time fire-fighter who was on duty for a couple of days, followed by a couple of days off. That left just me. I did the best I could to adjust to the expectations that were placed on me. *I needed this placement to work. I wanted a forever family. I didn't want to be an orphan.*

Dad signed me up for bowling. That was a lot of fun and a great distraction! Over time, I began to understand how the game worked and got more than just gutter balls all the time. Our league had a fundraiser, and I remember going around our neighborhood asking for donations. My donation sheet filled up very quickly. Later that night, I figured out why. I had just gone down Josh's paper route and taken donations from his customers. Since they knew Josh, they donated very well to me, but Josh got practically nothing. He was very upset that I had received a second place trophy for the most funds raised. Josh was very angry and kept telling me that the trophy should have been his, not mine. I felt bad for hurting him but on the other hand, this was my first trophy. I was awarded for something good, but now it felt like I didn't deserve it. *Maybe I didn't. Maybe I didn't deserve to be happy or do anything right.* That was the message that Daddy had given me, and the Roberts, too.

After a month or two, my mom decided that my adjustment period was over and that I needed to start doing more chores around the house. So, at this point I started cleaning every room in the house except the two bathrooms and the weight room. Josh only had to clean the weight room (they were afraid I might break something) and to keep his own room picked up. I was required to vacuum and dust his room. When asked why he couldn't clean his own room since he was older than me, the response was that he had a paper route that wears him out. Trevor was "too young" to do any chores. So, at the age of thirteen, I was cleaning almost an entire two-story house, plus a basement, all by myself. To top that off, it all had to be done before I could start on any homework. I was getting more and more upset. I found myself staying up later and later to finish homework. Playing with friends was practically unheard of. I felt more and more alienated. More and more isolated. I tried talking to my caseworker. She talked with the Smiths. Mom was so upset that I had said anything to my caseworker that she made a chore chart for me to fill out from that point forward. It kept track of which job I was doing, when I started it, and when I finished it. Yet, what no one understood, was that before I began filling it out, she cut my chores by more than half in order to not appear bad to the courts.

CHAPTER 21

When school was out, we traveled out-of-state for a family reunion. That reunion was the most fun I had had with the Smiths. There was so much laughter as I played with other kids and actually had the opportunity to be a kid for once. One of Mom's sisters gave me her phone number to call her if I needed anything or if I just wanted to talk. I was unsure of why she would do that, but I took her number and tucked it in my pocket for safekeeping.

A couple of weeks later I found myself completely distraught, so I called her. I told her about all the housework that I was expected to do and how she demanded perfection with everything I did. If I didn't do something correctly, then I was to correct it WITHOUT marking it on the chart. Her reasoning was that I should have done it correctly the first time. My aunt felt so bad for me, that she told me the truth about why her sister wanted to adopt. Apparently, Mom only wanted to adopt a daughter to help her with the housework.

From that point forward, I determined in my heart that this adoption was NOT going to happen; that I would do whatever was needed in order to make this adoption not go through. I would not become part of a family just to be a personal slave. I didn't know much, but I knew that this was wrong. I deserved a family that would love me for ME and not for what I could DO for them. Unfortunately, I found myself always questioning why people loved me. Was it because they loved ME or because they loved what I DID for them? My caseworker was not listening to me and refused to do anything about my statements that explained that I didn't want to stay in this placement. She kept telling me that I needed to try harder to make this placement work, or she'd give me the "give it more time" line. *Was there something seriously wrong with me, that not even my OWN case worker would listen to me? Was I not worth fighting for? Did I not have any rights? Would I be forced to become a part of this family?* After being completely ignored by my case worker, I acted in the only way that I could think of in order to get out of this home. I started to take things off my dresser and pack them away in boxes in my closet. Dad asked me one day where my things were that used to be on the top of my dresser. I told him that I had packed them away. He actually paused thinking about what I had just said and asked me if I wanted to stay in their home. As tears began to silently fall from my eyes, I told him that I did not want to stay here any longer. I wanted to leave. He told me that he would talk to the caseworker tomorrow. As Dad walked away, I curled up on my bed and allowed the tears to fall. *I was an orphan.* For once, that didn't scare me any longer. I would soon be leaving this place. I would no longer be used as a slave. Maybe my next place would be better. Then again, maybe I would be stuck in the system for the rest of my teen years. I was older now and it would get more and more difficult to find a family to adopt me. I was an orphan. It looked like I would always be an orphan.

CHAPTER 22

Soon after that, my case worker took me to an emergency shelter home until a more permanent foster home could be found. This placement was just over seven months in length. Once again, I returned to my birth name. *I was an orphan. I was alone. I couldn't count on anyone to be there for me. Would I ever be loved for who I am, not just what I can do?* As I sat on a bed in this shelter home, trying to find a quiet moment amongst so many girls, I couldn't help but think about the things that had transpired over this last year. I thought this adoption thing was supposed to be a good thing. Maybe I need to think about this again. *Do I really want to continue seeking a forever family to call my own, even if it might mean going from home to home? Maybe it would be better to just remain an orphan in the system.* There were so many questions about what I wanted to do and how much more hurt and pain I could endure.

Sitting on that bed, I tried to find answers to the questions that swirled around in my head. *Why did others keep treating me like an object to be used? Then when my usefulness had been used up, then they'd just throw me away? I had been used for as long as I could remember. My daddy used me for his sexual play toy. The Roberts used me as a playmate who would play nicely with their precious daughter. The Smiths used me as a free personal maid. The Johnsons were the only family that hadn't used me. Maybe they were the exception instead of the standard? Were my experiences an indication of how kids were supposed to be treated? Was I so messed up that I would forever be an orphan? Was I incapable of being loved? Then again maybe being loved always required a sacrifice of some sort. Maybe allowing myself to be used was my sacrifice? If that was true, then why did it feel SO wrong deep down on the inside? If it wasn't a sacrifice, then maybe it was a punishment. The things I did with my dad must have been so terrible that I'm still being punished for participating in them--for desiring them. This inability to find a family was all my fault. I was an orphan. From the looks of things, I would always be one. I was alone. But maybe, just maybe, I didn't have to be completely alone. Maybe I could change my destiny. Maybe I could make myself wanted. Maybe I could make myself lovable. Maybe I could make myself undamaged, or at least appear to be undamaged. If I could pull that off, then maybe, just maybe, I could find a family to call my own. I had to do better. I had to prove to others that I was worthy of being loved, even if I didn't feel that I was. I had to bury these feelings deep down inside.*

No one must ever know that I was the cause of the evil things my dad did. No one must ever know of the secrets that took place in my past. I had to bury it deep inside my heart and mind. No one could ever find the map to the treasure of secrets that were my life. I would bury them deep. I would put them behind walls. I would lock them behind doors. I would put guards at each of those doors to make sure no one ever got on the other side. I must have layers and more layers of protection. I must be perfect so I can find that family to call my own. It really was the only way I could survive. My past must never be known. It couldn't appear to affect me in any way. That way I wouldn't be damaged goods and then someone might adopt me. Then someone would choose to love me. I would be the perfect daughter. I got off that bed, a changed individual. The secrets were securely hidden away within my mind hopefully to never be discovered again.

The girls apparently had asked me a question, but I was so deep within my mind burying the secrets that I hadn't heard them. *I needed to get better at that. No one could ever know. I needed to be able to respond normally.* They had asked me if I wanted to go swimming. Sure! Let's go! We went swimming many times during the month that I was there. It was a way to pass the time when there wasn't really anything to do except for a list of chores that the girls who lived here rotated amongst them.

One day, encouraged by the other girls, I decided that I needed to shave my legs. So, for the first time ever, I shaved away the baby hair on my legs. My legs burned for days, though I didn't let any of the girls know! Apparently, you need to use something other than just the razor when you shave. I had just started to feel at ease in the shelter home, when my worker informed me that I was moving. *Would my life ever be normal? Would I ever be allowed to stay in one place for more than six or seven months?* More walls went up, as I couldn't allow anyone to see that those words were so hurtful.

CHAPTER 23

I left those girls and entered yet another shelter home. I was only at this house for four days before I was moved again. I have no idea why I was even moved to another home for only four days. *Why couldn't I have just stayed in the other home and move once instead of twice?* The constant moving fed the belief that there was something wrong with me, though I had to make sure that the hurt and pain were secured behind the barriers. No one could see or know about the hurt and pain.

This time I entered what the system called a long-term foster home. As school was getting ready to start and I knew that I would be entering yet another system, this meant making new friends and entering new classes. I was SO tired of this process. My studies were always the same no matter which home I was in, so I always poured my heart into. It was a way for me to escape the pain and heartache that was actually acceptable to the world. In light of all of the changes that had taken place over the last year, I told my adoption worker that what I wanted more than anything was to finish an entire year at the same school. *I wanted stability. I wanted more time when being introduced to a prospective adoptive family. The second adoptive family was done completely without my knowledge and that was unacceptable to me. It was MY life and I needed to have a voice in what that was going to look like. Others were always dictating decisions for my life, and I was powerless to do anything about it.* I left the meeting with my adoption worker with a new sense of power. It was very a weird feeling. I could hardly believe that she agreed with my terms. Finally, I had some power and control over the decisions that were made about MY life. It was a victory for me. I had a smile on my face that was real for the first time since I had left the Johnsons' home. I wanted a family that was like theirs. The love flowed so freely in that home, and I longed to live in that kind of environment once again.

My foster parents took me to my adoption meetings. I had been attending them since my first adoptive placement. The kids would meet with a counselor in one room, while the parents meet with a different counselor in another room. The meetings lasted about an hour to an hour and a half. Even though I wasn't in an adoptive placement at that moment, my worker wanted me to go because I was still on the potential adoption list. I had a few friends that I had made in these meetings. One of them, Chellie, and her parents would have me over for play dates occasionally. It was fun to get away for a while and visit with a friend.

While at this long-term foster home, I played on the local soccer team. This deepened my love for soccer. School became a struggle socially, though academically I excelled. It was frustrating and challenging to make friends, because I never knew how long they would be a part of my life. I couldn't take the chance of allowing them full access to my heart, because my fragile heart couldn't handle the abrupt ending of the friendship when I was forced to move away. Every friendship over the last couple of years had ended abruptly, breaking my heart over and over again. *Did those friends miss me? Did any of them lie awake at night wondering what happened to me? Did I make an impact on their lives, or was I just something that blew out of their lives as quickly as I blew in? Could anyone blame me for not wanting to allow others to get close to me?*

CHAPTER 24

Slowly over the course of a couple of months, I finally started to make some friends. Some of them were just friends at school. Some were from the neighborhood that I now lived in. Some of them were soccer teammates. I even had my very first sleepover since I was taken away from my daddy. This was a huge deal for me. I felt I had betrayed my friend all those years ago, and I didn't want to hurt or betray yet another friend. This foster family seemed to be normal enough that I felt my friends were safe to enter my home. This time there were three of them! We had pizza, played games, laughed at the silliest of things, and watched movies until really late. I was not used to staying up late and, apparently, I fell asleep first.

In the morning I woke up to strange smirks on the faces of my foster parents. I wasn't quite sure why they were looking at me that way. I was then prompted to look in the freezer. That is when I found my bra strung across the opening of the freezer! Apparently, it was a sleepover tradition (that I was totally unaware of) to pull a prank on the first person who fell asleep. I laugh about it now, but back then I was so embarrassed. Especially when I found out that it was my foster dad who had found the bra! Life was going surprising well for a change as it seemed almost normal. One could get used to this kind of simplicity.

CHAPTER 25

Despite the fact that life was feeling more balanced at my new foster home, the walls and defenses that I had erected on that bed in the shelter home were still holding…most of the time. My foster parents were previously married and had their own children. Now that they were married, their children would come on for weekends as put forth in a custody agreement. For the majority of the time, I was the only child in this home, except when my foster parents' children came on weekends. Those were puzzling and insecure weekends. I fought for the attention of my foster parents, not wanting to share their love and attention with other kids, not even their own children. That created tension within the home, but my foster parents decided to stick it out and help me work through the issues. Having the other children in the same home felt threatening to me. It made me feel that my foster parents would change their minds about having me in their home. If I were being compared to their children, I would fall below par and then be asked to leave. I didn't want to leave, so I fought hard to be the perfect child. I always had to be better than the other kids. I had to make sure that my place in the home was secure. We eventually settled into a rhythm and worked things out, but it was still a huge stressor to have them home for certain weekends.

My foster mom tried to help me "fit" in by allowing me to experiment with different hair styles. I wanted a new look, so she took me to get my hair done. I was so proud of my new hairdo! Until I went to school… It was there that I was made fun of and found myself at the receiving end of many jokes and laughter. I had gotten a perm. I used a hair-pik to style my new "do" thinking that it wasn't supposed to look pressed in on any side. The result was a pale white girl with an afro haircut, and now my whole perception of it changed. It was awful! I wanted nothing more than to erase every photo ever taken. What was I supposed to do? I didn't have my mommy around to help me figure things out or instruct me on how to best style my hair, or even to suggest what might look the best for the shape of my face. I was swimming upstream with no instructions in the world of beauty. This was the first of many lessons that had to be learned the hard way because I had no mom to help guide me.

At thirteen years old I started to babysit the kids in my neighborhood. It was a way to make some money for the first time. It was fun to be able to take care of small children. I simply played with them and made them the center of my attention. It was good to shower younger kids with love, time, and affection. That was what I had always wished my parents had done with me, and I found it easy to give others what I never had. It made me feel better to give that to others. I hoped it would help me to understand what it feels like to have the time, love, and affection of someone safe. The kids loved me, and it wasn't that hard to get babysitting jobs.

I had occasional visits with my biological family--well at least my mom's side of the family. I was allowed visits with my Aunt Linda, Grandma Becky and Bill, Grandpa George, Cousin Cindy, Cousin Donnie (when he was home), and occasionally my brother (whenever he was at Grandpa George's house when I came to visit). It was nice to see them. Apparently, Grandpa George tried to adopt me, but they said he was too old and in poor health. Aunt Linda had expressed interest as well, but she never followed through with the required classes. The visits were the best that I could do at this point, which were only a couple of hours here and there. It was about all that I could handle anyway. I loved them all, but I always lived in fear that my daddy would show up when I was there visiting. He knew where my mom's family lived and I wasn't sure if I could handle seeing him in person at that point. Seeing him in my nightmares was enough! Those tortuous nightmares seemed to never go away; sleeping wasn't something that I enjoyed or looked forward to. I dreaded the nights and tried to stay awake so I wouldn't have to sleep. The nightmares were like my own personal torture chamber that seemed to have no way of escape.

School continued to be my great outlet as it was the only stable and constant factor among all the different changes in my life at home. That is why my schoolwork always came first and why I did so well academically. I joined a group at school that welcomed and gave tours to new students. It was something that I was very good at, especially since I had been a new student so many times. I simply welcomed and included the new students the way that I had always wanted to be welcomed and included. I also volunteered in the library as an aide. The organizational aspects of the library, in addition to my love of reading, made this a perfect opportunity for me. My circle of friends was continuing to increase, and I was truly settling into my new school very well. Life was beginning to look quite sunny for once.

CHAPTER 26

I was still being transported to the adoption meetings every month. It was a welcome sight to see my friends and hang out with them for a couple of hours, but it was also very painful. All those kids had a family to call their own (though many struggled to see the bright side of that) and I didn't. It was difficult to attend and hear them talk about the things that I only dreamed of having. Some of them just complained about their new siblings or their parents. It was difficult at times, because I remembered the feelings that I had at the Roberts and the Smiths. Some of them were very similar at times. It made things challenging and difficult to process. I wanted these kids to be thankful for the family that they actually had, but was I thankful when I was in the two prior adoptive placements? I realized that, in some ways, I was being very hypocritical and decided to simply stop sharing my perspectives. Overall, my defenses and my walls held strong and, in actuality, these meetings only reinforced those defenses as I longed to have what seemed forever out of my grasp. That was very taxing on my emotions. I was still friends with Chellie. Her mom, Kathy, came with her to the meetings and she was always so kind to me. One day, Kathy asked me if I'd like to come for a sleepover to hang out with Chellie. I was excited! It was the very first invitation that I had received to sleepover at someone's house!! I said yes and Kathy said she would make arrangements with my caseworker.

CHAPTER 27

The day of the sleepover arrived and I could hardly stand the excitement. I entered the house which was huge! Later, I found out why: Chellie had two brothers, Paul and Marc. That was a big family. The boys were playing on a game console when we walked in. I hadn't seen one of those before and I was intrigued and wanted to stay and watch, but Chellie wanted to head to her room. Chellie and I played all night. We had dinner together as a family, which was something I was still trying to get used to. After dinner we continued to play together until bedtime. The next day, Kathy took me home. It was a wonderful experience that I truly enjoyed. She even told me that Chellie had really enjoyed having me over and wanted to know if I would like to schedule another sleepover, maybe for a whole weekend. *I just couldn't believe my ears! They wanted me to come back and hang out with Chellie for an entire weekend? Hanging with my friend and her amazing family for an entire weekend? YES!! Chellie was SO lucky to have the Rosenbooms as her forever family!*

A couple of weeks later, Kathy and Chellie picked me up for the weekend sleepover. I couldn't believe that any parents would allow their daughter to have a friend over for an entire weekend, but I wasn't complaining. It was good to get away from my foster family and be someplace in which I was wanted. It was hard to express how I felt, so I just didn't try to explain it.

Things were going well over the weekend. Then in the middle of the night, I started to feel sick. I got up and ran to the bathroom. On the way there, I threw up on the bathroom floor as I tried to make it to the toilet. I hated throwing up and did everything in my power not to. After I was finished throwing up, I quietly started to clean up my mess. Man, I was scared! My daddy didn't tolerate such things, and I always had to clean it up before he found out. I needed to move quickly but quietly so as not to wake anyone up. A little while later, Kathy came into the bathroom. I cowered in fear expecting her to get angry about the mess that I made. Instead, she expressed such sympathy and care about my well-being. She asked me if I was feeling okay and told me to go back to bed and that she would finish cleaning up the mess. She even told me that I should have woken her up and let her know that I wasn't feeling well. *I was SO confused! Why did she care so much about me? Why wasn't she yelling and screaming about the mess that I had made? Why was she willing to clean up that mess without complaining?* I was very baffled because I hadn't received the reaction that I had expected. I crawled back into bed with the realization that Chellie really did have an amazing family. As I drifted off to sleep, I dreamt that if I were even half as fortunate as her when I found my forever family, it would be wonderful. That is, IF I found them. Chellie and I continued to have playdates throughout the next couple of months, which I greatly looked forward to and enjoyed considerably.

CHAPTER 28

My adoption worker told me that she was coming over to my house to discuss a new possible adoptive placement. I was a bit concerned, because I had made it very clear that I wanted to oversee selecting my new family. Yet my caseworker assured me that I already knew this family, and that we would discuss it upon her arrival later that afternoon. I stewed about it all afternoon! *Who could she be talking about? I already knew them.* My mind worked triple time, like trying to solve a Rubik's Cube, as it processed the information and tried to deduce who she was talking about. Suddenly the colors all aligned, and there was really only one possibility that I could come up with. *Could it be possible? I had to be dreaming.*

As my adoption worker pulled into the driveway, I ran outside breathlessly. With excitement and hesitancy, I asked, "Is it the Rosenbooms?" With a calm voice she told me to come inside and we would talk. With my foster mom, adoption worker, and myself sitting at the kitchen table, I was told that the Rosenbooms had indeed expressed interest in adopting me. I was so excited I could hardly sit still. As my heart thundered in my chest, I told her that, yes, I approved. Exuberantly I asked, "When can I move in?" She politely reminded me that I had told her that I wanted to stay in one school for an entire school year. I told her, as my heart raced, that I didn't care anymore. I knew that family, and I wanted to move in as soon as possible. *My dream had come true! I had found my forever family. Yet, I have to keep those caution flags up. I must keep all those secrets buried behind all the barriers and layers of protection because that is the only reason that you have a family that wants you. They don't know you completely and neither do you know them completely! It is an entirely different thing to be a part of their family versus just coming over for sleepovers. BE CAREFUL!!*

My adoption worker explained that Kathy had wanted to adopt me for quite some time, but the family wasn't sure as they didn't know me. She wanted to make sure that I would fit in well with the entire family before uprooting me once again. So, my sleepovers were actually mini trials, so to speak, for the family to get to know me and for them to determine whether

I would be a good fit for them. They didn't want me to know the true reason for the sleepovers, because they didn't want to get my hopes up or hurt me with yet another failed placement. They were always thinking about me, and that was something that would take some getting used to. There was still the mandatory waiting period before the adoption would be final. *They could change their minds just like the others had before them, so I couldn't allow myself to get too comfortable. If I get too comfortable, then the walls could fall and they will know the truth. It will only make it harder once they realize who I truly am, what I've done, and change their minds about adopting me. This could all end as quickly as it began. Fear gripped my heart at the idea of my secrets being found out and my dreams falling like a house of cards. I must tread softly and quietly! Please adopt me! I want to be a part of this family! Please adopt me!*

CHAPTER 29

Now the paperwork and the moving process began. In the middle of March, I would officially move into my new adoption placement. I would be enrolled in a new school to finish out my eighth grade year. The process was not easy. The goodbyes at my old school were intense and sad, but at least I had the opportunity to say goodbye this time. I had forgotten what it was like moving into a new school and it wasn't easy: new teachers, new classes (that were always at different places even though it was the same class), new friends, all while trying to adjust to a new family. It was overwhelming, but I tried hard to not let anyone know just how much. But I had started the process of settling in. In a couple of my classes, the new school was ahead of where my old school was at, so I had to catch up in some of the classes. I had made a couple of close friends rather quickly for the first time, especially Amy, as she and I had so much in common and spent a lot of time together. It was a good feeling to know that I could actually remain friends with her for many years--if the Rosenbooms didn't change their minds that is. Life was finally feeling good, almost as if the dawn was approaching on the nightmare of my childhood. The Rosenbooms took me to church each week. It was a Catholic church, but it was church. They had a different way of doing things, but I soon adapted and adjusted to the changes.

About a month after moving in, we were told that my adoptive father Lee had his job transferred to another state. When school was finished in a couple of months, we would be packing up and moving to Michigan. My siblings weren't too happy about moving. I was so used to moving that it didn't faze me very much. However, troubling thoughts still intruded. *Would I be allowed to go with them? Or would I be placed back into the foster care system? Would my dreams die as quickly as they were given? IF I was allowed to go, what would happen in five months after they changed their minds? Not only would I be abandoned again, but this time it would be in a completely different state! Would Michigan send me back to Iowa once that happened? Or would they just place me in the foster care system in Michigan? If I was stranded in Michigan, it would be impossible to visit Grandpa George and my brother.* I didn't know what was going to happen. My anxiety was super high, and I didn't know how to process all of these questions flowing through my head at such high speeds. All of the possible scenarios were playing in my mind almost non-stop. The main question for which I desperately sought an answer was whether or not I was worthy of having a dream actually come true. I had to prepare my heart just in case the answer was *no*. At that point, Kathy picked up on my anxiety and reassured me saying, "You will be going with us to Michigan." That brought me considerable relief, but it didn't stop all of the questions or negative scenarios running through my head.

The rest of the school year seemed to fly by. Kathy and Lee took weekend trips to Michigan to look for a new house. Since the company offered Lee a job transfer, they were paying for our relocation, and movers were constantly in and out of our home the weeks leading up to our scheduled move date. They packed up almost the entire house over the course of a couple of weeks. It was interesting to see how they worked. My anxiety rose as we neared our moving date, but I worked extra hard to bury that anxiety so no one would notice. There were struggles with some of my siblings, but I was used to that since I'd lived with so many different families.

CHAPTER 30

Moving day arrived and we made the long trip to Michigan. We arrived to another huge house in the country sitting on ten acres. It was such a wonderful and beautiful home. I definitely was not used to having the luxury of such nice houses! My parents had the master bedroom on the main floor and all of us kids had bedrooms on the upper floor. The boys each got their own room, and Chellie and I had to share the biggest room. Sharing close space began to cause a few issues. Things started to get more and more difficult with my sister/friend. It was slowly becoming apparent that we were going to struggle with living in the same room.

Chellie had Fetal Alcohol Syndrome and epilepsy. These conditions made it difficult for her to process things, and she would most likely never mature past a certain age (which was different for each person). It became quite evident that I was quickly moving past her regarding maturity and development, and our common interests were slowly decreasing. She was extremely messy and threw her clothes and things all over the place, while I had to have order with all of my things. I could not function within the chaos of that environment. My entire life had been chaos, and I wanted no part of it if it was within my power to control. I even had gotten to the point of taping a line on the floor dividing our room into two parts (each of us had our own entrance door). I needed to have order, so on my side of the room I created the order that I desperately needed. The order around me provided a sense of stability and peace as the constant chaos raged within my mind.

Eventually Kathy and Lee allowed me to move into a small room in the basement. I had to deal with spiders and cobwebs all the time, but it was a small price to pay for the order that I so craved. It also significantly decreased the number of arguments that my sister and I had with each other, and it was convenient to have my room away from everyone else in the house. It provided me with a place to escape from the family when I just needed to be alone because I had reached the overload point. It was the first time that I had a space to myself that no one could invade. It was convenient that no one ventured downstairs unless they were accessing the freezer or the pool table, which unfortunately was in a room that was a tad too small. Playing pool in the basement was definitely more challenging now as you could only truly line up your shots a fraction of the time. If anyone wanted me, then they just called from the top of the stairs. So not only had I gained my own room, but a tremendous amount of privacy, which I treasured as well.

The first couple of months after we arrived in Michigan, we had lots of things to do in order to make the house our home. Unpacking box after box seemed to go on forever. Then we cleaned out the huge barn and the garage, helped Lee set up his garden, planting trees, and mowing all those acres! It was a lot of work, but eventually the workload began to wane.

CHAPTER 31

This move brought Kathy much happiness, as she was closer to her family then we were previously. I had the opportunity to meet my aunts, uncles, cousins, and grandparents for the first time. I was a bit nervous to meet them. I didn't have the best experience with extended family. *Would they accept me? Would they be as safe as my immediate family appeared to be? Would I be treated as part of the family or as an outcast? Would they be like my biological grandparents? Would they be mean or abusive? How did they treat their grandkids? Would they have unspoken rules that must be followed?* Kathy told me that her family thought she was crazy for wanting to adopt another child after their adoption experience with Chellie. Kathy told them that I was different and that they would understand after meeting me. *Would they even want me to be a part of their family? Would they reject me like the other families had?* I just didn't know what to think, so I was quite shy and hesitant.

To my great relief, Grandpa and Grandma were unlike anyone I had ever met! They were SO kind and loving. I kept expecting the axe to fall, but it never did. They were different than any of the grandparents I have ever met, biological or within the adoptive families. Grandpa George had been the closest to these people than any of the other ones. Grandpa loved to tease his grandkids, and it was nice to be treated just like the others. However, the teasing was always in fun, never in a mean way. I'm not sure Grandpa had a mean bone in his body! Grandma had such a sweet presence about her. They were absolutely nothing like my biological grandparents. Neither one forced me to do anything that I didn't want to. Their home was filled with peace, love, and laughter. Was this how grandparents were supposed to be? It was such an adjustment and, at times, I simply didn't know how to process it all. Grandpa was nothing like my biological grandpa, which was the only measuring tool that I had. Maybe I needed to change the standard by which I measured grandparents. All that I knew was that, for the first time in my life, I always looked forward to visiting them. My new grandparents brought smiles to my face and joy to my heart.

CHAPTER 32

That summer we also packed up the van and took a huge road trip to Washington/Idaho for a reunion on Lee's side of the family. Lee was the youngest and his family was HUGE. He was an uncle the day he was born! It was very strange for me to suddenly have such a large family with such strong bonds. I met so many relatives that summer, it was overwhelming at times. My siblings and I camped outside with the other teenagers in the family. We went swimming, boating, fishing, hiking, played volleyball, went huckleberry picking, ate huge family meals together, played games, ate popcorn, and had the family's famous Coke Cake.

This week had so many firsts in it. It was the first time that someone took the time to teach me how to fish without strings attached. It was lots of fun. It was also the first time that I was trusted enough to swim across the lake with cousins. I wasn't the best swimmer (as I had never taken formal swimming lessons), but I knew enough to keep myself above the water and to get by. My adult cousins kept an eye on me and offered a couple of times to go back or to give me a ride in one of the boats, but I refused. Unbeknownst to them, I could not admit to these nice people that I had never been trusted to swim this far before, and I didn't want to disappoint any of them or make them return just because of me. So, from the depths of me, I pulled strength from places I didn't know I had and pushed forward. Afterwards, I felt a lot of pride in myself. I prayed that my cousins didn't see my weaknesses and tell my parents. I was still trying to show them the best side of me so they would want to adopt me. These feelings of a close-knit family were so strange and foreign to me. I had never seen a family that was so close to one another that didn't abuse or hurt each other. I was indeed very blessed to have found this family. I just needed to keep myself together so they wouldn't change their minds like the others had done. Soon our family reunion had drawn to a close, and we took the long drive back to Michigan.

CHAPTER 33

Eventually the honeymoon period of this adoptive placement had come to a close. I had chores and responsibilities to finish, which for the most part I did willingly. After a while, I received the same reminders that my siblings were getting. There were times when Kathy and Lee would talk to me and I dissociated mentally and checked out. I went to the safe place inside, hoping that they didn't notice. My safe place was where I went when I felt threatened or triggered by events that typically brought hurt and pain. My safe place was an amazing waterfall with birds chirping in the trees and beautiful flowers that grew along the banks of the waterfall. There was no one else there: just me. It was safe. No one could hurt me here. While I was in this safe place, a part of me would simply reply to whatever questions were being asked. When the perceived threat of danger was gone, then I would return from my safe place. They were never mean, but the sternness in Lee's voice was at times too triggering to my biological dad's tone of voice. *Daddy would always start with a raised voice and then the hitting would begin. If not hitting, then the abuse would begin. I don't think that Lee would do those evil things, but I must be sure. I must protect me at all costs.* I tried hard to stay present and pay attention, but many times I retreated to my safe place and went to auto responses in the hope that it would not escalate into violence. It never did, but I never knew if this time would be different. I would operate on autopilot until I felt it was safe enough to come back out.

CHAPTER 34

When school began again, it didn't seem that much different from the other schools that I had attended. New schools required much guardedness. At least my new parents had no objections to me being serious about my school work. They never questioned my studies, and for the most part I was allowed to spend as much time as I desired on my homework, as long as I came to dinner with the family and did my chores.

I really liked my science teacher. He was quite knowledgeable and made science interesting. I thoroughly enjoyed his class. I still remember the day he found out I was from Iowa. He always had an open grade book policy, which meant that we could always look at our grades before or after class. One day he passed back our quizzes and on the top of my paper was a note that said, "Hawkeye fan -2," and my score reflected a drop in points. I wanted to see the grade book to see if he actually subtracted points just because I wasn't a Michigan State fan! He wouldn't allow me to look at it, stating that the bell would be ringing and there wasn't enough time. I had to sit through the entire class wondering about my score. After class, he assured me that it was just a joke and showed me the proof. He told me later that he was just trying to get me to relax a bit and have some fun. I understood, but he didn't understand that I couldn't let my guard down. There was too much at stake.

CHAPTER 35

The start of school brought another aspect of my adoption that I greatly disliked: mandated counseling. According to my social worker, there was no way I could have gone through what I had experienced without needing someone to talk to about those traumatic events. Honestly, they couldn't even begin to fathom the depths of the trauma that I had endured. This part of the adoption process was extremely difficult for me. I hadn't told a single person the details of the trauma that I had experienced. Most of those memories and feelings were locked away behind many, many barriers, hopefully to never be accessed for fear of being rejected once again.

I could not allow any counselor to know my secrets, so the games began. I shared surface emotions and events. I talked about my current adoptive placement. I talked about my mommy's death. I talked about being separated from my brother. I talked about the many moves and the different families where I had been placed. I talked very briefly about the abuse from my daddy, but it was just molestation. That's all I could safely admit to anyone. In these counseling sessions I created timelines, projects, and completed some journaling exercises. I cried and made it look like I was dealing with things, but the real memories and the real pain were buried way too deep to be accessed in these sessions.

After a while, my counselor would tell Kathy that I was "cured," and she would then take me to another counselor and the games would repeat. Over and over and over, we repeated the same process. *I just want to be left alone! Didn't these people understand that I can NEVER tell the whole truth? No one would believe me even if I did speak the truth. They would lock me away in a mental hospital for conjuring up such crazy scenarios. I would be considered an outcast and NO family would ever want to call me their own. I carry too much baggage for a family to want me if they knew the whole truth. The secrets must be kept secrets at all costs! There can be NO deviation from the original plan!*

I kept private journals that were hidden in my room that contained the darkest of my thoughts and feelings, the things that I couldn't share with anyone. It was such a huge burden at times but, when I thought of the alternatives, I had no other choice that I could see. So, I wrote in those journals about some of the secrets, the isolation, the buried pain, the buried anger; all things that would never see the light of day. It was an outlet for me to share all the things that I wished I could share with the counselors and my parents. I wrote letters to my mommy, to God, and even to my dad. Sometimes those letters would be filled with angry rants, and other times tears spilled onto the pages as I poured out my heart with the hurts and pain of my secrets. The journals were a lifeline to me. It gave me an avenue to explore the thoughts and emotions that were buried beyond my ability to express them openly.

CHAPTER 36

I had become accustomed to rural schools in Iowa in which the kids were from the same economic status. At this school the kids seemed quite different, and it was very clear that the economic differences played a huge role for the majority of the student body. You either had wealth or you didn't. The majority of the students in this school were accustomed to things being handed to them on a silver platter, so to speak; they really didn't have to work for anything. The cliques were very strong, and they created great divides. I made new friends, though most were among the older students. They were much more mature than the kids my own age. I didn't see the point in foolish behavior or practical jokes that were played on others by my peers. It was such a waste of time and, unbeknownst to them, it was hurtful to the recipients! The older kids had more awareness of the consequences of their actions and acted accordingly. Some of my new friends were on the same bus as me, and those friendships flourished for whatever time we had until we arrived at school. I made good friends with quite a few band members, but since I had decided to not take band my freshman year, Kathy would not allow me to switch into band. She said I had made my decision and would have to wait until the following year. She told me that I could use the time to adjust to my new school and family. That made me quite angry. I had developed friends in the band and wanted to be a part of it. For the first time in a long time, I felt like I actually belonged somewhere and it seemed like Kathy was keeping me from those friendships. I just couldn't understand why she would hold me back, but she wasn't budging and I had to wait.

CHAPTER 37

A couple of weeks into school, I was eating lunch in the lunchroom and found myself choking on a piece of food. I flashed back to years ago when I couldn't breathe while with my dad, but he was laughing at me instead of trying to help me. Most of the time he was the actual cause of my choking. Panic started to rise in me as I couldn't breathe and felt a sudden onslaught of unwanted memories. My hands flew to my throat and chest as I tried to gasp for air, but relief wasn't coming. My friends were beginning to get concerned as I continued to cough and couldn't stop. My science teacher happened to walk by at the time. He asked me if I was choking and needed assistance. I nodded frantically. He quickly reached around me and efficiently performed the Heimlich Maneuver. The stuck object flew out of my mouth as I sucked air into my deprived lungs. After I could talk and he could see that I was going to be alright, I thanked him and tried to continue with my lunch with a manufactured calmness. Even though this incident made me feel very vulnerable and embarrassed, I attempted to blow it off as no big deal. I didn't want to be dependent upon anyone for anything. Choking like that in front of dozens of other students put me in the spotlight--and that was NOT where I wanted to be. I needed my friends to go back to their conversation so I could have a few minutes to stuff the memories and feelings that had surfaced down deep once again. I tried to change the subject, but all my friends wanted to talk about was what had just happened!

After school was over that day, I promptly stuffed this incident down deep along with all the other trauma and just went about my daily routine. I never got around to telling Kathy and Lee about that lunchroom incident. A couple of months later, they found out about it from my science teacher at parent-teacher conferences. They weren't too happy that I didn't tell them about something so important and that they had to find out from my teacher. *I screwed up with that one. I should've remembered. They just don't understand that when I stuff traumatic events, I don't remember them in my conscious mind. Please don't let this be the cause of me leaving this family.*

CHAPTER 38

My parents allowed me to play AYSO soccer in the fall season. American Youth Soccer was something that I had done before, and I felt fortunate that they would allow me to continue playing. I made some friends on the team and looked forward to seeing them each week at practice and at the games on Saturday mornings. I really enjoyed playing soccer and was actually pretty good at it. I often played as the goalkeeper and did a great job blocking most of the shots. It was almost therapeutic for me. As the players from the other team tried to attack the goal and score, it was my job to stop the attack. Playing goalkeeper gave me with ability to control something for a change. Throughout my life, I felt as if I was the brunt of endless volleys of attacks. Even though I couldn't stop the attacks as a young child, playing goalkeeper gave me some of that control back. It was very empowering to grab that ball and then to punt it far from me. *Take that! Get out of here! You're not welcome here.*

In a lot of ways, that was what I was doing with my entire life. I would decide who to allow into my heart and the secret places that it contained. Sometimes I would allow Kathy in (it was always easier to allow her in than it was to let Lee in), and other times I would push her away as hard as I could. The logic behind this waning and waxing didn't make sense to my parents. I could tell that it upset them, but they never seemed to want to give up. Sometimes I pushed them away simply to see if they would push back. Would they pursue me or would they just allow me to continue to push them away over and over? It was my way to check the strength of their desire to adopt me.

CHAPTER 39

After being a part of this family for close to six months, I had expected the axe to drop, and for my parents to change their minds just like all the others had before them. Yet they didn't seem like they were heading in that direction. The fights between my siblings continued. It was never anything huge, just constant competition. I had to show myself as worthy of their love and attention. I had to prove that I was worthy of being adopted. I was scared that if I were compared to their children, that I would fall below par and then I'd be asked to leave. I didn't want to leave, so I fought hard to be the perfect child. I always had to be better than my siblings. I had to make sure that my place in the home was secure.

This constant battle in my heart seemed to go on for months. I tried to prepare for the inevitable: being told that they decided against adopting me. One afternoon after school I found myself alone in the living room with Kathy. Suddenly, she said, "Jenny, it doesn't matter what you do, we are not changing our minds. We are going to adopt you." That simple statement made me realize how much I was worried about them changing their minds. I had been attempting to give them reasons to change their minds. Yet my efforts to hadn't worked. *No matter what I do? They are going to adopt me? They are GOING to adopt me. All this time I have been thinking that it was time to pack up and go. Yet, she doesn't want me to go. She wants me to stay. Maybe my dreams will actually come true!* That statement hung with me and echoed in my heart for months to come. Maybe I would be lucky enough to beat the odds and have the gift of a forever family as a teenager.

CHAPTER 40

Freshman year flew by and I found myself in a weird position. Some of my dearest and closest friends were graduating, and I would be left behind trying to make new friends yet again. That seemed to be the story of my life.

The summer that followed was spent helping Lee with the garden and the new trees that he wanted to plant. I did a lot of mowing with the lawn tractor. It was soothing and therapeutic for me. The monotonous task of mowing was quite refreshing, and it gave me the ability to escape into my own mind and think without the distractions of siblings or being forced to interact with others.

Kathy drove my siblings and I to Iowa for a couple of weeks during the summer, just as she had done for spring break. My sister went to stay with her biological grandparents. My brothers went to stay with friends from our old school. I went to stay with Grandpa George on my mommy's side of the family. Due to the uncertainty of the location of my biological dad, I didn't see or visit with anyone on my dad's side of the family. Grandpa George would always make sure that my favorites were in the house: Pepsi in glass bottles, sweet pickles, Brach's Milk Maid Royals, and apple butter for my toast. It was a very strange compilation of things to ask for, but my grandpa didn't mind. My cousin lived right below Grandpa, so I got to visit with her and her kids as well. My brother would often come over to visit while I was there. Grandpa would take me to see Grandma Becky at least once during my visits. He would also drive me to see the Johnsons. That was a big highlight of my vacation. Dianne had been so close to being my mom that it was healing for my heart to spend some time with her and her kids. I always dreaded having to leave, but Grandpa would be so desperate for a smoke, and Dianne wouldn't allow him to smoke in the house. It was a great couple of weeks, though nightmares still haunted my sleep. These nightmares consisted of my daddy hiring someone to find me, kidnap me, and force me to return to the constant abuse and torture. Being in Iowa, I was so much closer to my daddy that it was unnerving at times. So, despite the fun times I had with my biological family, it made me feel safer to increase the distance between my biological dad and myself.

CHAPTER 41

In the summer just before my sophomore year, I went to marching band camp. It was a lot of hard work, but it was also a lot of fun. I quickly learned that I didn't like playing my clarinet and trying to march at the same time, let alone memorize all the music! YIKES! They asked if any band members might be interested in being part of the color guard. I gave it a whirl and found out that I seemed to have a natural ability for it and really enjoyed spinning a flag. It was SO much better than memorizing my clarinet music. So, I switched from the woodwinds to the color guard for marching band season. It was lots of fun learning how to spin and twirl a flag. It was hard work, but it was something at which I seemed to excel. We had to memorize our flag routine and our positions on the field for the show. The tricky part was putting the two together and spinning a flag while moving around on the field. We could not drop our flags or our band would receive a deduction in points during competitions. I had a great time and soon became a "teacher" to some of my fellow classmates who couldn't quite remember the routine. I was able to grasp the technical skills required for this position rather quickly.

After band camp was over, school started. While I didn't have my favorite science teacher that year, I still tried to excel at biology. I found biology to be very interesting and enjoyed dissections the most. I found myself helping quite a few classmates with both algebra II and science. I tried to do well at writing and English, but it was a huge struggle. Over the years, many teachers told me the same thing over and over: my grammar needed improvement and my vocabulary was limited. I struggled with understanding big words and breaking those words down in order to spell them. I managed to do okay, but it wasn't easy nor did I enjoy it very much.

CHAPTER 42

My time with the Rosenbooms had exceeded the dreaded six-month mark, but since my case was transferred from Iowa to Michigan, my adoption would have to follow Michigan's rules and guidelines instead of Iowa's guidelines. Therefore, I had to live with a prospective adoptive family for an entire year before an adoption could be made legal. As my tenth grade year began, that one-year time frame had come and gone. We were now waiting for paperwork to be transferred from Iowa to Michigan. The process seemed like it would never end, that I would remain an orphan and a ward of the state forever. I tried to go on as normally as I could, but having that unknown element just hanging in the air was very difficult to live with on a daily basis. In my mind, the longer I waited, the more it increased the chances that my parents could change their minds about going through with the adoption.

School progressed rather slowly at times, but at other times it felt like it zoomed past. I still struggled to maintain control over the emotions raging through my heart and mind. I continued to write in my secret journals. It was the only place in which I could be totally honest. The counseling sessions continued, but I couldn't possibly be truthful in those sessions! If I actually told the truth, then my prospective parents would definitely change their minds, and I would remain an orphan forever. I'd be lucky if they didn't commit me to an insane asylum!

Those journals were my only lifeline at the time, and I kept them hidden away in places where no one would find them--even by accident. When things became too much to handle and the journaling wasn't quite enough, then I would revert to soothing myself once again. It was a habit that I just simply couldn't break. I would fight the urge, but then the memories would come flooding in and my resistance was drowned out by those flood waters. After I succumbed to the temptation, I would then be overwhelmed by wave upon wave of self-hatred and disgust as I curled into a ball wishing that the flood would recede and I could forget.

CHAPTER 43

My new family went to church each week. It was definitely something to get used to once again. Previous families didn't really go, so it was good to be back each week. I found some comfort in attending church, yet I still didn't understand why I felt that way. Since I was of the proper age, my parents took me to catechism classes. There was a lot that I didn't know, but it was fun and enjoyable learning more about God, the Bible, and the Catholic Church. My teacher, Michelle, made great connections with the kids in her class. We would gather in her home for our classes on occasion, and she would always have snacks for us. Michelle was very knowledgeable about the Church, but more than that she was down-to-earth and easy to converse with. I had many deep discussions with her and learned an incredible amount in the process.

Occasionally she would have us play a game in order to make learning easier. One of these games was called "Sword Drills." She would call out a topic or a particular passage and we would race to see who could find it first. For some reason, I did quite well with this. The others struggled with their Bibles, whether it was from apathy or simply not caring to look at it, but I enjoyed learning more about it. I didn't understand a lot of what I read, but that didn't stop me from trying.

There were lots of rules with the Catholic Church; some I didn't understand very well, but I kept my opinions to myself trusting that in time the answers would follow. When I completed catechism classes, then I participated in Confirmation. Confirmation is a sacrament in the Catholic Church that confers the gifts of the Holy Spirit (wisdom, understanding, knowledge, counsel, fortitude, piety, and fear of the Lord) upon the recipient. After my Confirmation, there was a small party with my family and extended family. It was a great day. I can't really explain what this day meant to me. I simply enjoyed being in God's presence and felt incomplete whenever I would leave the church. I tried to understand what it meant, but it was one of those things that I had to just put aside in the back of my mind to address at a later time.

CHAPTER 44

A month into the school year, we received a court date for the adoption. My heart was so uncertain of what to do with that news. I wanted to jump up and down and shout it from the mountaintops, but I wanted to keep my composure as I couldn't look like I was desperate to be adopted. I lived in a state of complete anxiety as the October 12th court date approached. I spent a lot of time battening down the hatches, so to speak. I made sure that the secret doors were protected and that no secrets would escape. I spent lots of time journaling with the hope that it would ease the desire to open the floodgates. I tried very hard to not allow myself to get too excited--just in case they changed their minds at the last minute. This moment was a lifelong dream. *Would it finally come to be? Would I actually be a part of a forever family?*

October 12, 1988 had finally arrived. Since it was a Friday, my siblings and I missed school that day. We all dressed up and headed towards the courthouse. The thoughts flowing through my mind were constant like a tidal wave as I sat in silence in the car while we drove to the courthouse. *Would I really be adopted today? Was the search for a forever family finally coming to an end? Would my internal struggle finally be over? Would I finally be able to drop the walls and barriers after all these years? Would I finally be chosen and accepted? Would this family become my own family?* We arrived at the courthouse and were greeted by the adoption worker who escorted us into the courtroom.

The last time I was in a courtroom, the courts were trying to terminate my daddy's parental rights. Those memories caused my feelings to fluctuate up and down as my heart filled with a combination of fear and anticipation. We sat around waiting for the judge to enter the room. After a little while, he entered the courtroom, took a seat behind his bench, and greeted everyone. He asked each person to enter their name and age into the court's record. This was so different from the last time I was in court. The butterflies within my stomach grew with each question. I couldn't believe I was standing on the edge of my biggest dream coming true.

The judge said that it looked like this adoption process had taken a long time. He then asked my parents if they had changed their mind or if they wanted to proceed with the adoption. My heart stood still. Did my ears hear the judge correctly? *Did he just give them an option to not adopt me?* It seemed like my entire life flashed before my eyes at that point in time. So many questions flooded my heart and soul. *If they say no, will I remain an orphan forever? I'm fifteen years old and my chances of finding another family will be near impossible. If they say no, then what will become of me?* I felt so powerless in that moment as my entire future was in the hands of what I hoped to be my soon to be parents. It seemed like time had frozen in place.

They told the judge that they had *not* changed their minds and that they still wanted to go through with the adoption. I tried so hard to breathe normally and not let on how that question had filled me with fear and anxiety.

He then asked me if I wanted to be adopted by the Rosenbooms. Time was still frozen as my mind churned a thousand miles a minute. It suddenly dawned on me...I had a choice. I really had a choice. My entire life had been filled with others telling me what to do and where to go. Yet here stood a judge who gave me a choice. The gravity of the situation was not lost in the moment. I had a say in my own future. In one moment, it felt as if he had stripped all power away from me and made me feel so powerless. Now he had given me complete power to control my immediate future. I tried to keep my voice level as I said that I wanted to go through with the adoption.

The next few minutes were filled with legal jargon, and then the judge said that it was time to end the court hearing and finalize the adoption. He said that since it wasn't his adoption but mine, I needed to come up to the bench and close the court proceedings myself. I slowly stood up and approached the bench. He told me to sit in his chair behind the bench and pick up his gavel. He told me that when I was ready, I could say whatever I wanted to make the adoption final as I brought the gavel down. I sat there turning the gavel over and over in my hand as I contemplated what to say. *There are so many things I want to say, but now isn't the time. Will I be laughed at? Will I even have a voice if I opened my mouth?* There were so many thoughts vying for a chance to be spoken out loud. Yet, the only words that I managed to mutter aloud were, "It is finished," as I brought the gavel down with a bang. The searching was finished. The unknown was finished. The moving from one family to another family was finished. The pain of being rejected by a potential family was finished. I was officially adopted. I had finally found my forever family.

The next few minutes were filled with lots of pictures with the judge and my new family. *MY new family!* Those seemed like such foreign words as they rolled around in my head. My mind wondered back to the past as it revisited all of the families that I had been a part of: the broken birth family, the many foster homes, the failed adoptions. This family didn't seem like they would be anything like the other families that I had been a part of over the last fifteen years. *I finally found a family to call my own, and they call me theirs. I am part of a family. I am accepted. I am chosen. I am no longer an orphan. Or am I?*

This family had just adopted the girl that I pretended to be, the one that I allowed them to know. They knew nothing that had happened to me. They knew nothing about the secret journals. They knew nothing about the secret addiction. They knew nothing about the things that I had buried deep within behind so many doors, walls, and barriers. They fell in love with and adopted THAT girl, not me, not the REAL me. I still had too much baggage for a family to accept ALL of me. If they knew the real me, they would not know what to do with me. They would probably commit me to an institution or revoke their decision to adopt me. I would be rejected once again. That rejection would hurt even more now than before, because I had now tasted what it was like to be a part of a family that had wanted me. I had finally experienced what acceptance meant. Even though that acceptance was not the acceptance of the REAL me, it was still better than the complete rejection that I had experienced up to this point. I could not imagine having the feeling of acceptance torn away from me, so I came to a decision that would be very hard to keep. I realized that I could never allow those walls to fall. I had to maintain the charade that I had created. I would never be allowed to be the girl behind the walls and barriers. Ever! I was an orphan. I would always be an orphan. The silence behind my smile was absolutely deafening.

PART III – MY ADOPTIVE FAMILY

CHAPTER 45

Over the next couple of months, I had a difficult time adjusting to the fact that I was adopted, yet there was another "secret" me. In order to cope with this dichotomy, I had to create more defenses and more walls. *I must not allow any of the secrets to escape the inner sanctuary of my mind.* For the most part, those defenses held in place with only a few things escaping here and there--but nothing major. Everyone saw my life proceed as a normal teenager. I fought with my siblings. I failed to do my chores as requested all the time. I got into trouble--though nothing too serious or very often.

Since I was officially adopted now, I had to begin the process of calling Kathy and Lee Mom and Dad. Calling Lee "Dad" was fairly easy to do. I didn't have any person in my life who had fulfilled my idea of a dad, so that transition was somewhat easy to make. I know that at times I expected more from Lee than was reasonable. I had pictures in my mind of what a father was supposed to be and Lee didn't fulfill all of those ideals. Please don't get me wrong; Lee was a great dad. I simply didn't truly know how to connect with a male figure. I had been so injured by my own daddy, that it left a huge chasm that I was unsure how to cross. At one point, I decided to try something. Lee was always busy with work, maintaining our ten acres of land, cooking (Kathy didn't cook very often), and planting and maintaining our massive garden. At times it felt like he didn't have time for me because he was too busy doing everything that needed to be done. What I had mistaken for a lack of love was, in reality, a gigantic display of true love. This concept took quite a while for me to figure out. One day I decided that I would try to meet Lee on his own turf, so to speak. I spent hours in his garden weeding the carrots so they could grow bigger. When Lee came home, he was blown away to find that his carrots were already weeded. That simple act of kindness was the beginning of a solid relationship with my dad. It was definitely different than what I had dreamed, but it was a great relationship. I was truly blessed!

One of the hardest things I dealt with was the desire to call Kathy "Mom." I had called so many women "Mom," that over the years it had kind of lost its meaning. Yet, I struggled with the desire to call her Mom. *If I call her Mom, what will my real Mom think? Would she be offended by the fact that I had called SO many different people by that name already? Would she be happy that I felt comfortable enough to call someone that again? Would it be dishonoring to my real mom to call Kathy "Mom?" Would it be dishonoring to Kathy to NOT call her "Mom?"* So many questions flooded my mind as I struggled with the desire to call her Mom. She had done so many things for me and behaved in all the ways that a mom should, that it was simply not an option to call her by any other name. *Mommy, I am sorry if this offends you, but my heart must do what it must do. She deserves to be called Mom for all that she did for me; she deserves to be honored by me.* My heart had made its decision, though at times it flinched as the words flowed from my mouth. Eventually, as time went on, it got easier and easier to call her Mom and the memory of my real mom faded into the not-so-distant past. The look in this woman's eyes when I started calling her Mom would forever be etched in my memory. It appeared that I had made a decision that truly honored this woman.

Another way I could honor Kathy was to remember her birthday. I took special care to make sure that I was not a typical teenager who forgot to wish my mom a happy birthday. I had written the date in my calendar and made sure that I didn't forget. Her special day arrived, and I wished her a happy birthday. I wanted her to know that even though I had just become a part of the family, I respected her enough to remember her birthday. The look of confusion on her face made me realize I had made a huge mistake! It wasn't HER birthday, but it was my biological mom's birthday. Her birthday wasn't for another four months! *I just want to crawl into a hole and disappear! How could I insult her that way? It was extremely rude to wish her a happy birthday on the day that was actually my real mom's birthday. Could you imagine someone wishing you a happy birthday and the birthday was actually someone's who was dead?* I had written my real mom's birthday in my calendar so I wouldn't forget, but I didn't label which mom!. After battling the idea of calling her Mom, when I saw "mom's birthday" on my calendar, I had honestly thought it was *her* birthday. *I'm so angry and upset with myself! What is she thinking? Is her heart broken? Her new daughter had finally started to call her Mom and it must have made her heart swell in pride. Then I blew it by wishing her a happy birthday on the birthday of my birth mom. She must have thought that she was second string once again. Would she continue to love me? Would she still want to be my mom? Did I blow it forever?* It seemed that once again I proved that I would be an orphan forever.

CHAPTER 46

In the spring, Mom and Dad allowed me to try out for the softball team. I made Junior Varsity and enjoyed playing short stop. I wasn't the fastest runner, but I did okay. It was the first school team that I had ever played on. Up to that point I had only played in the summer on little league teams. It was amazing to see my skills growing from the last time that I played. However, I still felt isolated amongst my peers. I don't remember seeing my parents in the stands for my games. Since my mom was so soft spoken, at times it seemed like she wasn't there at all even though she was at most of them. Dad was too busy with work and his gardens that he wasn't able to attend every game. It was hard to show them reasons to be proud of me when they didn't seem to want to watch me in the things that I participated in. This made me feel very conflicted on the inside. I thought they loved me and wanted me to be a part of their family. This conflict was such a battle within my head. I would hear the other parents yelling encouragements to their kids, but I never heard those for me. Most of these feelings were colored by the lens of rejection that I had come to expect from everyone.

Before I knew it, school drew to a close for the year. I lost quite a few friends to graduation once again which brought a lot of sadness and loneliness. I had received an award for completing my sophomore year with perfect attendance. Some of my friends laughed at me and couldn't believe that I hadn't missed a single day of school all year. Yet it was something that I took pride in, because school had so much meaning to me. It was the one thing that no one would ever be able to take away from me. Families were taken away, schools changed, friends lost, abuse endured, but school was mine. It was my safe haven.

The summer months brought more loneliness and isolation, because I didn't have the security of school to occupy my time and thoughts. Typically, I read a lot during the summer to pass the time. This particular summer I was also eligible for driver's education. I fought having to take the course as I had no interest in learning to drive. Yet my parents forced me to go. The classes were boring and the videos they showed were stupid!

Any normal person would see the logic of wearing a seatbelt and driving safely, but I did what I was told and endured the classes. Driving times behind the wheel were not the best experiences for me. My driving skills were not in question as I had practiced those on the range, but I greatly disliked not knowing where I was going. My car mates knew the area and got around with ease, but since I had no interest in driving, I never paid attention when my parents drove around town. My nose was always stuck in a book. This was a great thing for my education but not so much when it came to knowing where I was going. The lessons were a bit challenging at times as I had to wait to be told exactly where to turn.

One summer day my sister came up to me and out of nowhere and tried to smash an egg on my head. I found out later that our older brother had dared her to do it. She was laughing, though all she did was crack it a little. So, I took the now slightly cracked egg and smashed it on *her* head! She had a gooey mess to clean up and I didn't. The plan had backfired on her, and in the moment it felt great! I still didn't understand why our brother would put her up to it, but I just rolled with it. I was proud of myself for the great comeback, but I also felt sorry for her because she didn't understand what was going on. She had been a pawn and it wasn't right. I should have taken the high road and simply thrown the egg away, but I was tired of being on the receiving end of countless jokes from mean-spirited kids all my life. It felt good to actually fire back, but I realized that, in that moment, I was just like those mean-spirited kids picking on someone who didn't understand. I tried to get control of myself. I must never allow this to happen again!

CHAPTER 47

My family had another reunion out west, but this year it interfered with band camp. If I wanted to participate in marching band, then camp was required. So, my parents made arrangements for me to stay with my grandpa and grandma for the week. This was the first time I would be with them alone with no other family around. I was kind of nervous and a bit unsettled to stay with them alone at first. I didn't have a good experience with grandparents when I was left alone with them. However, they took great care of me and took me to practice each day. I tried out to be a captain of the color guard and was chosen. Throughout the week, Grandpa would ask me questions, and most of the time my response was, "I don't care." When I answered like that his reply was always, "Brain damage!" At first, I was really hurt and offended by his comment. After a while, I realized that Grandpa was trying to teach me to speak my opinion and not be afraid of having one.

It eventually became our inside joke and kept us laughing. It ended up being a fantastic week with them, and I got to spend some one-on-one time with my grandparents. I got to know them better, and it also gave them an opportunity to get to know me. That one week created a bond with my grandparents that I treasured for years to come. It helped me realize that maybe this was how grandparents were supposed to be: kind, patient, loving, gentle, respectful of boundaries, teaching with love and patience, talking but also listening for answers, and having deep conversations about life. I really had been adopted into an amazing family. Throughout the week I also witnessed their deep love for God. Maybe that was the contributing factor that resulted in such a drastic difference between my previous grandparents and these grandparents. It definitely gave me something to think about.

CHAPTER 48

O ne of my English classes required me to be a part of a club called "Reflection." It was a group that wrote the school newspaper. Writing wasn't one of my favorite things, as there were too many rules for spelling, grammar, and formatting that were required, so it was a struggle all year long. My teacher allowed me some freedom, and with that I ended up publishing two or three articles.

I was in my third year of Spanish. One of the projects that I completed involved translating a children's book into Spanish. I also drew and colored the pictures to make it look like the original book. I received many compliments from my classmates on the finished project, along with many accusations that I traced the pictures, which I did not do.

In chemistry class we were instructed to find a topic and prepare a science project around it. I wasn't exactly sure what most of the possible topics had to do with science, but I went along with it. I chose a topic that was very close to me: suicide. I remember doing the research, gathering the statistics, creating the poster for my presentation, and even creating the note cards for my speech. After class on the day that I presented my topic, my teacher told me that he was very impressed with my speech, and it was very evident that I had practiced many times before class. I just nodded my head and thanked him before going to my next class. I did everything in my power not to blurt out, "I didn't need to prepare for that speech, because I was talking about me! Wake up!! Don't you see that all of those symptoms represent me and my life?" The secrets were so difficult to keep to myself; the weight of them was crushing at times. Yet they must be kept hidden away for no one to see. Many of my friends relied on me for comfort and advice through their difficult times, and I gladly gave all that I could. The major issue was that they couldn't reciprocate that for me.

CHAPTER 49

One day after school before a band performance, my band instructor overheard a conversation between my friend and me. I had shared how hard life was and just not wanting to keep trying anymore. She pulled me into her office and flat out asked me if I was contemplating taking my life. I had been caught, and she had gotten to know me well enough so that it would be impossible for me to lie to her at that point. So I told her the truth. Yes--I had thought about it. We talked for a bit longer and then she informed me that she was obligated to call my parents and let them know.

I dreaded the discussions that would take place after being picked up. Later that night, Mom talked with me and told me how heartbroken they would be if I took my life. As I listened to her words, I screamed on the inside and just wanted to break down and cry. *You have no idea how strong I have had to be! You have no clue what I've been through! I miss my mom so much. I never had the opportunity to really get to know her! Besides all of that, you would only miss the person that I have pretended to be!! You don't even know me!!* Mom was going on about how much they loved me. In my head I thought, *They love me. They chose me. BUT they loved the part of me that I allowed them to see. They chose the part of me that I had shown for all to see. They did not see the REAL me, so how could they love someone they had never met? How could they accept someone they hadn't met? Those words felt so hollow.* Instead of saying the things that I wanted to say, I told her that I understood, and that I wouldn't try to take my life. After she left I sat on my bed as silent tears fell down my face. *Would I ever be heard? Would I ever be fully understood? I don't think it's possible. I'm an orphan. I would always be an orphan.*

The ripple effects of the discovery of my suicidal thoughts seemed to never end. I didn't know how I was going to eliminate the suspicions that seemed to surround me everywhere I went. Mom and Dad tried counseling yet again. No one understood. I didn't know how I could explain why I wanted to die without exposing my deepest secrets that I had vowed to keep buried. If I told the reasons, then I would have to go find a new place to live because my secrets would be out. The internal pain of maintaining those secrets was too much to bear at times.

Since the potential to take my life was no longer an option due to the suspicions that now surrounded me, I found another way to release the internal pain: I started cutting. It allowed me to take my anger and frustrations out on my skin. Though it wasn't the best method, it did give me something else to focus my attention on besides the pain that I couldn't talk about. I had no clue as to what to do with that pain. After cutting, I took care of the wounds that I had created in an attempt to take care of the internal wounds that I had no clue how to heal. The wounds were never deep, as that would draw unnecessary attention, but just enough to draw blood and cause pain. It was like an exchange took place: outward physical pain for the inward emotional pain. Eventually things seemed to return to normal around the house. The magnifying glass had finally been put away, though the cutting continued on and off when things became too overwhelming for me.

CHAPTER 50

Now that I had completed driver's education and had turned 16, my parents left me with an ultimatum. I could either get my license to start driving myself to my activities or I could pay my friends gas money to take me, because they were done driving me around. I did not understand why they would force me to make that choice. *What was the big deal? Didn't they want to spend time with me? Did they not love me like they professed to? Aren't parents supposed to take their children to their activities? I guess they didn't want to spend that one-on-one time with me anymore. Had I done something wrong to force their hand?* I stuffed the feelings of abandonment, hurt, and confusion down deep inside. They must not see those emotions—I couldn't let anyone see them. I had to figure out what I did wrong so I could fix the situation. *I can't lose my parents after finally obtaining the right to call them mine.* So, I chose to take the test and get my license, which wasn't that hard. I could take the family car if I found work and also drive myself to school activities. It appeared to make my parents happy, so I must have made the right choice. I enjoyed the alone time, but my parents still didn't understand. Their choices and decisions made me feel unloved and unwanted. It was just like the first prospective families. I felt like an orphan once again. *I was an orphan and I would always be an orphan.*

CHAPTER 51

As I sat in class one morning, I heard an announcement about a family that was looking for a babysitter. When I heard this, I wrote down the information and followed up on the offer. I actually got an interview to babysit their son! They were quite well off, and whenever I went there to babysit I always felt that I was in a mansion! The little boy and I had a great relationship. After a few months of babysitting, I was asked to housesit for them while they went on vacation. I was allowed to eat anything I'd like, watch anything I wanted on their television, and I slept in one of the bedrooms. I was told that I could have a friend come over to keep me company if I desired. That week was very relaxing.

While housesitting, I received a call from my brother stating that he was passing through town and wanted to visit. I told him that I was housesitting and wasn't sure. Then I remembered what the family had told me: I could have a friend over to hang out. So, I allowed him to come in the house for a while. We hung out and talked, catching each other up on the events of our life. He told me that he was driving semis taking loads across state lines. He even took me for a ride in his truck! It was a lot of fun to ride around in the cab of a semi. After a bit, I had to ask him a question that was burning in my heart. Why didn't he believe that I was abused by our dad? His response was almost instant, and it took my breath away. "If I believe you, then I would have to hate Dad. He is all I have left." I sat there unable to breathe as I attempted to process what he had just said. *Dad is all he has left? What about me? Don't I matter to him at all? So, in essence he has chosen Dad over me--the man who tortured me with so many things that went way beyond the things that I have actually admitted to. He chose him over his only sister. I didn't understand.* As I sat in the semi staring out the window, it became abundantly clear to me. As far as my biological family was concerned, I had no family that wanted anything to do with me. *I was an orphan. I would always be an orphan.* I stuffed these thoughts and feelings way down deep inside as I attempted to regain control. *My brother must not see how his words stung and hurt my heart.* We headed back to the house to hang out some more. It was getting late and, since he would be uncomfortable with my adoptive parents, I decided there would be no harm in allowing him to use the spare bedroom. So, he spent the night and then took off in the morning. After he left, I proceeded to wash the sheets and then made the bed again.

The family came home and, in the spirit of total honesty, I told them that my brother had arrived in town unexpectedly to see me. I told her that since she had stated that I could have a friend visit, I didn't think she would mind that my brother came over. She was so totally NOT okay with that. She was mad that I didn't tell her that my brother would be coming into town ahead of time. I told her that I didn't know that he was coming. She said, "Family just doesn't show up unexpectedly." I tried to tell her that it was my biological family, and I didn't have much contact with them. I never knew what they were doing. She was totally offended that I allowed a boy to spend the night, almost as if we had slept in the same room. I went on to explain that he was my BROTHER, and he stayed in the guest bedroom and I stayed in her son's room. She paid me, thanked me, and sent me on my way. I thought maybe she finally understood. On the following Monday at school, I heard an announcement for a babysitting opportunity. At that point, it was quite obvious that she had not understood. She must have thought that I had lied to her and had a boyfriend spend the night instead of my brother. Oh well, life goes on. Her life was too perfect to even begin to understand the family that I was born into and the life that I had lived up to that point. It was their loss, not mine.

CHAPTER 52

I had to maintain the appearance of enjoying the independence of being able to drive so as not to raise suspicions about the way that I really felt deep inside. So, I bought my first car on a payment plan from my brother. It was an awesome little car. I enjoyed the freedom that it brought. I could go places by myself without having to depend on others, reestablishing my independence. I could never rely on others, and this time in my life appeared to be no different. Having my own car created some independence in its own unique way, and it provided me the privacy that was needed at times in order to keep everything below the surface. After a while, Mom and Dad allowed me to start driving to school. It was fantastic to not have to ride the school bus every day!

Winter arrived and I was a bit nervous about driving in the snow, but I couldn't allow that to be seen on the outside or Mom wouldn't allow me to drive. I had driven a couple of times and things had gone well. One morning, a week before Christmas vacation, there was a big storm that blanketed the area. Despite the fact that the roads were covered in snow and it was still snowing, school had not been cancelled. The night the storm began, I had homework in each of my classes which had required me to bring every textbook in my locker home in order to complete it all. Chemistry proved to be quite a challenge, and I needed help from my teacher in order to finish my assignment. My teacher had a very strict policy and would only allow questions before or after school, so I asked Mom if I could head to school early. She questioned whether I would be allowed to go since the roads had not been cleared yet, and she was concerned that school might be cancelled. But I was very stubborn and set in my ways.

Eventually after it was clear that school would still be in session, she gave in (against her better judgment) and allowed me to drive to school. She warned me to stay in the tracks made by the other cars and to take it slow. I remember the discussion that we had awhile back about driving in the tracks that previous drivers had created versus creating my own as I drove to stay in the center of my lane. My logic was: why would I stay in the tracks of other vehicles if it was obvious that they were set on the very edge of the road? If you started to slide even a little bit, then there would be nowhere to go except into the ditch. Mom told me that if I tried to drive in the center of my lane outside the previously laid tracks, then my tires could get caught in the buildup of snow in the center of the road, and it could pull me off to the side and into a ditch or possibly into oncoming traffic. I nodded my head and agreed with her, but on the inside, I thought that her thinking was flawed. I would drive the way that I wanted since it was my car, and she wasn't there to correct me.

I packed up my backpack with all of my schoolbooks, my bass clarinet, and the bags of Christmas cards with candy canes taped to them that I had prepared for my friends. Then I headed off to school to get my chemistry questions answered, and afterwards to play Santa to my friends. I heard my mom's words echoing in my mind, but I chose to ignore them. I thought my way of thinking was more logical. Besides, I thought I knew better.

I kept my car in the center of the lane, even if it wasn't in the tracks of the other vehicles. About five miles from home, my front tire got caught in the thick snow and started to pull the car right across the road! As my car was heading towards the ditch, I thought maybe Mom did know what she was talking about. I should have listened to her! The next thing I knew, my car had hit the ditch. I thought I would simply go into the open field and coast to a stop. Instead, my passenger tire found the only dip in the ditch which caused the car to start rolling. Then the passenger window was broken by the only rock in the entire ditch! My car rolled one and three quarters of a roll before it came to rest on the driver's side door. As I sat there strapped in by my seatbelt, I could hear the wheels of my car spinning as fast as the wheels of my mind. I couldn't believe I had been in a car accident. I couldn't believe that I had rolled my car. I should have listened to my mom. I was grateful to be alive and breathing. *How was I going to tell Mom? How was I going to get my chemistry questions answered now? How I was going to get out of my car? Why wouldn't the tires stop spinning? Maybe I should shut off the car.* Finally, the wheels of the car stopped spinning! Peace and quiet came-- at least outside my mind.

The next thing I heard and saw was a stranger looking down through my broken passenger window asking me if I was okay. I responded that I appeared to be okay, I just couldn't move my legs. I realized that my legs were pinned and I couldn't seem to move them. Thoughts dashed into my brain faster than I could count to ten. *Am I paralyzed? Is there so much damage that I'm pinned in the wreckage? Would I be able to walk again? My brother told me that the guardian angel pendant was good luck--how could this be considered good luck? I haven't even made my last payment!* Upon looking down at my legs, I was expecting to see the engine crushing them, but instead I ended up chuckling to myself. My backpack was literally stuck between my legs and the steering column making it impossible to move! It was such a relief to know that I would be okay. I pulled my books out of the way and my legs became free. The kind gentleman helped me get the belongings out of my car, and then he helped me get free from the wreckage as well. The gentleman offered me a ride to the gas station around the corner. I questioned if I would get in trouble for leaving the scene of an accident, but he told me it would be okay, especially since it was only my own car that was involved and it was extremely cold outside. So, going against my better judgment, I allowed him to give me a ride around the corner to the gas station so I could call the police and my mom.

The police and Mom arrived at about the same time. The police asked me what happened. After listening to my account of the events, and since no other cars were involved, he decided not to issue me a ticket and I was free to go. He then told me that he was glad that I had worn my seatbelt. He said that if I hadn't had my seatbelt on, then I would have gone through the windshield and would have either been crushed by the car as it rolled over me, or I would have rolled around within the windshield. I didn't understand why he would say those things to a teenager! I tried to push those thoughts out of my head, but it was hard to do. The feelings and thoughts coursing through my head were strange, because as push came to shove I was grateful to be alive. Despite the occasional suicidal thoughts, I was grateful to be alive and breathing. Even though I voiced many objections, Mom took me home instead of to school. She said that I needed to rest and make sure that I was okay, and that maybe in a few hours I could go to school.

After asking her for almost an hour or two to take me to school, I finally got my way. I arrived shortly before chemistry class and tried to ask my teacher the questions that I had intended to ask before school, but he wouldn't budge. Questions could only be asked and answered before or after school. I even told him that I had tried to come early, but I was in a car accident. He said he was sorry to hear that I was in an accident, but his answer was still no to asking questions between classes. I was so angry at him. So, I submitted my homework, partially completed.

The next day I woke up extremely stiff and sore. My dad took me to school early so I didn't have to ride the bus and could finish something that I had accidently left there. My chemistry teacher approached me as I sat in the hallway leaning against the lockers and working on my homework.

He stopped and said, "Jenny, your accident was a bit more serious than you led me to believe."

I turned my entire upper body to look up at him and said, "I didn't lie to you. I was in an accident."

Then he continued on his way. I think I received a bit of leniency with my assignment once the extent of my accident was known. It even made the local newspaper. I had become "famous" simply because I had shown the world that I didn't know how to drive a car on snow covered roads in the middle of a snowstorm. *Never again.* That's what I told myself. I would not allow anyone to intentionally make fun of me again. I had to be above the bar in all areas of my life. I could not permit myself to give other people any reason to tease me, reject me, or make jokes about me.

CHAPTER 53

One spring evening, my Grandpa George and my brother showed up at the house. They had driven all the way from Iowa to Michigan in one day just to pick me up and go back the same day. My cousin had committed suicide, and his funeral was in a couple of days. They wanted me to be there. They were insistent that I come with them, but my mom wasn't going to force me to go if I didn't want to. I chose to go with them. My grandpa even allowed me to drive his car while he and my brother got some sleep. It was my first driving experience traveling so far, let alone driving at night! The drive allowed me to think about what had happened and why I was returning to Iowa. This whole situation had raised many questions in my head and left me contemplating my recent thoughts. We arrived at Grandpa's house early the next morning. I managed to get some sleep before the visitation began.

The wake was very difficult on me. The casket was closed because my cousin had shot himself in the head. I was grateful that the casket was closed, as the memories of my mom's funeral and visitation came flooding into my head and heart. I stepped outside to get some fresh air and clear my head. One of my cousins came out after me. She started talking to me, telling me that I looked like my mom. Then she asked me if I remembered my mom. *Did I remember her? How could I forget her! I spent so much time talking to her, writing about her, wishing I could see her again, wishing I could get to know her better. I couldn't admit to her or anyone that her memory was fading.* Instead, I politely asked her to tell me about my mom. The stories I heard next made me miss my mom even more and only increased my anger towards my dad. My mom had been married to another man before my dad. They couldn't have children together and, since my mom wanted children, they ended up getting a divorce. Then she met my dad and got married. Mom and Dad fought often and Mom tried to leave when my brother and I were young, but she could never get away from my dad. When she would get away, he would sweet-talk her and she would return. My dad told her that she could never leave him. The news that rocked my world was the fact that my mom had had chest pains before the heart attack that took her life. When she had the previous chest pains, the symptoms went away without medical intervention. So, when my mom started to have chest pains again, my dad refused to take her to the doctor claiming that the pains went away before and they would go away again. Only they didn't. Instead, the chest pains turned into a full-blown heart attack that took her life. Upon hearing these things about my mom, I missed her all the more! I wanted her back. This news also made me hate my dad even more! He was the reason that I didn't have my mom around! He basically killed my mom! I wondered what my life would have been like if Mom hadn't died. *Would the evil things he did after her death still have happened? Would Mom eventually have left my dad?* So many questions swirled around in my head and heart that would never be answered.

My heart ached for my mom, and yet I couldn't escape the fact that I was at a visitation for someone who took their life. *What would my funeral be like if I actually succeeded in taking my own life? Would there be people who mourned my death? Would family be at each other's throats? Would there be tears or anger? Would anyone really know the secrets that were stored within my head and heart?* I had to return to the visitation, so I stored these thoughts and feelings into the recesses of my mind. Afterwards, we went back to Grandpa's house; the burial was the next day. I don't remember too much about the funeral. My mind had retreated within itself, and I was suddenly six years old again. I saw my mom in the casket, not my cousin. Then I snapped back to the present.

After the funeral was over, everyone went back to Grandpa's house. People were gathered in small groups as they drank away their sorrows. There was a lot of fighting and yelling going on after a while, and I just didn't understand why family was at each other's throats instead of supporting one another. I escaped into the comfort of a chair in another room in an effort to avoid all the discord.

My aunt came by and asked, "Why are you in here when everyone is outside?"

I spoke my mind as I answered her question, though I probably shouldn't have, given her response. "Because everyone out there is trying to drown their sorrows with alcohol and fighting and bickering with each other instead of supporting each other during this time of loss. How is that honoring my cousin?"

She didn't like what I had to say. With anger in her eyes, she proceeded to shout at me. "You are a spoiled, snot-nosed brat who doesn't know anything!"

Her body language suggested that she was doing everything in her power not to strike me. I sat in Grandpa's chair totally shocked and silent as the walls of protection rose around and within me. I couldn't believe my very own flesh and blood had just said those words to me! This was the very aunt who had expressed interest in adopting me a few short months ago. So many thoughts coursed through my head that I simply chose to retreat within my mind instead of responding to her. There were parts of me that wanted to strike her, but I could not allow those parts to actually act out in anger. I would be no different than my dad if I permitted them to surface. It took considerable effort to restrain myself, but simply retreating within was the best option.

In that moment, I realized just how much I missed my new family, and how much I wanted to just be home and away from this place. I couldn't believe that family actually behaved like this. Tomorrow I would return home. I just had to make it through this day, and then I would be home again. I decided to venture outside to visit with some of the other family members who had arrived, though I steered clear of my aunt. I was told by another family member to cut her some slack as she was simply in pain. I understood that she was in pain and that she was my elder but being in pain does not justify striking out at others, either verbally, emotionally, or physically. *I live my entire life in pain and no one knows. I don't strike out at others-- at least not intentionally.* She buried a child that day. *I know I can't possibly understand the depth of pain associated with losing a child, but I know what it's like to have buried my mom. So, I understand in more ways than she can possibly know. I live with pain and secrets that no one knows about--secrets that often threaten to swallow up my life--secrets that have me standing at the brink, ready to give it all up--many times. The only way that they haven't done so is because I bury them deep within my soul where no one can see them, let alone even know they exist.* Family slowly started to disperse, and the day from hell finally ended. I would return home in the morning. I was so grateful that I had a different home to go to, an escape from the reality that the people I spent time around these past few days were my "family." It could have been my daily environment, but thankfully it wasn't any longer. My family in Michigan might not know my secrets or the "real" me, but at least they treated me with respect, and there wasn't any yelling and screaming at each other as they drank themselves into oblivion.

CHAPTER 54

U pon returning home, things settled back into a steady rhythm, and I was extremely grateful for it. Softball season came and went. I enjoyed playing on the JV team. I was not the best player, but I learned skills and improved as time went on and had a ton of fun. I played infield and was efficient at that position. During one game, the batter hit a ball directly at me; it took one bounce and was headed straight into my glove. I was so busy thinking ahead of the steps needed to throw out the batter at first base that I fielded the ball incorrectly. Instead of trapping the ball with my throwing hand, the ball bounced up and out of my glove right into my face! That was a very painful way to learn how to properly field a ball in the infield. Needless to say, I never made that mistake again!

During another one of my games, I was up to bat and hit a grounder. I made it safely to first base, but I accidently rounded the base in the wrong direction and the other team tried to throw me out at first. I ran back and slid, but my cleat caught the edge of the base and stayed put as my body kept sliding. Even though I was safe, I was in quite a bit of discomfort. I messed up my ankle and my knee. I received permission from the umpire to walk it off. After a few minutes, I returned to the game and continued to play, though in pain, until my coach noticed I wasn't doing well. He ended up benching me with ice packs on my ankle. After that I had my ankles taped by the sport medicine person before each game for the duration of the season. I eventually purchased supports to help stabilize my ankles while I played. My knee seemed to be okay for the most part. It ached every once in a while, but not enough to keep me down.

CHAPTER 55

To make money, I found some babysitting jobs for kids in my neighborhood. It was an amazing job. I would get paid to play with kids and give them my undivided attention. I just had to love them and make them feel like they were the most important person in the world. I treated them as I wished someone would have treated me. One night I was watching two kids who lived behind my house. It was going to be an easy night. The parents had already fed the kids and one was already asleep. I just needed to play with the oldest who was about four years old. After about an hour I could put her to bed. Then the rest of the night would be mine to do whatever I wanted to do. I looked forward to having some uninterrupted time to read my book.

As we played, she started to get sick. I picked her up and ran to the bathroom. As I held her over the bathtub, she threw up her entire dinner…macaroni and cheese. After she was done, I washed her up and then laid her down to sleep. Then I had the privilege of cleaning up the mess! I cleaned out the tub and then scoured it clean with sanitizer. Next, I had to clean up the spots where she had thrown up on the carpet and floor before we made it to the bathroom. So much for an easy evening to myself! I spent most of my evening cleaning and trying hard to not to get sick myself, and periodically checking on the little girl. She seemed to be just fine and was sleeping soundly. I had finally finished cleaning the house and had just started reading when the parents returned. They apologized over and over, but what does one say? Kids get sick, and most of the time it's not anyone's fault; it is simply a fact of life.

Overall babysitting was fun, but it didn't provide the consistency of income that I desired, so I found a job at the local grocery store. I started out bagging groceries and taking care of the bottles and cans in the back room. This was before the automatic bottle machines were installed in my local store, so the customers would bring their bottle returns to the service desk and they would be counted into a metal cart. When the cart was full, it would get wheeled into the back room where baggers would be responsible to sort those bottles and cans into machines then returned to the respective companies to be recycled. There were days when I would arrive to work and the back room was filled with full bottle carts. Though most of my fellow associates hated those days, I absolutely loved them. It was a personal challenge to clear the back room and still perform my bagging responsibilities when it got busy. I would get into a rhythm and those bottles and cans disappeared into the machines as the carts were emptied one after another. I escaped into my own personal world while working those carts. It was pure heaven for me. My mind would wander while my hands sorted the bottles and cans. I had become the master of multi-tasking, as it was the only way that the feelings I had buried deep inside could be checked and managed by a semblance of order and organization.

My co-workers knew that I was hard-working and relied on me to help clean up the back room when I was scheduled to work. Eventually I ended up working in almost every department within the store before I left for college. I bagged groceries, sorted bottles and cans, filled the dairy department, wrapped produce to put out on the shelves, restocked the grocery shelves and frozen coolers, took out old magazines and put out the new ones, worked the HBC totes, cashiered, worked the service desk, and restocked the beer case. I was versatile in almost every department!

CHAPTER 56

As the school year drew to a close, I finished with several honors. I worked so hard in school and wanted the acknowledgement and praise of my parents but never seemed to obtain what I needed from them. As a consolation prize, I received the acknowledgement of the school system and the teaching staff. I had been inducted into the National Honor Society based on my grades and overall academic performance as well as the personal responsibility that I exhibited. I had been inducted into the Spanish National Honor Society as well.

As I sought after the acknowledgement of my parents, it seemed like it was always just a quick phrase of "good job" but that it lacked depth of meaning behind those words. It felt as if the good grades were expected of me. It seemed so unfair when my siblings would obtain a B or even a C and get praised on a job well done, but my straight A's barely got acknowledged. It was like I wasn't worthy of being praised. *Don't they see the countless hours of studying that I do to maintain those grades?* My nose was always stuck in a book, whether for studying or just plain reading. The reading was a way to escape into a different world than my own and to dream of the way things could be: where the good guys always win, the guy always gets his dream gal, and justice always prevails. It felt like my parents were oblivious of the work that I poured into school. Even as I kept up my grades, I also held down a job and completed my chores around the house. It seemed that it was all just expected and therefore not worth acknowledging. The apparent double standards made me feel that I wasn't a part of their family, simply a permanent guest. It reinforced that idea that I was still an orphan. *I would always be an orphan.*

CHAPTER 57

The last two years of high school were very busy. I worked at the store twenty to thirty hours each week. I had a full load at school in addition to college prep courses. There was marching band, color guard, concert band, and different clubs that I participated in that kept me running from one thing to another. During that time, I pretty much kept to myself. Since I had no one who could possibly understand the things that had happened to me, let alone the result of those events, the same thoughts continued to plague me: *I was an orphan. I would always be an orphan.* Being an orphan brought with it a certain amount of natural independence--and I was extremely independent. I had attempted to rely on others and felt that it failed every single time. Due to the circumstances of my upbringing and the experiences that I had been through, I came to the conclusion that I couldn't trust or rely on anyone except myself. Therefore, I didn't ask for much help with things. The maturity that I had was way beyond my physical years, as I had to grow up so much faster than any of my peers. As time went on, I grew away from my sister as I matured and her disabilities prevented her from maturing at the same rate. So, we didn't "hang out" and play the same things very often. Occasionally when I wasn't working or doing homework, we would play a game or watch some TV together. During this time, my older brother moved off to college which reduced some tension in the home, especially since it felt that I no longer needed to compete against him.

CHAPTER 58

Throughout my childhood and school days, I did all that I could to avoid looking "pretty." I didn't want to draw any unnecessary attention to myself that might cause me to get hurt once again. I didn't enjoy wearing dresses, as it would make me look like a girl and, if I was ever placed in a bad situation, it would make me so vulnerable. Thus, I had a very strong hate and distaste for dresses. The only time you would see me in one was on very special occasions that required it or if they were ankle length.

I also avoided wearing makeup. Even though almost all of my friends wore makeup, I didn't. Then one day I decided that I should give it a chance. So, I went to the store and used some of my own money to purchase what I thought I would need by looking at the pictures on the products and reading the directions on the back of the items. I left the store pretty proud of myself for accomplishing something so important with no direction or help from anyone else. I didn't have any close friends to ask about how to apply makeup, because that would require me to admit that I didn't know how to do something that most of them had probably been doing since they entered middle school. I also didn't feel that I could ask my mom how to apply it. I thought I should just know how to do it and thus to ask for help would be a reflection of my inadequacy. It might give them another reason to question their decision to adopt me. So, I simply read the labels and tried my best to follow the pictures and directions.

I felt very proud of my accomplishment and headed off to school. I arrived a bit early and went to hang out with my friends before school officially started. They asked me if I had been out in the sun, as it looked like my face was sunburned. I told them I hadn't been in the sun. I told them how I had applied my makeup. Amongst the laughter and teasing, I realized that I had no clue how to do this and reading labels wasn't enough to do it right. With each comment and jab, my heart was hurt and walls went up even higher as I had to bury the hurt and pain of their teasing. They had no clue how their words were tearing me apart and causing such damage. After enduring the teasing for a few minutes, the conversation moved to something else, so I silently slipped away. I went into the bathroom and scrubbed my face clean as tears silently fell.

I decided at that point that it wasn't worth it. Wearing makeup was not something that I enjoyed. I wasn't like any of them! I wasn't from a high privileged family. I didn't have someone to tell me how to apply makeup. I didn't have the example to follow from a young age. I didn't have a mom who showed me how to put it on, nor did I even know what to buy in the first place. I didn't have loving parents from birth that gave me everything on a silver spoon. I didn't know what it was like to grow up watching my mom and how she "groomed" herself every morning. I didn't question her steps along the way nor did I dream of following in her footsteps. I would never be "beautiful" like them. They lived what seemed like a perfect life. I did not. *I'm an orphan. I would always be an orphan, an outsider that would always stand out as a sore thumb.* From that point forward, I stuck to a little eye shadow, blush, and mascara, if anything at all. I would not allow anyone to make fun of me again. I would either be accepted for who I was and the way I looked or they weren't important enough to be in my life. The wall was in place, and I wouldn't allow anyone to hurt me in that way again. My defenses were set.

Fixing my hair turned out to be very similar to my attempts at wearing makeup. I had no clue how to use a curling iron or how to do fancy things that the other girls were doing with their hair. Back in eighth grade, I thought getting a perm would be so cool! I remembered my foster mom taking me to get the perm and thinking I would get so many compliments. Instead, I was teased because it looked like I had an afro hairstyle that was so odd on a little white girl. Well, time hadn't been a good teacher. I still had no clue how to wear my hair and rarely did I venture out with a new style. I refused to allow myself to be placed in a situation where I could be the center of another person's cruel jokes and teasing.

So, I chose to keep my hairstyle simple. I grew my hair long. I wore it up in a ponytail, pulled back at the base of my neck, or up in braids. At band camp one year, I taught myself to do a French braid. Occasionally I would wear it down. My dad had liked my hair long when I was a young girl. Parts of me wanted it long to please him just in case I ever ran into him. Other parts of me liked wearing my hair down because I could "hide" behind it without being called out for actually hiding. I saw it as an extra level of protection. At times, I really wished I knew what else to do with it because it was so thick. I could take a shower in the morning, towel dry it, and then put it into a French braid. I even slept with the braid. The following morning, I would undo my braid only to find my hair still damp! I hardly ever blew my hair dry because it took a really long time. All of these were issues about self-care that I struggled with alone.

CHAPTER 59

At school one day, around midmorning a popular boy asked me to meet him after school on the stage that was located in the cafeteria. Since I had to stay after school for a sporting event and didn't need to take the bus home, I thought, *Why not?* I didn't know what he wanted but thought it couldn't hurt to just meet him. The rest of the afternoon I kept wondering why he wanted to see me. I most definitely wasn't one of the popular kids, so I couldn't figure it out.

School was over and now I could figure out what this boy wanted, so I went to the cafeteria and waited next to the stage. He finally arrived and stated that he needed my help on stage, so I joined him behind the curtains. I was trying to figure out what we were going to do because I didn't see anything up there that would require our assistance. Confusion gave way to a little bit of panic. *What's going on? Why isn't anyone else around? No need to worry, this is just a boy of my own age. I just need to relax and ask him what's going on.*

The next thing I knew this boy was forcing me to do things that I didn't want to do. After he finished using me to satisfy his needs, he laughed as he said, "Thanks." I tried to collect myself after he left and to figure out what had just happened. *What happened? He didn't need my help. He just wanted to have something to laugh about with his friends. How could I have put myself in that place and that position to be used that way in my own school?*

As I sat on stage behind the curtain hugging my knees and rocking back and forth, I asked myself over and over what had just happened. I was confused beyond belief. *He said he liked me. Then his "thingy" and his hands were in places they shouldn't have been.* I wanted to throw up. I felt so dirty. I needed to brush my teeth and take a shower. I needed to feel clean. In my mind it was as if I was a little girl once again. I wasn't safe here after all. I couldn't escape the things that happened to me as a child. Was there an invisible sign on my back that I didn't know about?

Should I tell someone? Should I tell the administration or my parents? No, I couldn't tell anyone what happened. I would get into trouble for being on stage without permission. If I told my parents, would they think that this was normal behavior for me? Would they even believe me? Would they talk to the police? Flashbacks of sitting between the police officer and my dad overwhelmed me. If I told my parents, then they would insist that I go back to those stupid counselors to talk about what happened. *It's my fault; I should have known better. I should have insisted that other people be present before going on stage with him.* If I told my parents, would they think that I was too much trouble and send me back to the foster system? I had to be the perfect child in order to maintain my adoption status. If I told my parents, would they tell the school administrators? Since I wasn't one of the popular kids, would they even believe me? It would be my word against a popular boy who had grown up here his whole life. I couldn't tell my friends, because it would make them think that I was the type of girl who played around and that would probably ruin my friendships. *No, I can't tell anyone what had just taken place.*

So now I had to get myself together and continue on just like I used to do as a little girl. *No one can know what just transpired on the stage. It must be stored way down deep along with the other things behind the barriers.* So, I retreated disassociating as I went deep within to hide the thoughts and feelings. They couldn't surface or it would ruin my reputation among the administration, the teachers, my friends, and my family. I couldn't control what the boy was going to say among his friends, but I had to control what I could. So once the thoughts and emotions were buried down deep and locked behind the barriers, I pulled myself up off the stage floor. After making sure that I was put together and collected all my things, I walked away as if nothing had happened. I went to a drinking fountain and swished some water to clean out my mouth the best I could, then I went off to complete my homework while I waited for the sporting event to begin. *Normal and ordinary must be maintained so that no one suspects that something is wrong and begins to ask questions. I'm alone in these matters. I'm an orphan. I would always be an orphan.* I didn't have the luxury of sharing with other people or relying on anyone other than myself.

CHAPTER 60

During chemistry class we often had work days to complete the reviews at the end of each chapter. Our chemistry teacher didn't permit us to simply talk the hour away. My desk was in the front row of the classroom--right in front of "his" desk. I enjoyed the front row seat because it was easier to pay attention without the distractions of my classmates. On these workdays, the teacher would sit on his stool and watch us as we worked or he would walk around the room. He was one of those amazing teachers who always monitored our progress and made sure that we were working and not wasting time. There were a few instances when I'd catch him staring at me. I'd smile at him and then get back to work.

Later on that day after school, I went to his classroom to ask a couple of questions since I had to wait for some event later that afternoon. When I got there I was the only student in the room. As I pulled out some materials, he asked me a question that totally caught me off guard.

"Where do you go?"

I replied, "What do you mean?" A look of confusion fell across my face. I felt panic start to rise up.

He continued, "Sometimes when you are working in class, you get a blank expression on your face and your eyes drop down about five degrees and you appear to stare into space. Where do you go?"

My mind spun out of control as it attempted to find a place to land that would satisfy his curiosity without compromising my integrity. "I guess I just daydream."

I could tell that my answer didn't completely satisfy his curiosity, but he didn't pursue it further as another student entered the room.

This teacher was the first person to ever notice me disassociating, and I had no idea how to deal with that. No one had ever called me out on it before. I had to be more careful of when and where I slipped into the depths of my mind. Since another student had entered the classroom, it gave me the perfect opportunity to change the subject back to the matter at hand, which was the chemistry homework, without making his head spin with the speed at which I'd abandoned the conversation. He seemed to go with the flow, though I could tell he still had more questions and didn't really believe that I had simply been daydreaming. That had been a close one! I had to be more careful in the future. This could never happen again.

CHAPTER 61

One lesson that I learned early on in life is that I was incapable of having a close relationship with anyone. Every time that I began to get close with someone one of two things happened: they would either betray that relationship by hurting me, or they would leave me. From all the different homes to the friends who graduated, life continued to prove to me that I was incapable of maintaining a close relationship. Fear would arise in me whenever I felt any closeness developing. *Would they leave too? Would they hurt me like the others?* At first, I ignored the fear, but when one is continually devastated by others, it begins to create a barrier. The walls rose out of hurt and fear. I didn't like being abandoned by others, so walls were erected in order to protect my heart from further injury.

At this point in my life, I had so many walls up and so many layers of protection that it looked like a labyrinth inside my head and heart. If you managed to get close enough, then there was a huge moat that would need to be crossed. That moat was wider than those in any fairy tale! My heart had to be protected at all costs. Yet, a part of me held on to the thought: *Would anyone ever find a way to cross it? Would I ever find that one person who could make their way through all of my defenses? Would there ever be someone who knew the real me?* I dreamed of a time and place that would allow me to live outside of all the defenses that I grew up with and had cemented into place. However, that place was only going to be found in the dream world, and I was continually cautious of any close relationships. I knew a lot of people and had quite a few friends during high school. Some were closer than others, but none of them knew the real me. *No one does. I am an orphan. I would always be an orphan.*

CHAPTER 62

T he week before my senior year started like every other. I attended band camp with long days in the hot sun practicing routines and marching drills over and over. It was amazing the things that we could accomplish in a week! We still had much to fine tune, but we had the basic maneuvers down. I was elected color guard captain again. It was a ton of work, but a lot of fun as well. I had a knack for learning the routines quickly, so I would spend time slowly going over them with those who struggled. Even though I spent a lot of time instructing others, it was developing my natural teaching abilities, and I loved the challenge. Seeing the facial expressions on my fellow guard members when they finally learned the routine was all the thanks that I needed. Those looks were priceless and worth every minute we worked together.

As part of a civics class, I was selected along with a few classmates to participate in a Teen Jury. We had the opportunity to actually be a jury for other teens who had been accused of breaking the law. It was up to us to listen to the evidence, decide on a verdict, and then help with the sentencing, though a judge helped us with that one. Their future rested in our hands, and we had to do our best to provide a fair and just trial and to weigh the evidence with care and diligence. Having been in court for the parental rights determination and the adoption, and also wishing that my father would be prosecuted for the things he did to me, this experience brought me a unique sense of fulfillment as I helped determine the future of these young teens. When we found them guilty, the judge helped us determine the consequences of their actions. Would rehabilitation work or did they need a harsher sentence? Were they remorseful for their actions? Did they deserve a lighter sentence or were they in need of a harsher one?

So many thoughts swirled in the depths of my mind as we worked together to come up with the correct sentence for each defendant. *What would it look like if my dad was sitting there? Would he act and or look remorseful? Would the jury and judge throw the book at him? Or would he get off with just a slap on the wrist?* The memories of all that my dad had done, and thoughts of how the jury would respond, left me pondering the gravity of the decisions before me. It allowed me to not judge too quickly and to remain very thoughtful for these young people. What if they received the right intervention at this stage in their life? Would it make a difference? *What was my dad like at this age? Was he a troubled teenager? Or did he start down the wrong path later in life? Would he be different if someone had intervened early in his life?* So many questions swirled in my head.

These young adults needed love and the right mix of attention and discipline. Maybe the decisions that this jury made could forever change their lives for the better. We had the opportunity to change the future right here and now. With these thoughts flowing through my heart and soul, I realized that we were given a high level of responsibility, and I took this job very seriously. I didn't want to make the wrong decision. I also realized that it was ultimately up to the person standing in front of the jury. They had to make the final choice to change or not to change, but I needed to do my due diligence for the individual before me.

CHAPTER 63

Prom: that word in and of itself was very nerve-wracking. The idea of getting all dressed up, applying make-up, going out with a guy, and dancing--none of it sounded appealing to me. However, since it was my senior year, I decided that I would go, if only for the experience and tradition. First issue: what would I wear? How could I afford a prom dress? *I hate wearing dresses, but maybe I can find one that isn't too bad since prom is a special occasion. I know that I can't afford to buy one myself. I can't ask Mom and Dad to buy me a dress. I'm pretty sure they would just say no. So how else can I get a dress that is modest and cheap? Maybe I could ask my friends if they have any ideas.* I ended up borrowing a dress from a classmate that she had used the year before. Problem solved. The next issue: who was I to go with? I didn't have a desire to go with anyone from my school, so I thought that I would ask a friend from youth group. He said yes. Problem solved.

The big day arrived. Since, my friends knew that I didn't know a lot about hair and make-up, they offered to assist me in getting ready. Before I knew it, the guy from church arrived to pick me up. We did the standard picture taking at the house before we left. My friend was acting a bit strange, but I couldn't figure out exactly what was different. We arrived at the prom and there was a photo station, food and, of course, the dance floor. We did a bit of everything and hung out with my friends simply talking and laughing. The night came to an end, and I was thankful that I had decided to go. I had fun even though I hated wearing a dress! It felt great to get home and to put on my PJs. Over the next couple of weeks, I finally figured out what was so off with my friend from youth group. He was attracted to me and thought that since I asked him to prom that I had feelings for him, too. Oh boy! *What had I just done? Couldn't two people simply go to a prom as friends? I had no desire to date him! He was just a friend!* Well, over the next couple of weeks, I had to fend off flirting and other subtle attempts to be more than just friends. I finally had to just flat out tell him that I wasn't interested in anything more than friendship. After talking with his sister, I learned that I'd apparently broken his heart. He was devastated. I chalked this up to total inexperience with a huge learning curve.

CHAPTER 64

My senior year wrapped up with many accomplishments: perfect attendance, Spanish club, Spanish National Honor Society, National Honor Society, Presidential Academic Fitness Award, JV letter in softball, varsity letter in band and color guard, and an acceptance letter into Lee's Honor College on Western Michigan University's campus, as well as a scholarship to Western Michigan University. I was asked to play my clarinet in a quartet for another school's baccalaureate ceremony with other youth group members. I was quite honored at the privilege of playing with them. We had many rehearsals the weeks before the ceremony.

One day after school, I was heading to rehearsal and running a bit late. The route that I normally took was a long stretch of straight, flat, back road. Typically, I always sped down that stretch of road as visibility was great and I could see any potential obstacles. For some reason on this day, despite the fact that I was running late, I did not speed. Up ahead I could see a minivan with their blinker on indicating that they were going to turn into a driveway on my side of the road. I didn't think anything of it until the van started to turn into my lane directly in front of me! Time slowed as my mind ran a thousand miles a minute while I searched for alternatives to T-boning the van. I swerved to avoid it, and then I tried to avoid some mailboxes. I thought that I had enough room, but I was wrong as we ended up clipping driver to driver in a head-on-head collision. Her van stopped in the middle of the road and mine continued across and came to a stop in the ditch.

What just happened? Why did she turn in front of me? Now, I am going to be really late! I was just in an accident. Will my parents kill me for being in a second accident? How can I get in touch with Michele to let her know I wasn't going to make rehearsal? Did she really just pull out in front me? Man, my car! How was I going to get back and forth to school? Those tires need to stop spinning! I'll turn off the car. That's better. My mind would not stop spinning, but at least the tires had stopped. I released my seatbelt and opened the door.

The other driver was approaching my car clutching something to her chest. With a second glance, I realized she was holding a baby in her arms. She was hysterical. She kept repeating the same two sentences over and over. "Are you okay? My baby, my baby." I struggled to actually get out of the car. I took one step and tried to stand up. Instead, I collapsed onto the ground. I hurt all over and my head was spinning. My head and neck were really sore. I couldn't believe I just hit a car with children in it! Besides the crying infant in front of me, I could hear other kids crying in the van. What just happened? Why did she turn when I clearly had the right of way?

A lady from the house across the street came running over to check on us. She asked me if I was okay. I told her I thought that I was, but that my head and neck hurt. She informed me that she had called the police and an ambulance was on the way. She asked me if there was someone she could call for me. I told her probably my dad. I started to crawl around my car to get to my backpack where the number was located. It was so painful to move. The lady kept telling me that I probably shouldn't move too much and should stay still. If I told her where the number could be found, then she would get it. I leaned against the back of the car trying to get my bearings.

A school bus slowly passed by as they steered around the accident. The next thing I heard was the ambulance in the distance as the sirens grew louder. They came up to me first. After assessing the situation, they immediately put a neck brace on me and then slowly lowered me onto a back board. They placed cushions on either side of my head and strapped me down to the board so I wouldn't move. They then lifted the back board onto a stretcher and strapped me to it, then loaded me into the back of the ambulance.

As they drove me to the hospital, tears were silently falling down my checks. The EMT noticed the tears and kept telling me that I was going to be okay. I wanted to scream at him! *Didn't he understand? I just hit a car with kids inside of it! Were the kids okay? Would the baby be alright? Were they hurt at all? I couldn't care less about me; I just wanted to know if the children were okay. They had whisked me away so quickly, that I didn't get to find out if the children were harmed or not. I knew the accident wasn't my fault, but it didn't erase the fact that I had hit them. What would have happened if I hadn't tried to swerve? I would have T-boned the van and rammed right into the children!* I was grateful that I had attempted to avoid the accident. Still, the tears seemed to flow without end. One spot on the back of my head was beginning to hurt a lot more than I could handle. I tried to lift my head slightly to ease the pressure on that one spot, but the EMTs had secured it too tightly. I couldn't move even a little bit.

I arrived at the hospital and they wheeled me into a room. The nurses and doctors brought in portable x-ray machines to make sure that I hadn't broken any bones in my neck. I laid there strapped to the back board for what seemed like forever while they waited for the results. My head would not stop asking the same questions over and over: *Were the children okay? What would the police say, as I had left before they could even speak to me? How would I get my backpack out of the car? Where was the car? Did anyone else come to the hospital? I was alive. Did I break my neck? I don't think I did as I could move my hands and wiggle my toes or at least I thought I could. I couldn't lift my head to look as the straps were still in place. My head really hurt. I wish they would take this strap off or at least loosen it a little so I could tip my chin down a bit to relieve the stress on that one spot on the back of my head.*

Then I heard my dad outside my room as he was talking to someone. My dad was here. Tears continued to fall down the sides of my face. After listening a bit, I realized that my dad was talking to the police officer. The officer told my dad what happened and that it wasn't my fault. The other driver had admitted total fault. She didn't see my vehicle until it was too late. She was a bit sore and had promised to go get checked out later this evening. She just needed to calm down and make sure that her kids were okay. Thankfully they were fine. As the impact of those words fell upon my ears, I felt myself relax for the first time since the accident. *They were okay. The kids would be okay.* The tears continued to flow, but now they were tears of relief and happiness. My dad came into the room followed by the doctor. The doctor asked me how I was feeling. I told him that there was a spot on the back of my head that hurt from being strapped to the back board and asked if they could at least loosen the strap so it would take the pressure off of that one spot. After a few more questions, he took it off as long as I promised to not move it too much. This brought me instant and very welcome relief.

After some other tests and quite a bit of time had passed, they finally gave my dad permission to take me home. They told me that I would be sore for a few days following that type of head-on- collision. It had been a very emotional afternoon. I was sore all over and exhausted. Apparently, Mom had contacted Michele to let her know what had happened and that I wouldn't make it to rehearsal. My backpack was returned to me, and my car had been towed away.

Later that week, Dad and I went to see the car. The insurance company had totaled it. Taking one look at the damage made me so grateful to be standing there. *How did I manage to walk away from that accident? The car was smashed up pretty good. Now I understand why everyone was so concerned about me! How did I walk away with no injuries? The hood and front grill were partially pushed into the front seat. I'm not even sure how I managed to get out of the driver's seat. I think that accident was worse than I thought it was.* However, I was fine. I had a headache for a couple of days, and my body was extremely sore, but I had no broken bones and no lingering medical conditions. I was alive and I would walk in my high school graduation ceremony the following month.

CHAPTER 65

Graduation day arrived, and I was beyond excited. Grandpa George and my brother traveled to Michigan. Everyone braved the very hot gymnasium to attend the ceremony. After playing Pomp and Circumstance with the band for the previous graduating classes, it was wondrous to actually hear someone else play it for me. I ended up graduating thirteenth in my class of 187. I thought that was impressive, as most of those in the top ten had taken Advanced Placement courses, which were weighted classes, and had GPAs that were above 4.00. *Were my parents proud of me? Was Mom proud of me?* I strived to gain approval from my family and those in authority. It was as if no amount of praise was enough to actually convince me that I was loved and accepted. I had this void in my heart that demanded to be filled. The void may not have been obvious from the outside, but on the inside every praise and compliment I received helped plug up that hole in the darkness. I tried so desperately to replace the void with self-confidence and the love of others. Yet deep down inside it always felt as if I wasn't loved and accepted. On some level I knew my parents loved me, but it simply couldn't bridge that void inside my heart and mind. *It feels like I will always be an orphan.*

Time seemed to stand still during my graduation ceremony. It was a bit surreal that I was actually graduating. There were the speeches by my classmates and awards were distributed. I was called forward to receive a pin for perfect attendance during my senior year. The choir performed a couple of songs. Then each of us was called up onto the stage to receive our diplomas. I had made it. I was officially done with high school. In a couple of months, I would be doing something that very few in my biological family had ever done: I would be going to college. I was given the opportunity to break free from the pit of my past, and I was determined to make a positive difference in this world. I wanted to become a teacher and help other hurting kids like myself survive in this world. I wanted to be able to give them hope and help them achieve a feeling of success. I knew that some teachers really stood out and made a difference in the lives of their students by offering them that kind of support, and it changed my life forever. My chemistry teacher had been one of those teachers for me. I wanted the opportunity to do that very same thing for other kids. After the graduation ceremony, we met up with friends and family for pictures before boarding buses to take us to "Grad Bash."

The next several hours were going to be the last opportunity for our class to be together before we went our own separate ways. The PTA was sponsoring our drug- and alcohol-free evening of food, fun, and fellowship. The venue that was chosen offered many different options for activities with my classmates. There was a dance floor with a live DJ, games, food tables, and free gifts. The evening was filled with laughter as we all celebrated the end of our high school career and all that we had accomplished over the last four years.

Even though there were lots of classmates that I knew, there were very few that really knew me. I greatly disliked huge public gatherings like this and just wanted to find a corner where I could sit comfortably and observe everything around me. It was still very difficult to feel that I fit in with everyone. Quite a few of the things that some of my classmates said or did seem childish to me. The experiences and abuses that I had been through had matured me way beyond the pranks and jokes that they enjoyed. Basically, I kept to myself or spent time with the few close friends I'd made.

Several movies were shown in a separate room throughout the night with bean bags and pillows to sit on. One of the movies was *Arachnophobia*. I had absolutely no intention of watching it because I hated spiders, but my friends talked me into it. This was one instance in which peer pressure made me stay and do something that I really didn't want to do. In instances such as this, it was as if my voice was taken away from me, and I was a little child once again with my daddy ordering me around. Back then I had no options but to stay put and endure the things he did to me. Now those feelings emerged once again, and I felt I had no option but to stay put and watch the movie. I tried to close my eyes several times, but my friends nudged me hard until I opened them. I was so grateful when it ended.

For weeks afterwards I had nightmares of spiders taking over or lurking in every corner waiting for just the perfect moment to jump out. It took me a long time to get over the instinct of looking over my shoulder and being afraid of everything that moved. It gave me an even greater hatred for spiders since that day and turned a simple dislike into an almost paralyzing fear. I couldn't allow my friends to know, but it was extremely traumatizing for me. The night soon came to an end, and we all gathered our prizes and new backpacks to board the buses that would take us back to the school where our families were waiting to pick us up.

CHAPTER 66

T he next couple of months were filled with lots of long hours working at the store trying to build up some money for college. Mom and Dad wanted me to attend a local university or college simply because my older brother had gotten a bit homesick when he had chosen to go away. So, I had to choose something close to home on the off chance that I would get homesick as well. I didn't feel that it was a valid line of reasoning considering that I had only been a part of the family for just over four years, but I didn't argue too much. I accepted the scholarship and offer to attend Western Michigan University.

Western was a great school with an excellent secondary education program that was well-known. I also chose to move into the dorms so I could have a richer experience of campus life, and to avoid the thirty-minute drive one-way to get to work. It also gave me a certain amount of independence. I dreamed of having a place where I could be myself and not have to pretend to be something that I wasn't. It was a very exciting time. Before I knew it, the summer was over, I resigned my job, and prepared for this next adventure in my life.

Once again, I found myself packing my possessions. As I placed each piece of clothing, it brought back so many different emotions: *packing to get away from abusive people; packing to move into another home because I was unwanted in my current home; packing when not knowing what was in store for me at a new place; packing not knowing who would be in the next home let alone where I would lay my head to sleep; packing because I was an orphan no one wanted and too damaged for anyone to ever truly love.* However, this time the reason was so different from any of the previous reasons.

On move-in day for freshmen at WMU, I realized that I was making a mark in the history of my biological family and attempting to make my adoptive family proud: I was heading to college. We packed up the car and drove to the campus. I was assigned to a room in Valley III. We pulled up to the dorm and saw car after car, each filled to the max, lined up and unloading. There were upper classmen there to help us find our way and load up carts to carry our possessions up the elevators to the correct floor. I thought that I had packed so much compared to my previous moving experiences but, as I watched the other freshmen unload their belongings, I realized that I had packed barely anything by comparison. Some of them were unpacking mini-refrigerators, lamps, furniture and other things that made me feel very out-of-place.

It seemed like things hadn't changed after all: *I was still a misfit among my peers.* I had my clothes, my school items, bedding, winter gear, bathroom items, desk supplies, and my boom box. I didn't feel that I needed a ton of things, so I had a very simple list of items for my dorm room. Yet the sheer volume of possessions that a lot of the kids brought with them made me feel like an orphan among them. It took me back to the days that I would pack my things into a bag and stand in front of a stranger's door with a social worker as I waited to be let in. Then I would be shown to a room or a bed and would be left to unpack in a state of isolation and unworthiness as the adults discussed me in quiet whispers. After my parents had finished helping me unload my things, they said goodbye and took off for home. I spent the rest of the day unpacking and settling into what would be my new room for the next eight or nine months. As I set up my things, I realized that I was alone in a strange environment unpacking once again. *I've been in these types of situations so many times; I've actually lost count; I'm an orphan. I would always be an orphan.*

Western sent notification to the dorm residents as to whom their roommates would be so they could communicate with each other over the summer and determine who was bringing what. I was getting excited to meet my roommate in person. We talked a couple of times the weeks preceding our arrival. After she arrived and her family left, my roommate discovered that one of her good friends was just down the hall. She went to the Resident Advisor to see if she could change rooms. So, just like that, I had been abandoned once again. I know that it had nothing to do with me, but it still stung. It made me feel like there was something wrong with me; otherwise, people wouldn't be walking out of my life all the time. Eventually they moved someone else into my room, and we ended up getting along just fine and became friends.

CHAPTER 67

Within the first couple of weeks, I was hired to work in the cafeteria. It was a convenient, and I didn't have to travel for a job. That became very helpful once winter arrived. I washed off tables, took care of trash, ran the dishes through the dishwasher, and I restocked the dishes at the beginning of the food lines.

On occasion, I would even work the door. That job was a walk in the park. I sat at the entrance and verified the cards of each person who entered. The job also afforded me time to study or read an assignment because it was quite slow at times--at least when I had the opening shift.

After a while, they taught me how to take care of the drink station. I learned how to change the milk, refill the juice machine, and how to change out the soda pop concentrate. They even taught me how to clean the nozzles for the pop dispenser. One thing was definitely true: I built muscles working the drink station! The milk bags had to be placed into crates, and then those crates had to be lifted into the machine, all while having a two-foot ledge for the trays in front of you. The first couple of times it was extremely difficult to lift it up, but over time I became very proficient at it. I used to love the rush hours in the cafeteria. Everything moved so fast. You had to make sure that everything remained stocked. I always made it a personal challenge to see if I could go my entire shift without making a fellow student have to stand in line waiting for something to be replaced.

Aside from providing a job, another benefit of working in the cafeteria was receiving free food. Then, over time, I became a shift supervisor who was put in charge of other employees.

CHAPTER 68

L iving in the Valley dorms did have some downfalls, one of which was walking up a huge hill to get to classes. The most direct way was over the pond's bridge, up a dreaded hill, and through woods. It was a very steep route. The other option was walking around the pond. That hill was more gradual and a bit easier to climb, but it was a longer route. Due to the length of the walk to most of the buildings, it was best to make sure that you had everything you needed for the day when you left the dorm.

As a part of the Honor College, classes were held in an amazing building with leather couches that were extremely comfortable. I made some new friends there, and we studied together on those couches. I loved having a place to gather with my friends in-between classes.

Even though I was having a great time at college, there were still many struggles. I continued to suffer with nightmares of my dad. The dreams were always the same: he wanted me back, so he hired a private investigator to locate me; the investigator would track me down and then share that information with my dad; dad would show up and force me back with him. I would wake up startled and unable to breathe, with a choked scream in my throat. After one of those nightmares, it was impossible to go back to sleep. The memories were overwhelming to say the least. It was almost too much to handle. I wanted nothing more than to stop the flow of never-ending memories. So old solutions resurfaced. The only way that I could think of to do was to take my own life. Suicide seemed like the only plausible way to get the nightmares and the memories to stop. Thoughts of how I could end it all were constantly going in and out of my mind. The dreams were terrifying. I would simply lie in bed hugging a stuffed animal until it was time to get up for the day. The lack of productive, restful sleep was beginning to take its toll on me, on my ability to get my homework done, and to study for my classes. Honor English was killing me. I wasn't a writer, and I hated being forced to write a certain way. Because I was in the Honor College, it was expected of us to write well, and we were responsible for a ton of papers. When one doesn't get much sleep, it's extremely difficult to think about the proper way to write a paper. My mind just couldn't focus.

One morning after about two or three days without much sleep, and another horrendous nightmare that had so many details of the ways that my dad would torture me because I left him those years ago, I found myself stumbling into the Honor College. I saw my friend Beth working in the office where she'd taken a job and went in to see if I could get a hug. She suggested that I snuggle up on one of the couches and try to get some sleep. She said that it was safe there, and that she would make sure that I was awake for my next class. I decided it was worth a try. I had about four hours until my next class. I went into the lounge and settled down on one of those leather couches. With Beth's words of safety swirling in my mind, it wasn't long before I was sound asleep. I woke up a few hours later and found that free sandwich samples had been distributed in the lounge promoting the new store that just opened off campus. I devoured it and fell back asleep. The next thing I knew, Beth was waking me up to say that my class was starting in about twenty minutes. It was the best sleep that I'd had in about two weeks, and there were no nightmares. I felt like I could accomplish anything.

CHAPTER 69

One of the things that I did early on at college was to locate the nearest Catholic Church. There happened to be a student parish just off campus. I enjoyed going to church there each week. I couldn't explain why I felt so at peace there, but I did. The only bad thing was that the peaceful feelings never seemed to last all week. I joined the choir and found myself at the church multiple times a week. I would even read the Scriptures during mass on Sunday. The feelings that were kindled within me when doing these readings were difficult to articulate within my mind and heart. I simply didn't understand. All I knew was that it was a good feeling, so I wanted to continue reading them.

Our choir ended up doing a couple of recordings. I was going to be "famous!" Well, maybe not famous, but my name would be on the label of an album! That would be something that I could look back on later in life with a great sense of pride.

While walking throughout the campus, I would see these sidewalk writings that said *InterVarsity, Check it out!* This referred to InterVarsity Christian Fellowship. As I walked over those chalk messages repeatedly, I became curious as to what it meant. I felt a pull to know more about it. However, my mind kept repeating the same single thought over and over: *It's for Christians and I'm Catholic.* I thought it wasn't for people like me, so I simply dismissed it.

CHAPTER 70

T he memories were still running rampant in my head, and I was struggling to keep them under control. This season of my life I had so much alone time that the walls would come down, and the memories would come rushing at me. Then when it was time to interact with others, it would be difficult to put those barriers back into place. I was all over the place. The suicidal thoughts were almost uncontrollable when I was alone in my room. My mind had been going and going all day and when I made it back to the dorm, it was shut down time for any higher level of thinking. The protective gates of my mind were overpowered by the memories of the evil things that had happened to me.

Among all those memories, my mind just couldn't release one important thing, my mom. *Who was she? What exactly happened to her? It was my fault that she was dead. If I had just prevented her from sitting down, then she would still be here. I need to know more about her. I want to be just like her.* It was an idolization that was unquenchable. All the while these thoughts were going on, the suicidal thoughts were continuing.

My RA--Resident Advisor--and I had become friends, and we had many discussions about life and college. During one of those conversations, the defenses fell just long enough to mention the suicidal thoughts that ran rampant at times in my head. The RA was under obligation to inform the dorm supervisor. I was called into her office one day to discuss the situation. She told me that if I continued with these thoughts, then I would not be allowed to stay in the dorm as it was too high of a risk. Then she asked me a question.

"Why do you want to die?" My answer was quite simple: to find out who my mom was so I could be just like her. The next question that the supervisor asked me really made me think more than any other.

"After you discovered who she was, where would you be like her? You would be dead."

She just punched the biggest hole into my thinking that I couldn't plug no matter how hard I tried. She was absolutely right. I sat there with my mind racing a mile a minute as I tried to figure out a response. Then she asked me to tell her about my mom. I told her how she died, and how it was my fault that she was dead. She then asked me another question that punched a humongous hole into my thinking that had been in place for years.

"If your mom was having a heart attack, medically speaking, what difference would it make if she was sitting or standing?"

My response was, "I guess only the distance that one would fall before hitting the ground."

I was blown away. She has just totally dismantled the thinking that had placed mounds of guilt and blame on a little girl so many years ago. *It wasn't my fault that Mommy had died? It wasn't my fault!* I left that office a different person. I had to promise to stop talking about suicide.

I kept replaying those two questions over and over. *If I was dead, then where would I be like my mom? If your mom was having a heart attack, medically speaking, what difference would it make if she was sitting or standing?* That conversation had unlocked such freedom for my tortured mind—so much freedom from the constant torment of the voices within my head telling me that it was my fault Mom died. I slept very soundly that night as a blanket of guilt and shame had lifted. Deep in my heart, I knew that there were still a lot of memories that would require my attention, but for now I would simply relish in the layer of freedom that I had experienced.

CHAPTER 71

That freedom only seemed to last for a small period of time. Even though there was relief from the guilt of my mom dying, it did nothing to relieve the unreconciled memories that flowed without regard to my well-being or my schedule. One evening, I couldn't take much more and I decided that I needed to clear my head, so I took off for a run through campus. I ran all the way to Miller Auditorium on the complete opposite side of campus and back. Upon my return, my friends were upset with me because it was night, and I could have been hurt. I was mad at myself as I could barely walk because I had pushed myself beyond physical limitations. My old injury from high school and the previous year had acted up, and my knee was killing me. I had a friend get some ice for me, and I proceeded to ice my knee as I focused on some homework.

That night I decided it was time to place tighter reins on my mind. I needed to install even more walls and security layers. These memories needed to stop, and the only way that I could do that would be to add walls and layers of protection. I could not allow my mind to continue to run free without restraint. I may have been on a huge campus where not many people knew me, but I still had to focus on the reason that I was there. I finally found the freedom from the memories that I was looking for. When one would occasionally push past the barriers and sneak its way through the layers of defense, I would attempt to deal with it. If it was too painful, then I would cut my arm to ease the emotional pain. It was a transfer from the emotional to the physical. That seemed to help quite a bit. Even though the suicidal thoughts never went away, I did stop talking about them as I had been doing. Those thoughts were always in the back of my mind as a way to finally end the pain once and for all. If things got too bad, then it would be something to resort to, but no one would be warned about it.

CHAPTER 72

My coping methods had allowed me to make it through my first year of college. I moved back home for the summer. I found a job at K-Mart. My mom worked as a pharmaceutical technician there, and I became a cashier. I was able to save money for my return to college. There was one part of my training that really stood out to me. They told us that the perfect way to spot a counterfeit bill was not to study the types of counterfeit methods but to study the real thing, so when you ran across something that wasn't the real thing, it would stick out. That statement struck me in so many different ways. You study the real thing so that when a fake is presented you know right away that it's not genuine.

One day I finished ringing up a customer's purchases, and they went to pay for their order with cash. They handed me a twenty-dollar bill. I went to put it into my register when I noticed that it seemed different. I looked at it and checked for the security features that proved it was a real bill. The customer finally asked what was wrong with their money; I told them that it didn't appear to be real. They took it back and examined it. They said that it was an older version and that they wanted to keep it. So, they paid with a different bill. Whether it was an older version of a bill or counterfeit, my training had paid off. That lesson stayed with me; it would be something that I would never forget.

CHAPTER 73

Summer went by way too fast and soon I found myself packing for my sophomore year of college. I would be moving back into Valley III and would be working back in the cafeteria. I was on a different floor of the dorm this year. There was a new feeling on this floor than what I experienced the prior year that was hard to explain. I knew that something was different, but I couldn't put my finger on it. I chalked it up to the fact that I was now surrounded by students who were a little bit more experienced, but it still felt odd. A few months later, I would know the difference in the students that resided on this floor.

I started back at my job in the cafeteria as a supervisor. I worked closely with the director and the union workers who prepared and served the food on the lines. They taught me how to prepare the scrambled eggs, and it was a lot of fun using the huge stove. Often on Saturday mornings when there weren't quite as many union workers on duty, it would be my job to make the eggs and ultimately to teach some of my workers how to prepare them.

The workers even showed me a card game that they played on their breaks. It was called "Hand-n-Foot" and was difficult to pick up when I only had three or four minutes at a time. Eventually, after I figured it out, it became one of my favorite games. I loved the strategy--and luck--that went into the game. The only downfall was that it took many people to play, typically six. Then you played with seven decks of cards. On really slow days, I would sneak in a couple of hands with them in-between my responsibilities. Though it was not a quick game, it was a great one that allowed for lots of conversation and laughter.

CHAPTER 74

I went back to the student parish on campus. It felt good to be back in the church with so many young people in it. There were so many things, though, that I simply didn't understand. *How could I feel so whole while at church, yet the moment I left the doors I felt so empty and alone?* This question haunted me. It made no sense to me. *How could a simple building create such strong emotions, such relief for my troubled soul? Why did that peace leave after I was away from the building?*

Classes started out pretty well. One thing was definitely true: I loved math and science and greatly disliked English and writing papers. It is a good thing that I was studying to be a high school teacher focusing on math with a minor in chemistry. As I walked to my classes every day, I kept seeing those chalk writings on the sidewalk about InterVarsity Christian Fellowship. The messages kept grabbing my attention. One day I decided that I was going to stop by on a Thursday evening and check it out.

When I arrived at the meeting, there were a lot of college students there, including some of my floor-mates from the dorms. I sat with some of them as the meeting got underway. Even though there were a lot of people, I felt so alone. *What was I doing here?* Apparently, this was the first meeting of the year, and everyone was catching up with each other from the summer. The meeting began with everyone singing some songs. I hadn't heard of most of them, so I simply listened. Then a speaker got up who used the Bible to teach us a short message. Afterwards, there was some fellowship and mingling while everyone took time to sign up for small group Bible studies around campus throughout the week. Since I was having a good time, I decided that I would try a small group. I figured that if I didn't like it, I would simply stop going. I joined a group that met in my dorm once a week.

CHAPTER 75

I was very nervous when I went to the first Bible study meeting. There were a couple of people from my floor and others I didn't know. I happened to sit right next to the leader. He asked us to go around the circle and state our name, when we became a Christian, how we became a Christian, and what we wanted to get out of our Bible study. He gave us a couple of minutes to think about our responses and then, since I was new to him, he started with the person on his right. I listened as each person spoke. It was difficult to process what they were all talking about. They described a specific time and place that they became a Christian. Their answers highly confused me. *Was I actually a Christian? Could a Catholic be a Christian? Why did they talk like Jesus was one of their best friends? The personal relationship that they described with Jesus was confusing to me.* By the time it was my turn to speak, I completely changed my answer from what I had written down. Figuring that honesty was the best policy, I decided to tell them that my answers had changed completely after hearing their responses. Their responses made me question whether I was "saved." I didn't even know what that meant. I had not experienced a conversion experience that they all had described. I guess I wanted to simply find out what they were all referring to and get to know more about the Bible. My church never encouraged us to read the Bible, so this would be a completely new experience for me all the way around. The group asked one favor of me: if they used words that I didn't understand, that I would ask for clarification of what they meant. I figured that I could do that.

As the weeks progressed in our small group, I interrupted numerous times asking for clarification on things that I didn't understand. After a while I started to feel guilty for interrupting so much, but they reassured me that it was good for them to explain and remember the foundation of their beliefs.

In addition to attending weekly Bible study meetings, I was also attending the weekly large group sessions. They had the same basic format as the first meeting that I attended. One week during large group the speaker did something that seemed a bit strange to me. After he finished teaching, he asked if there was anyone in the room who wanted to have a personal relationship with Jesus. I remember sitting there feeling as if he was looking straight at me and talking to only me. The thoughts that went flying through my brain at that point in time were extremely rapid. *Was he talking just to me? Do I want that relationship with Jesus? Will it really make a difference in my life? Is this the reason the peace was with me at church but not outside the building? Was Jesus the answer? Can He really be trusted? If I said yes, would I then be able to maintain that peace everywhere I went? What would happen within my walls if I invited him in? Would He dismantle my walls and my defenses? Would I even need those defenses anymore? What would other people think if I raised my hand? Oh well, I missed the opportunity, the speaker was moving on.* Maybe next time I'll be ready to raise my hand. Wait! The speaker asked again. He said that he felt like there was someone sitting on the fence and was hesitant to come forward, but that he was going to wait a few minutes more. I decided that he was talking about me. I very shyly raised my hand. Then he asked us to stand and follow him as he prayed. I hadn't talked to God before, so that was new to me. I had been in church for years, but I had never prayed like he did.

Afterwards, my entire small group approached me and congratulated me. They told me that if I had looked around at all during the invitation, then I would have seen every single one of them with their heads bowed praying for me! I didn't know what to say. I felt so important and special, yet that was conflicting with what I was told my entire life. *I was an orphan and I'd always be an orphan. So how would this decision affect those thoughts?* The internal peace was overwhelming. I had never experienced the peace that I felt at that exact moment.

Later that night when I was alone in my room, the peace still remained. *What had happened? How did praying one simple prayer bring such peace? How would it affect the memories? Would it make a difference if I let down my defenses and my barriers? I better not take any chances with that one! It had taken me too long to finally get a handle on all those memories and to place them all behind strong defensive barriers. It was something that I simply couldn't risk. In the meantime, I would enjoy the freedom that I now had within me.* I fell into a deep and peaceful sleep with a smile on my face completely unafraid. When I awoke the following morning for class, there was a bounce in my step and a joy that couldn't be explained in words.

CHAPTER 76

One of my coworkers in the cafeteria asked me out on a date. He wanted to take me to a performance at Miller Auditorium on campus. I thought it might be fun, so I said yes. He said that he would pick me up, and we would go to dinner first, and then to the performance. I was pretty excited and, as the day approached, my friends helped me get ready. They talked me into putting on a dress, despite my great distaste for them. Then my friends helped me put some makeup on. We took extra time with my hair by curling it so I would have long curls that draped past my shoulders, as my coworker had only seen me with my hair up in ponytails or braids because of work. I slipped on my high heels and then proceeded down to the lobby to wait.

I waited for almost fifteen minutes as my date was very late. Not a very good first impression! He walked in and his jaw dropped and so did mine. He was blown away with how beautiful I looked and kept repeating the same remarks over and over. I was blown away as well. Here I was all dressed up to attend an event at Miller Auditorium, and he arrived in jeans, boots, and a sweater! I was SO overdressed compared to him but had no time to change as we would never make the performance if I did.

We walked out to his car and he opened the door for me. I was blown away once again. His car was a mess!! He had trash everywhere, and I had no choice but to smile nicely and get in. I attempted to find a place to put my feet among the trash on the floor. I wasn't sure where he was taking me for dinner, but I was still kind of excited. The next thing I knew, we had pulled into McDonald's parking lot. *Was he really taking me to McDonald's for dinner? Could this evening get any worse? Mind you, I was a college student and I liked McDonald's--but for a date?* I was screaming in total disbelief on the inside but put a smile on my face and attempted to enjoy myself. We went into McDonald's and, as we waited for our food, all the patrons kept staring at me. They were probably wondering why I was so dressed up. Mind you, I was the ONLY one dressed up in the entire restaurant! My shoes echoed through the lobby with every step that I took, which only drew more attention to us. I ate my food wondering what everyone was thinking. I simply could not wait for the meal to be finished so we could leave. That moment finally arrived and we left for Miller Auditorium.

He pulled up and noticed the huge lines of traffic and decided that he knew a short cut that would get us closer to the doors. He turned off on a deserted road and headed to some parking lot on a different side of Miller Auditorium. He parked and I opened my door to get out. I had no idea where we were and had no choice but to follow him. He started trudging through the snow towards the back door of the auditorium completely unaware that I was in dress shoes and freezing! What a sight we must have been: a boy with boots, jeans, and a heavy coat creating a path through the deep snow with a girl behind him in a dress and high heels with just a light weight coat on. We trudged through the snow, ducking under tree branches here and there, for about ten minutes, as the distance between us grew because he didn't even think to stop and assist me. By the time we arrived at the doors, we were late and I was freezing and shivering. My stockings were soaked and I couldn't feel my feet. I had almost lost my shoes in the deep snow multiple times and my hair was a mess as it had snagged on a couple of trees along the way.

I don't even remember the performance. All I could think about was the heat that was slowing returning to my body, and the fact that I would have to go back the same way in order to return to his car after the performance was over! When he dropped me off at the dorms, all I could think of as I headed up to my room was that it was the date from hell! My friends all wanted the lowdown on my evening, and we had quite a few laughs as I told them about it. The next day, this coworker said to me, "I feel like I messed up really bad. Would you give me another chance?" I politely declined as the voices in my head screamed, *There's no way in hell I'm going out with you again!* Things were a little awkward for a few days at work, and then they settled back into a rhythm as if nothing had happened.

CHAPTER 77

In-between my classes, I spent all my extra time reading the Bible. I was drawn to the Bible like two magnets are drawn to each other; I simply couldn't stop reading the words on those pages. I found so many incredible things there. My life had completely changed when I accepted Jesus into my heart. I was joyful, content, and happy for the first time in a very long time. I started attending daily prayer meetings with InterVarsity. I'd come bounding in and immediately start sharing about all of the things that I had read in the Bible. It was simply so exciting to me that I couldn't help but tell others about it. Others told me that my excitement was contagious, and they were always smiling and laughing when I would come into those meetings. It reminded them that reading the Bible was important and that they needed to do more of it.

One afternoon it was raining pretty hard outside and my friends wanted to play in the rain. I had never played in the rain. As a child, I was told that it would make me sick or I'd get in trouble, so I never played in the rain. They asked one more time and I decided *why not?* I went outside with them. We laughed as we ran through the rain and jumped in the puddles and danced together.

About thirty minutes later, absolutely soaked to the bone, we went back inside. I jumped into a warm shower and then snuggled up in bed with my Bible and read. My roommate didn't understand why I was spending so much time studying the Bible instead of my schoolwork, because she never saw me study for school. I did my homework and I attended my classes and took notes, but other than that I was reading and studying the Bible. Even though I didn't study much for my tests and exams, I still received excellent marks that semester! In regard to my faith, I was learning and growing so much. I had an insatiable hunger for the things of God.

CHAPTER 78

I continued to attend the Catholic Church on campus. I was a part of the student group and was active in the choir. As my knowledge of God continued to grow my questions increased as well. My small group leaders were awesome and helped answer a lot of them as they came up. Yet there were some questions that simply couldn't be answered by them, and I knew that I couldn't ask them those questions.

One of my small group members, Jenny, started meeting with me one-on-one each week. She showed me how to read the Bible and find answers to my questions within its pages. I looked forward to these meetings, as I was learning faster than my mind could keep up. We got along very well and had many in-depth conversations over the weeks. As I studied the things that I read in the Bible, I found that they were conflicting with the beliefs of my church and it was beginning to bother me. I began to question the foundation beliefs of my church and why we were expected to do certain sacraments. *Why did I need to go to confession? Why did I need to tell a priest the things that I did wrong? Why not simply talk directly to God? Why did I have to say this many "Our Fathers" and this many "Hail Marys" to be forgiven? The Bible never mentions having to do those things in order to be forgiven. It states that I simply ask and He forgives. How could the communion elements actually become the actual body and blood of Jesus? Wasn't it something that we were to do as a reminder of the sacrifice that Jesus made for us?* I kept reading and studying the Bible to see if I could find answers.

After a while I decided to make an appointment with one of the priests at church and ask him my questions directly. I asked him why I had to participate in confession and why I would have to say X number of prayers in order to obtain forgiveness? I told him that the Bible says that we can go directly to the Father in prayer and ask for forgiveness, and that when I ask He forgives. Saying five "Our Fathers" and ten "Hail Marys" was almost like I was "earning" my forgiveness. It was as if I had to do those things in order to be forgiven. The Bible states nothing of the sort! Why go through a middle man when I could go directly to the Father? These things made no sense to me.

The priest told me that confession wasn't mandatory. The frequency of confessions that the church calls for is simply a guideline to help people examine their hearts. The act of confession was because some people were afraid to talk directly to God, and it was easier to speak to a "middle man." In regard to the prayers that we would be told to say, it was a way for people to feel that they were forgiven. I argued with him! We can't EARN our forgiveness--that is why Jesus came in the first place! So, it is actually deceitful to make the people believe that by saying prayers they can be forgiven. I was shocked that he actually agreed with me. He stated that most parishioners don't read the Bible and don't know these things. In my head I started thinking back on my many years of being in the church and couldn't recall one time in which we were encouraged to read our Bible, or even to bring our Bible to church with us. But I was mentally getting off track and needed to get on with the issues I came to discuss.

The last point was a huge one. I asked the priest if it was the Church's belief that the bread and wine actually became the body and blood of Christ. He stated that the communion elements are transformed into the body and blood of Christ. I asked him to show me in the Scriptures where it states that. I wanted to see the Scriptures that supported that belief. He showed me a passage, and we discussed it back and forth. In the Scriptures that he showed me, Jesus said, "Do this in remembrance of me." I asked him "If Jesus hadn't actually died yet, how could the bread that he broke with his disciples actually be transformed into his body? How could the cup of wine that he lifted actually be transformed into his blood? He hadn't died for us yet!" The priest stated that it was a symbol of what was to come. I stopped him. A SYMBOL! It's a symbol, not a transformation. It is supposed to be something that we do to remember what he did, not to actually eat and drink the body and blood of Jesus. He wasn't budging, and we finally agreed to disagree on that point. I thanked him for his time and made the long walk back to my dorm.

As I walked home, I couldn't help but talk these things over with God. I didn't know what to do. Some of the foundational beliefs of my church were contradictory to what I believed the Bible said, and I didn't know what to do about that. I poured my heart out to Him and asked Him what I should do. After a couple of days, I ended up calling my friend who was discipling me and we discussed it some more.

After much prayer, I made a very tough decision. I just couldn't be a part of a church in which I disagreed with their foundational beliefs. Therefore, I had to find another church. It was the only way that I could resolve the issues within my mind and heart. *What would my parents think? Would they be upset that I was walking away from the church that they brought me up in? Would they disown me because I was rejecting their church and their beliefs? The fear built up inside of me. Would they still accept me even though my beliefs were different than theirs? I prepared my heart for yet another rejection. I don't know why I expected things to be different. I was an orphan. I would always be an orphan.*

CHAPTER 79

I continued to attend the weekly small group meetings, the large group meetings, the one-on-one meetings with Jenny, and the daily prayer meetings. I slowly started to pull away from the Catholic Church as I sought other possibilities. Despite my involvement in all these things, I still spent quite a bit of time studying for my classes. I found myself in the library at all hours of the day studying both my Bible and the books for my classes. After the large group meetings, there was a handful of people that would gather at a local restaurant and share a few orders of cheesy garlic bread as we just laughed and hung out together.

Over the span of a couple of weeks, one of those people, Aaron, became my first official boyfriend. Aaron was unlike all the "men" in my life up to this point. He would open doors for me. He walked me to my classes when he had the opportunity. He would walk me back to the dorms after a study session in the library so I wouldn't be out by myself late at night. We had lots of fun together and deep conversations about the Bible and our plans for the future. I was very careful about sharing too much of my past. I didn't want to scare him away and, besides that I wasn't one hundred percent sure that I could trust him with the secrets that were buried beneath the layers of protection that I had installed in my mind and heart.

Aaron surprised me one night with a poem that he wrote for me. I was blown away with how romantic he was! He even created my own personal mix tape. It had a whole bunch of amazing songs that he had recorded in order to offer me some encouragement throughout the week. Creating that tape must have taken him hours upon hours. He was always so thoughtful in the things that he did. You would often see us hand in hand walking around campus. He did confuse me though. *If my dad was right, then why wasn't he trying to move faster? Why wasn't he interested in my body? Wasn't that all I was good for?* Yet, the messages that I was receiving from him was a resounding NO. I was quite confused on the inside, but I never mentioned any of these conflicting internal thoughts. I simply continued to try to figure him out.

One weekend Aaron asked me to come with him as he went home for a family party. I agreed to go and had the opportunity to meet his family for the first time. So many things had crossed my mind on the way to his house. *If he was bringing me home, was this relationship getting serious? What was his family like? Would they like me? Would I like them?* His parents greeted us at the door and welcomed me with hugs and smiles. They seemed like genuinely nice people. We visited in the kitchen while final preparations were completed. Aaron's grandparents arrived, and they also greeted me with hugs and smiles. This family was quite friendly and very functional, unlike the dysfunctional family that I grew up in. They said something that intrigued me and also scared me to death. They told me that they had been praying for Aaron's future wife since the day he was born. It was awesome to see such dedication to family and good solid Christian principles. Yet, that statement still scared me. *Why did they share that statement with me? What had Aaron told his family about me? Did they think that I was going to be his future wife? If I was that person, then that meant that these people have prayed for me my entire life!* That thought was way too much for me handle at the moment, and I was extremely grateful that extended family started to arrive.

We spent the remainder of the evening laughing and having a wonderful time of fellowship in one of the most peaceful environments I had ever experienced. His family played a game of spoons. I was warned that they were very competitive when they played, and I decided to join in the fun. They were not joking! People were scratched and hands were hurt as they fought over the remaining spoons. It was a great time! This family actually played real games together. I had never experienced this before. There was nothing even close to this at my family gatherings. It was getting quite late, so Aaron and I headed back to campus. That day had turned out to be wonderful, and I was grateful that I had come along. It was evident that Aaron's entire family loved the Lord and each other. This family gathering of his had left me with so many internal questions that I would need to process later.

CHAPTER 80

InterVarsity had scheduled a winter retreat and I was one of the first ones to register. I was looking forward to spending an entire weekend away with worship sessions and workshops on a variety of topics. It was a wonderful chance to learn more. One of the sessions that I loved the most was entitled Inductive Bible Study. This session taught me how to go beyond the surface of what the passage stated and to dig deep into what God was really trying to convey to us. I remember being handed a packet and asked to set our Bibles aside. We were handed an entire book of the Bible with no chapters or verses or heading labels--basically no man-made interpretations. It was designed to take us to the Word itself so we could draw our own conclusions and not rely on how other people had interpreted it. That session ended way TOO fast! I absolutely loved this approach to studying the Bible, and the things that I learned in that session stayed with me forever as I developed a love for dissecting the Word, figuring out what God was trying to tell us, and how I could apply those things in my life in the present.

One of the other things that I enjoyed about the winter retreat was the simple beauty that surrounded us. The leaders took a few of us who were interested to the beach, and we were able to climb on the huge boulders that lined the shoreline. It was a blast. I could sit there for hours just watching the beauty of the waves as they crashed on the rocks below us. We took lots of pictures as we absorbed all the beauty around us, both in nature and with the privilege of spending time with one another. It was a wonderful weekend get-away. I didn't want it to end!

It was difficult adjusting back to the usual day-to-day living. Others attempted to explain that it was always difficult coming home after a retreat. They described the retreat as a mountaintop experience, and it was difficult to come back down from the mountain and live in the valley. I understood what they meant, but it was deeper than that for me. The learning, fellowship, and deep conversations were all things irreplaceable to my heart. I realized I thrived on these things. I was at my best when those things were a part of my everyday existence. I greatly disliked moving through life as I had done for my entire existence so far. I had just gone through the motions of trying to survive one horrible thing after another. But in this place and with these people, I was actually thriving! My heart and soul were starving, and I just simply couldn't absorb enough to satisfy the internal hunger that existed. Growing up as an orphan didn't provide the people necessary to feed my heart and soul with love, acceptance, worthiness, and a sense of belonging and purpose. That lack of vital food for my heart and soul left it empty, and the hunger pains only grew and grew. Occasionally there would be someone who would feed me, but because my heart and soul were nearly empty, it appeared as if they were simply tossing scraps my way. More times than not, I would be forced to shove the hunger aside and ignore it or the desire alone would have killed me. When one is starving, you purposefully don't think about it or it makes the hunger worse. However, in this place, I was being fed and I couldn't get enough. The ironic thing here is that I didn't know that I was starving until people took the time to pour love, acceptance, and worthiness into me. My heart and soul were like hungry animals in front of a feeding trough, trying to take in all that they could before the trough was removed. One thing that I was extremely grateful for was the fact that I had been given the tools necessary to at least feed myself spiritually moving forward. Though, sadly, nothing could duplicate the deep conversations that had taken place. I had left that retreat so full, and little did I know that the food I had consumed wouldn't last as long as I thought it would. When one's heart and soul is fed, it begins to crave even more!

Many years later, my first foster mom, Dianne, told me that I was like a funnel: no matter how much love and attention she poured into me, it just poured right back out because I simply didn't know how to accept it. It seemed that I rejected the very thing that I craved. The love, affection, and affirmation that my heart was starving for, and so desperate to receive, was rejected in my head because I had believed the lies my father fed me as a small child when he told me that I was unworthy of those things. I allowed others to attempt to soothe me with their platitudes, but it was way harder than anyone would ever understand. The really difficult part for me was that I had gotten a taste of something wonderful, and it was pure torture to not have a constant source flowing my way. So, once again, I stuffed it way down deep. *I am an orphan and I would always be an orphan. I must realize and accept that there was no one who could give that to me on a consistent basis. I had to push the hunger way down deep behind all the barriers and doors. I can't allow it to affect me like it did. I can't allow any weakness to show or the little that I do receive might be taken away. That would be the ultimate rejection that would put me over the edge of no return.*

CHAPTER 81

After much thought, I decided that I needed to find a different church. Karen, Jenny, Aaron and I went looking for a new church to call "home" while attending college. Together we tried out Southern Heights. I remember walking in on a Sunday morning hand-in-hand with Aaron. Out of the corner of my eye, it seemed as if a young guy was staring at me. I brushed it aside and kept walking and thought I was probably just imagining things. We found a seat and thoroughly enjoyed the service. Afterwards we all discussed the experience on the way home. We decided that we would go back. The worship was point on, and the messages were straight from the Word. It was really amazing to be in a group of people with similar beliefs. The first true test for me was when it came time to celebrate communion. I found that the Church's stance followed a Biblical approach that fell in alignment with my beliefs.

CHAPTER 82

Summer arrived and my friends returned home. Since I was local, that left me seemingly alone. I had met many wonderful people at this Church that helped me not feel so alone. One of those people was Deb. She and her family accepted me as a part of their own. I spent many hours at their house. Deb began mentoring me and teaching me more about Paul and his ministry. It was very eye-opening to learn about all that Paul had accomplished, and what he had taught to the churches through the letters that he wrote. We would get together to study, and I would stay to hang out with her kids and eat dinner with them. This became yet another family for me. I now had two little sisters and a little brother.

That summer was a busy one. I moved back home for the summer. I had a full-time job working at K-Mart as a night stocker and then slept during the day. Having a room in the basement helped tremendously when I went to bed at eight a.m. During this time, I also began to be discipled by a pastor's wife from another church. I don't remember how I was put in touch with her, but it was a very vital part of my growth. She went through the basics of Christianity and what it meant to accept Christ and become a believer. I looked forward to those weekly meetings. They laid a solid foundation for me and my faith in God. To this day I still have the workbook that we used and my original notes I recorded. I may not remember her name, but the impact she had in my life will never be forgotten.

CHAPTER 83

When school started again, I had saved enough to move out of the dorms and into my first apartment with Jenny. It was an amazing and liberating feeling to be on my own. The freedom was indescribable. We had a ground level apartment. You walked down three to four steps and you would be at our front door. The apartment was about five miles from campus. Even though I didn't have to pay the high cost of living in the dorms, I did have the new expense of purchasing a parking permit on campus. At least it was a yearly pass and not one that needed to be replaced every semester.

Jenny and I got along very well. We commuted together whenever we could to save on gas. We now had to prepare our own food as well. That was another change from living in the dorms and was a bit of an adjustment. However, I could still eat for free whenever I was scheduled to work in the cafeteria. Since my grades were not at the required levels, I was no longer in the Honors College. It was a great relief to not have the expectation of writing all those papers. I spent a lot of the down time hanging out in the Honors College lounge, even though I was no longer a part of the Honors College, as it saved me a trip back to the apartment. My friends were often there, and I enjoyed relaxing with them in-between classes.

I continued to love math and science classes. I loved the concrete definitive answers. There were no wishy-washy answers or thought patterns. It was logical. My mind enjoyed logical things; they just made sense. The method classes in the College of Education provided me with different ideas on how to help someone else understand the concept that I was trying to convey. It was fun because my brain could come up with multiple ways to express the same concept. That ability came in handy when I spent time helping some of my friends understand their math homework. It helped me realize beyond a doubt that I was heading into the correct field.

CHAPTER 84

Things between Aaron and I became increasing more difficult as the memories of my past kept popping up, and my self-worth took a nose-dive. I never let anyone know exactly how much I despised myself, and how much I blamed myself for all the things that had occurred up to that point. The truth of the matter was, I didn't believe that I could possibly deserve someone like Aaron; I wasn't worthy of being the answer to a family's prayers for over twenty years. He deserved--and they deserved--someone who wasn't so broken, someone who could truly love him the way he deserved to be loved. Aaron held a special place in my heart, and I wished that my life had been different--but it hadn't been. Therefore, knowing that he most likely would never understand, I broke up with him.

Things were very different after that. I missed the late-night walks, the romantic gestures, and the random emails or letters. Most of all I missed his company. In order to avoid the pain associated with those things, I just turned my attention and focus onto my studies and the Bible to avoid thinking about it. It worked to some degree, but for the feelings that remained, I just stuffed them even deeper behind the barriers. *Who was I to deserve a man like that? I was an orphan and no one could truly love me and all of the secrets that I held within. I was simply unworthy of that kind of love. I had been fooling myself to believe that I could possibly be the answer to his parent's life-long prayers.*

CHAPTER 85

While attending church at Southern Heights, we had heard about a group for young adults called Narrow Gates. They met at a local church and sometimes at the house of one of the young adults that attended regularly, Bill and Mary. It was like an InterVarsity meeting on steroids. The worship was performed by a live band followed by someone teaching from the Bible or giving their testimony of what God had done in their lives. After the teaching was over, we would eat food and fellowship with each other for a good hour. These gatherings were so uplifting, and I absolutely fell in love with this group of people. Listening to the testimonies and stories of other people my age, and how they overcame their struggles with the help of God, was extremely encouraging to me. It gave me hope that maybe He could help me. *Did I truly have to be an orphan? Could He actually assist me with all of the things that I had stuffed so far down? Would He accept me with all of the secrets that I held?* The weight of all the secrets had definitely began to wear on me. Every once in a while, tears would slip down my face as hope crept in. Then reality would settle in: no one could help me. *I was an orphan and I would always be an orphan.*

Narrow Gate was a lot of fun and the size of the groups varied from week to week. Yet there were always the few who were there almost every week. I still attended Southern Heights, and when at school I also attended the InterVarsity meetings as well. All of these things were a lifeline that I refused to let go of. It was something that I needed more than I really understood at the time. Deep down I knew it was a way to get closer to God and the peace of His presence. I developed some strong friendships through these avenues. About five or six of us decided to rent a house together just off east campus. It would be an awesome year!

CHAPTER 86

I started dating again. When I first started attending Southern Heights, this guy, Richard (name has been changed for privacy), was the one I had felt staring at me as I walked into the sanctuary. He was working at the sound booth. It was a strange feeling knowing that this man had been silently pursuing me over the years. We started hanging out together at Narrow Gate and at church. A friendship was starting to form that was beginning to change into something a little bit more. He asked me if I wanted to join him in attending a Bible study group that he attended. I thought it might be fun, and I loved learning more about God and the Bible, so I said yes.

As it turned out, Richard was the only male in the group, and he didn't seem to mind. The leader of the Bible study was a woman named Phyllis. There was something very distinctive about this woman, and I spent a couple of weeks trying to figure out what made her so different from the others. The meeting place was quite a distance away, but I never missed a study. It was another lifeline to my hurting and empty heart. The things that Phyllis taught were always found in the Word, and these were things that I had never been taught before. I felt like a little bird in a nest looking for more and more food. I just couldn't get enough. I watched and listened to people talk to God in ways that I didn't know were possible. These women talked with boldness and authority. There were times when we would attend, and someone would leave healed from a physical ailment.

At one meeting Phyllis taught about the Holy Spirit and the gift of tongues. She talked about Holy Spirit like He was a real person; a helper that came to assist us at different times; with a special language that I could receive to talk with God. She wanted to know if I wished to receive my special language right there that night. I was a bit nervous and unsure of what I should do. Yet, she had shown us in the Word of Mark 16:17 (NKJV), "And these signs will follow those who believe: In My name they will cast out demons; they will speak with new tongues," that it was Biblical and in alignment with the Scriptures. So, I decided to go for it even though on the inside I was a bit skeptical. I had heard the ladies speak in different tongues, yet it didn't seem strange to hear. They all laid hands on me and began to pray for me. Within a few minutes I had received a new prayer language and began to speak it out. That night was the beginning of a wonderful new level of relationship with God.

CHAPTER 87

Despite the advances that I was making in my relationship with God, I still struggled with the memories of my past abuse surfacing at the most inconvenient times, and my battle with constant nightmares continued. One night, I was lying in my bed almost comatose as the memories were flooding my mind and I was helpless to stop them. My roommates tried to carry on a conversation with me, and I just laid there curled up in a ball. Concerned, they reached out to my boyfriend to see if he might get through to me. This timeframe was quite strange for me as I could "see" what was happening but was unable to engage or speak to my roommates or my boyfriend.

After a while, I finally snapped out of it and all I kept saying was that I didn't want to live anymore. I just wanted to die. The pain was too much to deal with and it just needed to stop. The decision was made that it would be beneficial for me to be admitted to a hospital for treatment. I was then transported to the hospital and checked into the psychiatric ward. I was faced with medications and appointments. The doctors prescribed sleeping pills so I could get some real sleep. They also put me on anti-depressants. After being in the ward for about a week, I was released to the outpatient program. I had once again regained control of my thoughts and was doing much better.

The outpatient program allowed me the opportunity to discuss the things that were bothering me in a group setting, and it seemed to be working. During one session, the counselor commented that I had a pretty smile and my teeth were aligned well. I immediately responded that it was because I had braces for years as a teenager. She asked me why I did that. I had no clue what she was talking about. She stated that I justify away any compliment that was given instead of accepting it and saying thank you. Once everyone else arrived, she started a new exercise aimed at only me: we went around the table and everyone had to give me one compliment, and all I could do was look them in the eyes and say thank you. The next fifteen minutes were pure torture! I didn't want to bring any attention to myself and now I had everyone's attention. That program finally came to an end and I was so relieved.

CHAPTER 88

Soon thereafter I made the decision to actually pursue my own healing. So, for the first time, I wasn't forced into counseling but decided to go voluntarily. True counseling is lots of hard work that doesn't end just because the session ended. I dived into some of the basic level parts of my story and worked through details that were hard to discuss. Despite the hard work, I proceeded to push past the difficulties of bringing up stuff from the past in order to try to get the nightmares to stop.

It helped to be able to speak about the pain for the first time with someone who had good intentions and believed what I said happened. I wrote letters to my dad and worked on detailed assignments that my counselor asked me to do. The assignments were not easy, as they were of events that were never spoken about before. It took a lot of courage to complete each assignment, but I was faithful as I wanted to be free from the holds that my past had had on me. It took practice to only allow certain walls and defenses to drop without allowing them all to fall. *I still have to be careful. No one will be able to handle the complete truth., I have to be careful.*

CHAPTER 89

One night Richard and I were simply hanging out and talking with each other about the future and our dreams and plans. Then out of nowhere, he asked me to marry him. I remember time stopping once again. Would I receive another proposal anytime soon? He was a good guy. He loved the Lord and served Him at church. He read the Bible. *He will be okay, right? Will others approve? I have no one to ask whether this engagement will be okay. No one has said anything negative about him. He does have a few weird quirks, but don't we all?* The next thing I knew, I had said yes. We were going to get married! It was a surprise to everyone as it happened so quickly.

The next couple of days brought smiles to my face and also many questions to my heart, though no one would know the varying levels of issues that invaded my heart. *Will he believe my story? Will he stand beside me? What will he do if he knows the whole story? Will he run away? Will I even be able to share my story with him? Is he truly "safe"? Can I ever be safe enough to live with my walls down?* We went looking for rings and picked out a set with an engagement ring and a wedding band. He then allowed me to place the ring on my hand and keep it there. It was an exciting and scary time. My heart was all over the map.

During one of my counseling sessions, I decided to be brave. If I was going to marry Richard, then he had to know what happened to me. I took a letter that I had been working on and decided to share it with him. When I read him the letter, I was housesitting at the time just a few blocks from Deb and her family. When I finished reading the letter, he got up and left. I was so hurt. I was once again an orphan. *I would always be an orphan trying to deal with the past completely on my own.* I stared at the diamond on my finger as the tears fell silently down my cheeks as my hopes and dreams were crushed in that moment. I wouldn't have a husband who would allow me to be myself after all. If I wanted to continue with the wedding as planned, I would have to continue to pretend to be the perfect "wife." I would have to live the rest of my life with the walls firmly in place. Was I willing to make that sacrifice? Richard ultimately returned about fifteen minutes later. He said that he was overwhelmed with all that I had read and went to Deb's house to talk. They told him to go back and talk with me. *He didn't come back out of his own accord; he came back because someone told him that he should.* The reality of that decision was not lost on me. We embraced in a hug and I allowed the tears to flow though not for the reasons that he might have thought. *I was an orphan. I would always be an orphan.*

CHAPTER 90

During the next couple of weeks of counseling we discussed the events with Richard and how that made me feel and what I was going to do about it all. My counselor thought I needed to give him a break. I had my whole life to deal with and come to terms with what was done to me. He had received a massive download of the events of my life in a manner of minutes. She felt that I needed to give him some time to process the things that he heard. It almost felt like excuses were being made for him. Once again, it felt like this whole situation was my fault and not his. I was so confused as to why I was made out to be the bad guy because I "dumped" my past on him. I just accepted that if I wanted to continue with this engagement, that I needed to just "move on." So, despite how much these events hurt me, I chose to move on.

A couple of weeks later, my counselor told me something that completely rocked my boat. She told me that through my homework, she had been recovering incidents of abuse in her own past. That session left me with even more trauma. For the first time in a very long time, it felt that I was being used to help her recover more and more memories. It felt as if the assignments that I had been given were actually to help her and not me. I felt violated and very vulnerable. I'm not sure how, but the office found out what had happened. I was immediately switched to another counselor.

I spent the next couple of months dealing with the previous counselor's actions and fighting a battle within that I couldn't share with this new counselor. I had reached out to both my counselor and my fiancé and had been betrayed by both of them. I found myself in a very unique situation with my counseling and chose to repeat the same ideology that I had when I was in high school. I played the game and said the things that he wanted to hear just to be done. The parting words of my counselor made me furious: "When you get married, you will be back as no one who has gone through what you have would be able to handle marriage without some assistance." Those words created a deep hatred of counselors, and I vowed to prove him wrong, and not to ever return to counseling again. I was alone in dealing with all these stormy waters. *I was an orphan. I would always be an orphan.*

CHAPTER 91

After much deliberation, despite my desire to be married and to have kids, I made a very difficult decision. I determined that I was not ready to get married yet. I needed more time to become the woman that God wanted me to be. I needed to simply focus on God and try to get a handle on my past. I had been through so much in the last couple of months and knew that if I was to be the wife that I was supposed to be, it wasn't time yet. My decision would break my Richard's heart, and I knew that there was no easy way to convey the information other than to be completely honest. Therefore, I gave the ring back and broke off our engagement. I retreated into myself and tried to organize the mess of my internal world. My thoughts were all over the place, and I needed time to myself in order to reestablish my walls of defense, reorder my thinking, and place things back behind the doors that must never be opened again. *I was an orphan. I would always be an orphan.* I needed to get used to that fact.

Shortly after I called off the engagement, my parents told me that they were moving to California. The company my dad worked for was bought by another company, and it was stationed in California. He was one of the few who were offered a job with the new company. They packed everything up and moved away. It was a difficult time, because I enjoyed my parents being so close to the university. After they left, I felt so empty. I tried to tell myself that it was simply a job transfer. However, my heart perceived something completely different. It felt like I had been abandoned once again. *Why did I continue to trust them? If I had kept the walls in place and not allowed them into my heart, then I wouldn't be hurting right now.* It seemed like every time that I place trust in someone and allow those walls to fall, I would get hurt again. Why did I keep torturing myself? Here I was in Michigan all alone. My parents left with my sister. My brothers soon followed. *I was alone. I was an orphan. I would always be an orphan.*

CHAPTER 92

Over the next couple of years, I kept attending church and Narrow Gate and InterVarsity. I dived into my studies and work in the math department at Western Michigan University. The memories never stopped coming to the surface. Through these times, I learned the mastery of hiding the thoughts and feelings of my heart deep inside of me. No one knew what was going on. Then the struggle became too much to bear once again. A co-worker convinced me to check myself into a treatment facility where I could get some assistance and not feel so overwhelmed and suicidal.

She drove me to Grand Rapids, and I checked myself into a short-term intensive treatment program that was Christian- based. I spent the next week or two with psychiatrists and professional counselors who helped me deal with the reasons behind my suicidal thoughts. Even though I couldn't ever tell them the truth (or I might never leave the facility), it was very helpful once again to adjust my thinking and to get things under control. They started me on some different medications that would need to be monitored by a psychiatrist when I went back home. The medication really helped to quiet my mind and helped me to focus. Since they were working better than the last set of medications, I didn't mind taking them. For the next couple of months, I started seeing a psychiatrist back home and it was going really well. Things finally started to look up once again. I determined in my heart that I would live. I had dreams again that I wanted to pursue.

CHAPTER 93

One of those dreams was to be the first member of my biological family to graduate from college. The natural course of action was to finish my degree which meant that I would have to quit my full-time job as a technical editor in the math department of Western Michigan University. The only requirement left was to complete a semester of student teaching. I then graduated with my BS in secondary education with a math major and a chemistry minor. Grandpa George came to Michigan to see me graduate. It was awesome to have both of my grandpas there on my special day.

Soon after graduation, I was immediately hired as a long-term math substitute. Unfortunately, the math teacher had had a heart attack, and the students had many teachers come and go. As a result, they were extremely far behind the rest of their peers. I came in and, in the course of one month, I had each of these classes back on track with their peers. I loved every minute of it! Sadly, the one-hour commute each way was getting more and more difficult to drive day in and day out. I started applying for jobs that were closer to where I lived.

I now lived in a two-bedroom apartment with a friend and her two-year-old. One day we found her daughter trying to place her peanut butter sandwich inside the VCR! Looking back it was quite a funny memory but not so much at the time. My friend and I decided that, since we couldn't have cats or dogs, we would get a bunny. We drove up to Grand Rapids to the pet store and found an adorable bunny to bring home. We named him Callie, which was short for Kalamazoo, since we were from Kalamazoo. It was so much fun until the landlord found out. He made us get rid of the bunny as our lease stated no cats or dogs were allowed, but the landlord said it implied that no pets were allow. Either way, we had a great couple of months with Callie.

Even though things on the outside seemed to be going great, the inside of my mind remained in turmoil. I struggled so much with the memories and the maintenance of the barricades I had created. It was very difficult to maintain, and I was weary of the burden that it had put on me. I simply wanted it all to stop. I determined that the best way was to take my life for real this time. I made plans but knew that if I told anyone, then I'd end up at another treatment facility. This time around I said nothing. There was one friend, Beth, from college that had made such an impact on my life, that I felt I needed to write her a letter to say goodbye and thank you. I sent the letter to her and continued with my plans. I knew that since she was almost three hours away, that I'd be safe from interference. I had only a few days to go before I completed my plans, when I heard a knock at the front door. Beth was standing on my doorstep! After reading my letter, she got in the car and drove almost three hours to my house to talk with me. She wrapped me in a huge hug and the tears just began to flow down my cheeks. She came inside and talked for a few hours. After she was certain that I wouldn't follow through with my plans, she said goodbye and started the long trip back home. Beth didn't realize the results of her selfless actions that day. Whenever you gave Beth a compliment, she ALWAYS gave God the glory, not herself. I wanted a relationship with Jesus that was similar to hers. It was an inspiration to me. Her actions that day showed me in a tangible way that my life had value, that my life was important, and that I was worthy of being cared about. The prayers that she prayed over me that day set me on a path towards having a close and personal relationship with the Lord. My life was never the same after her visit. I began to speak to God and share my struggles with Him. Things hadn't changed, but my perspective had undergone a complete overhaul.

CHAPTER 94

R ichard, my ex-fiancé, began the courting process once again. It had been almost five years since I broke off the engagement, and I was ready to begin looking for a spouse. Since it appeared that he had indeed changed, I agreed to go out on a date with him. He took me to see "Cats" the musical at Miller Auditorium on WMU's campus. He arrived in a beautiful suit, apparently a recent purchase, and took me out to eat at a nice restaurant before we went to the musical. I had a wonderful time. This was the first time that he had actually planned ahead for a date. I was very impressed! My heart was left questioning all the possibilities upon my return home that evening.

After passing the state licensing board exams, I was officially offered my first position as a high school math teacher. I loved teaching and thought I was in heaven. This was most assuredly what I was made to do, and I was very good at it. During my evaluations, I had principals tell me that they rarely saw the level of maturity and mastery of a classroom that I exhibited. I disliked breaking up fights, but the teaching was something I truly loved.

During my first year of teaching, Richard proposed to me for a second time. I thought long and hard about the answer. No one else had even come close to dating me, let alone proposing to me. Maybe I was just too damaged, and this was the best I could do. He had changed, so things were different this time. After I said yes, he shared with me that he told his sister that the ring would go on no one's finger but mine. It made me feel very special and glad that I took the time to get myself into a place where I felt I could be the best wife that I could be. I knew that deep down in my heart all the same questions remained, but I was in a completely different place. My relationship with God was amazing, and I had some awesome friends. Last time around, I didn't really have a good support system.

CHAPTER 95

One of the things that I wanted to do as part of my healing was going to be really difficult, but it was something that I needed to do. I had to confront my dad, face to face. I asked my brother if he could arrange a meeting with him. He said that he would take care of that. I then asked Richard if he would like to join me. I wanted his support. I had made arrangements to spend Thanksgiving with my biological family for the first time since I was adopted. Richard and I would go see my dad one day of that trip.

Just before we were scheduled to leave, my grandma became very sick with cancer. My mom told me to go ahead and take the trip as no one knew how long Grandma would hang on. Reluctantly, we went ahead and left for Iowa. One of the first places that we went was to see Dianne. Every time I was in town, I had to stop by to say hello. We would order taco pizza from Casey's and simply catch up with each other's lives. It was a fantastic visit! They could never be too frequent. We stayed with Grandpa George while in town.

The day arrived that I would see my dad for the first time in sixteen years. I was extremely nervous, but I knew that I needed to face him in order for the nightmares to stop. We met my brother, and he told me he made sure that my dad was sober. It was the only way that my brother would agree to bring me to see him. When my eyes fell on my dad, all fear of this man fled and was replaced with sympathy. He was skin and bones, and there was absolutely no way that this man would ever be able to hurt me again, awake or asleep. It was so evident that he was drinking his life away and had no ability to hurt me. That meeting was so healing on many different levels. We simply chatted about life, and I stayed as neutral as I could, not giving any information about myself that was too personal. After a little bit, we politely said goodbye and left.

We went to my aunt's house for Thanksgiving dinner. After dinner started, it was quite obvious that I didn't belong there anymore. There was so much drinking and things got out of control very quickly. In the middle of dinner, I received a phone call that I never wanted to receive. It was my mom letting me know that Grandma had died. Mom said that family was surrounding her and praying together, and she peacefully slipped away. I was an outsider once again. Family was gathered around her, but I wasn't there. I tried so hard to not allow my thoughts to go there, but the struggle was real. I was so angry that I was told to go and she passed away while I was gone. I hung up and saw everyone was at each other's throats. There was such an enormous contrast between these two families that it made my head spin. I couldn't handle any more and got up to leave. Richard and I decided to head home early.

Shortly after our return home, Grandma's funeral took place. I missed her so much. My heart fought being mad that cancer stole her from us, and mad that I wasn't there to say goodbye. In contrast, I was happy that she wasn't in pain; happy that she was in heaven. This woman was so kind, gentle, sweet, patient, and loving. She loved with her entire heart. I missed her chili; it was a combination of chili and spaghetti. I had never tasted anything like it before, and I remember her cooking that dish specifically for me when I spent the week with her and Grandpa Arno back in high school. She bent over backwards to make me feel loved and special. Her smile would light up the room. I just wanted more time with her; I wanted my future children to know their Great Grandma Margie. However, that wasn't going to be. Instead, I had to say good-bye to those dreams. There were many tears shed, but I had to hold onto the knowledge that I would see her again when I made it to heaven.

CHAPTER 96

I finished my first year of teaching but felt that God was asking me to change schools. He wanted me to move to a Christian school and teach middle and high school students. I would be teaching science, math, and Bible class. It was difficult leaving my first school as I had made a great impression and had an amazing first year, but I had to follow His leading. In the fall of 1999, I started teaching at my new school. It was quite different teaching in a Christian atmosphere rather than in a public-school setting.

I also began wedding preparations at the same time. Life was quite busy and my defenses were held in place by sheer determination. I was so uncertain of what God was up to, as three to four months into the school year I distinctly heard Him tell me to return to the public school. I listened to Him. I applied for a job back at my previous school and then resigned my post at the Christian school. I began to question what was going on. Why did I switch schools after only four months? Why interrupt the education of my students at the Christian school? Was there a reason that I was only a part of that school for four months? I didn't understand, but I followed His leading.

CHAPTER 97

In preparation for our wedding, Richard and I attended marriage counseling with our pastor and his wife. It was a great time filled with many laughs but also solid Biblical truths. I learned so much during this class. There were parts of the teachings that scared me to death, but I decided to trust God with those areas. The sexual component of marriage was scary to think about. I knew that I had kept myself pure (if you don't take into count all the abuse I endured as a child), and I wanted to give myself as a gift to my husband. Richard wasn't much into the specific details of the wedding planning, he just wanted to know what he needed to do and left the rest up to me.

My best friend, Julie, helped me plan and prepare for my big day. We made a wishing well for the cards and gifts as well as my wedding veil. She was always there; we were inseparable! There were many times that I wished my mom was there to help me plan my wedding, but she was almost two thousand miles away. I simply stuffed those feelings way down deep and wouldn't permit them to come all the way to the surface. I knew that I couldn't dwell on those feelings or I might head into a downward spiral and not be able to get myself back out. Julie and I planned out the reception and bounced ideas off of each other all the time to add those special touches to each component of the event. I was only planning to get married once, and I wanted this wedding to be all that I had ever dreamed of. It was a very exciting time. Julie even helped me grade papers when she had the time, or she encouraged me to keep grading until it was finished so I wouldn't get behind with my work. One wish that I made to Richard was that we have a limo to take us to the wedding reception. I had always dreamed of riding in one, and my wedding would be the perfect opportunity to make that wish come true. He stated that he would take care of it. I was so excited as each and every puzzle piece slowly started to fall into place.

There were a couple of times prior to our wedding that Richard and I came very close to breaking our promise to wait to become intimate with each other. We were simply kissing each other, and the next thing I knew I would be pushing him off me telling him we needed to wait. He would leave my apartment to cool off, and I would feel so awful. We may not have had physical sex, but we did in our hearts. I knew that we hadn't broken the promise, but we could have so easily done so. I didn't know what to expect. I had no example to follow and no one to tell me what I should or shouldn't do. Looking back, it was one of my biggest regrets not to have had that input from someone.

The big day finally arrived. Grandpa George and Uncle Dave came to Michigan to attend our wedding. Things went as well as I had hoped. After the ceremony, the limo driver took Richard and I on a short trip through town with just the two of us before taking pictures back at the church. Uncle Dave and Grandpa George didn't understand the plan and followed us for a while, honking their horn the entire time! It was a bit embarrassing, but I knew they were just expressing their love. We came back to church for pictures, but Grandpa George and Uncle Dave didn't come back with us, they went straight to the reception. After the photos were taken, the entire wedding party filed into the limo to be taken to the reception in style. It was a perfect day filled with the love and support of many friends and family. Every last detail that we had planned played out perfectly. I even surprised my mom with a special dairy-free cake just for her--that she could actually eat. It was one surprise that I kept a secret in order to see her expression on this special day. It was SO worth it. The only glitch that day was our pastor had forgotten one little detail…to sign our marriage license! We had to track down a couple members of our wedding party after the reception had ended in order to obtain the needed signatures.

Richard and I had a hotel room reserved for our wedding night, and then we were to fly out to Colorado for our honeymoon the next day. The wedding night was not exactly what I had imagined it would be. I had many uneasy feelings on the inside, but I figured it was simply newlywed jitters and things would settle down after a little bit of time had passed. We spent our honeymoon in Colorado at Sundance Trail Guest Ranch. For the entire week we rode horses, hiked, climbed mountains, white water rafted, and sat around campfires. We had a great time. The dude ranch knew it was our honeymoon and placed us in a cabin by ourselves and even left a bottle of champagne chilling in our room. It was very thoughtful of them to consider our circumstances and to accommodate us. We were even taken on a honeymoon ride one afternoon. A wrangler came along simply so we wouldn't get lost in the mountains, but she pretty much allowed us to be by ourselves. It was a fantastic week full of many wonderful memories.

PART IV – MARRIED LIFE

CHAPTER 98

A couple of weeks into our marriage while Richard was at work, I called my mom in a dead panic. I told her that Richard was just like my dad. I was scared and honestly wondering what I had gotten myself into. My mom immediately came back with, "He's not your dad. He is completely different. To compare the two would be unfair to Richard. You need to give him a chance." I don't remember a single word of the rest of our conversation after that point. I was told to not compare the two men and I understood what she meant. However, to me it meant that the things that were happening must be normal for married couples. *Since Mom didn't even ask me why I thought that way, then the things that were happening must be normal. The bruises on my arms from when he grabbed me must be normal. The forced sex in the middle of the night must not be rape, but normal things that happen in a marriage. The silent treatments and verbal onslaughts must be normal. The way he blew up at me because he didn't want to discuss something must be normal. I must be the issue, not him. The things that were happening were all my fault. I had to change my frame of mind. I must have been doing something to cause him to react in this manner. The things happening were my fault. I needed to become a better wife.* After much soul searching, I determined that the issue was mine. I was simply being triggered because of the past abuse and the things that were happening within my marriage were simply an overactive imagination. *It was just in my head; my marriage was just fine. It was just fine.*

About a week later, I freaked out because my cycle was late. I thought I was pregnant already. I couldn't breathe. At church the following morning, I pulled Julie aside and began to sob silently as tears fell down my cheeks. I couldn't be pregnant already! I wanted kids, but I was not ready as I was still trying to adjust to married life. Thankfully, my cycle started a few days later. Richard and I wanted children, so we never really discussed birth control and when we would start our family. I was too ashamed of my reaction to actually discuss it with Richard, so I just stuffed the thoughts and feelings down behind my defensive walls. Things still were not any better between the two of us, and my mom's words kept echoing in the back of my mind. The other words that suddenly came into my mind were the ones from one of the counselors: "You'll be back once you are married." The combination of the two conversations made this an issue, and I needed to figure this out. So, I buried anything that even remotely felt like abuse further and further down, making sure that they went behind the barriers and doors. *They must not be evident to anyone. I must be the perfect model wife. If I pleased him in every way, then there would be no need to be on the receiving end of these actions.*

CHAPTER 99

O ne month later, I was late again, but this time I was pregnant. I made the decision that despite the things going on at home, I would love this child with every ounce of my being. He or she would not have a childhood like mine. The cycle of abuse would end with me. With this determination set in my heart and mind, I then started the task to reinforce the defenses and make sure that my child would have the best life I could provide. It was so much fun to plan for the arrival of a baby. The toughest part was thinking about leaving him or her in a daycare. We decided to find out the gender of the baby for better planning, and our bundle of joy was going to be a baby boy. Since Richard didn't have any names that he absolutely wanted to name our son, I was able to name him. I settled on Zachariah, which means "God remembered." We gave him the middle name of Scott, which was the same as my biological brother. I wanted some type of positive connection to my birth family.

I thought that being pregnant might change things between Richard and me. Yet, it couldn't be further from the truth! I was still hiding the bruises from his rough handling of me. One night, I went to Julie's house to hang out for some scrapbooking and scrabble. When I came home and looked through the big front window of our home, I saw Richard jump up off the couch and run to the television. As I parked the car, I was wondering what that was all about. When I got inside the house, I asked him why he jumped up so quickly and what it was that he was watching that he obviously didn't want me to see. He tried to avoid the conversation, but he had been caught, so he finally came clean. He told me that it was a porn movie. I was in complete and utter shock while bile rose in my throat and anger rose within me just as quickly. I couldn't believe that he would even look at that stuff. *Why did he feel the need to look at that stuff? Wasn't I enough for him? Why would he watch those things in our home? What about the son that we were bringing into this world soon?* After much arguing between us, he agreed to not watch them again. It still didn't settle the issue in my mind and heart, but at least he had agreed to stop watching that junk.

When Zach was born, my love collided with inexperience and instant motherhood. My focus became all about my son who would be dependent upon me for everything. I thought that maybe our son would bring us closer together as a family, which it did for a while. Before Zach was born, I decided that I would nurse him as it was the healthiest thing for him. As I struggled in the hospital to get my son to latch on and actually nurse, I began to feel like a failure. *I couldn't figure out how to satisfy my husband, and now I couldn't even feed my son.* The guilt and tension kept rising and I thought that I would drown. There were specialists that would try to assist me with the nursing. They showed me alternative positions and gave helpful tips. Nothing seemed to be working. Yet, in the back of my head I kept hearing the words my best friend Julie had given me in advance about nursing newborns: "A newborn can survive for two to three days with no food because they have the nutrients from the womb," and "When a newborn gets hungry enough, they will latch on and eat."

The pediatrician was really concerned about my son not getting enough to eat, and therefore was reluctant to let him go home unless I agreed to supplement his feedings with formula. I sat on the edge of the hospital bed with those statements running through my head on repeat, and I flat out lied to the pediatrician and agreed to supplement my son with formula. I simply wanted to bring him home and give him a chance before I gave up. He was already coming home with a Billi blanket. This is a special phototherapy device used to treat neonatal jaundice which is not uncommon. However, I didn't want anything else. The pediatrician agreed to sign off on the discharge papers and, since Richard was working, my mother-in-law brought us home from the hospital. Not having my husband there to bring us home from the hospital, felt like just another rejection. I wasn't worthy enough to have my own husband bring us home. I tried to keep his words in the forefront of my mind, "I don't have sick days. If I miss work, then it will count against me. If I get three absences, then I will lose my job." However, it felt like the ultimate rejection. *I must push those feelings aside! He is attempting to save his job.* Yet, in the back of my mind, I struggled to understand what company could fire their employee for having a child. There were laws to protect those workers. Despite the internal dialogue, I had to focus on this beautiful bundle of joy that lay in my arms. He was so perfect in every way.

Once home, I sat down in my rocking chair trying to get my son to stop screaming, to calm down and nurse. It didn't help matters to have my mother-in-law asking if there was anything that she could do to help. I politely told her that we were just fine. That I was just going to rock him and try to nurse him. I knew she was just trying to be helpful, but I only wanted to be alone. I had just left the hospital with SO many people telling

169

me what I needed to do, that I didn't want it within my own home too. After she left to go home, I just sat there as tears rolled down my cheeks. I surrendered my desires to the Lord. I was so upset as I sat in that chair completely frustrated and willing to do anything to get my son to eat, even if it meant never breastfeeding. As I willingly gave up my desire to breastfeed, I completely lost it, and my body was racked with sobs. At that moment of surrender, my milk suddenly dropped and my son stopped crying as it began to flow into his mouth. He latched on and finally began to nurse for the first time. It was the most wonderful feeling in the world to have that personal bond with my child. I sat there as my tears of surrender turned to tears of joy. As my son nursed, I began to praise my Father for helping me relax enough to allow my body to do what it was designed to do. My son didn't have any issues from that point forward, and I didn't need to supplement with any formula. It was the first time that I realized that my mood affected my child. If I was upset, he sensed that and so did my body.

CHAPTER 100

A couple of weeks after the birth of my son, my parents arrived from California to visit and to meet their first grandchild. It was a fantastic visit; I had missed them very much. While they were in town, we dedicated our son to the Lord in church. We each had a chance to say a few words of dedication during the service. My parents, mother-in-law, brother, sister-in-law and her family, Richard, and myself all spoke something over our son, whether it was a Bible verse or a prayer. After we all had a chance to speak, the pastor dedicated him to the Lord. It was a fantastic day of celebration. I loved having the entire family present. But before I knew it, it was time for my parents to return home. My heart fell when they left. I wished they were closer to us. I wanted my son to grow up knowing his grandparents. I would have to find ways to make sure that was a reality.

CHAPTER 101

When my maternity leave was over, I went back to work and left my son in the care of a good friend who had a home daycare center. It was so difficult leaving him while I went to work. It ended up being a great struggle trying to balance my full-time teaching job with having a newborn to care for. After a few months, Richard and I sat down to discuss our options. When I looked at the math, my income was mostly devoted to childcare, and gas driving back and forth to work, with just a little left over. So, we made a decision for me to stay home with our son. I quit my job. Since I was going to be home raising Zach, we decided to try to have another child.

Grandpa George moved into our house along with my brother. It was awesome to have my biological family here during these moments in my son's life. A couple of months later, I found out that I was pregnant for the second time. This pregnancy was no different than Zach's; both were very easy. Sixteen months after the birth of my first son, I gave birth to another boy. We named him Joseph, which means "He will add" or "praise." Joseph's middle name, Michael, was identical to his dad's middle name. I truly enjoyed having two children, though Joe definitely was a challenge at times. A few weeks after he was born, Mom and Dad flew into town again to meet their newest grandson. We all gathered at church once again to have another dedication service as we presented Joseph to the Lord.

It was pretty evident that things within our marriage were not really changing and were pretty stagnant. Richard went to work; after work he would go to sleep while I would try to keep the kids as quiet as possible. When he woke up, he would play a little with the boys while I prepared dinner. After we finished eating, he would watch television while "playing" with the boys and then go to work. I learned quickly when he had reached his limits and would step in and pull the boys away before he would blow up or lose his cool. It was a very stressful time, but I tried to focus on the amazing boys that I had the privilege of raising. We took many trips to the park and to the library where we would bring home bags of books. We had many adventures with Julie and her children. Since there wasn't a ton of "safety" within our home, I tried everything that I could to find that outside the house. I wanted the best for our boys and enjoyed the time that I had to shape them into the young men that God wanted them to be.

CHAPTER 102

About one year after Joe was born, Grandpa George became really sick. He suffered from congestive heart failure and his kidneys were shutting down, which required that he undergo dialysis. After his first dialysis, he decided that it wasn't for him. He had lived his life, and if it was his time to go, then it was his time to go. I remember asking my pastor to come to the hospital to see if he would talk to my grandpa and possibly pray with him to receive Jesus as his personal Lord and Savior. When the pastor arrived, he told me to go ahead and that he would be there for support. I looked at him in total disbelief. I had asked him to come lead my grandpa to the Lord, as I had never led someone to the Lord before. I turned around and spoke to Grandpa George like I had never done before. I shared with him what my faith in God meant to me, how important my relationship with Jesus was, and asked him if would like to ask Jesus into his heart. He turned to the pastor and told him that he thought I was hypocritical at times, but he knew that I was right. Then as tears of joy silently fell, I led my grandpa in prayer asking Jesus to forgive him and for Jesus to come into his heart. It was one of the most special moments in my life.

He left the hospital that day with Hospice. A few days later, he was rapidly going downhill, and since I knew that he wouldn't last much longer, I didn't leave his side. I had taken some college classes to renew my teaching certification and had skipped a few of my classes to stay with Grandpa. He was sleeping most of the time now with a few lucid moments. At one point, my brother told me to go ahead and go to class, as he thought that Grandpa would still be here. Against my better judgement, I decided to go to class. A few hours later, my brother called and told me that he had passed, and that I needed to come back right away. He wouldn't allow the funeral home to take him away until after I arrived. I quickly left school and drove to my brother's house. When I arrived, with tears falling, I said goodbye to Grandpa George. I never told my brother how important that was to me. I needed that opportunity, and he had given the greatest gift that day. I had a few moments alone with my grandpa to say goodbye.

In the next day or two, my brother and I transported Grandpa back to Iowa to be buried next to our mom. The funeral was quite difficult for many reasons. I was being triggered by some of the family that was present and didn't understand why. I had Grandpa's sisters, my aunts, asking me whether he had accepted Christ before he died. I informed them that he did accept Jesus a few days before he passed. They were so grateful to me. They told me that they were praying specifically that I would lead him to Christ before he passed away. At the graveside, I was smacked in the face with not only the death of my grandpa, but also my mom. My grandpa and my mom shared a double tombstone. Even looking at the tombstone resulted in a flood of memories that I was unable to stop. It was a painful day. I had lost a solid support in my life, and my heart was broken. I wished I had had more time with him, but at least it wouldn't be the last time that I saw him. My brother and I returned to Michigan and our families.

CHAPTER 103

One morning when Joe was about fourteen months old, I opened my bedroom door to find baby powder all over my hardwood floors. Upon walking into the living room, I found my oldest sitting on the couch watching cartoons on the television, and my youngest sitting in the rocker wearing only a diaper. There was baby powder all over the floor and electronics! As it turns out, he figured out how to climb out of his crib and take off his pajamas. He was able to reach the baby powder from the changing table and figured out how to open it. He had a great time watching the baby powder fly through the air when he squeezed the bottle. Of course, I was quite overwhelmed and upset. I placed Joe back in his crib and told him that he needed to stay put while I cleaned up all the baby powder. *Daddy would have beaten me black and blue for making such a mess.* I knew that if Richard was awake, that Joe would've been yelled at and harshly spanked. I need to get this mess cleaned up quickly. It takes FOREVER to clean up baby powder. You can't use a vacuum as it just sends the powder airborne. A broom will also send it airborne unless you take very small strokes. I don't remember how long it took me to clean up that mess, but he had definitely had a great time. As I was finishing up the last part, Richard woke up. I had managed to protect Joe from unnecessary punishment. Richard had no patience with the boys.

CHAPTER 104

My children were my life and the center of my focus. My marriage was still very difficult and full of abuse. I often found Richard on his phone looking at pornography, or I would come home to find him scrambling extremely fast to turn off the video player. I attempted to not take it personally, but over and over it made me feel like something was wrong with me. *I wasn't good enough for him any longer.* There were times that he couldn't have sex with me because he was too caught up with the images that he had been staring at on the phone or computer. Then the kids would often get on Richard's nerves. He would go to work in the morning, come home and fall asleep on the couch watching television. The boys would often climb all over him and wake him up to play with daddy. He would lose his temper at being woken up, and it would cause the kids to shrink back from him in fear. They were simply acting like children and something in that particular moment would set him off. It was like a volcano blowing its top. No one knew when or where it would blow. There were many times Richard would explode and yell and scream at the kids. Sometimes he would grab their arms and they would cry out in pain. At that point in time, I would raise my voice and say that he didn't know how hard he was gripping them and pry his hands off of the boys. When he gripped the boys' arms like that, most of the time, he left bruise marks.

One time he was extremely angry and was yelling at the kids for some reason. Something in me knew he was beyond angry, so I stepped in front of the boys and shut their bedroom door in an effort to protect them. He then started yelling at me and raised his hand to swing a punch. I know that his fist came so fast, that I flinched and ducked out of the way to avoid being hit. Instead of hitting me, he punched the door behind me and put a huge hole in the front panel. When I tried to talk to him about the incident later that evening, he pushed it off as no big deal. He told me, almost in an attempt to make sure that I knew that he would never have hit me, that's *why* he had hit the door. However, no matter how he chose to spin the incident, I found no comfort in the fact that he missed me only because I'd gotten out of the way. If he could take a swing in anger in the first place, then he could do it again. I felt that the kids and I were always walking on eggshells, trying our best to not provoke the bear. Shortly after this incident, I placed a poster on the door to cover up the hole so the kids and I wouldn't have the daily reminder of his anger. I knew that it didn't change our reality in any way, but I didn't want visitors to see the environment that the kids and I experienced each and every day.

Other times we would be discussing something and would come to a decision. Then the next day, he would totally deny the conversation making me think I had lost my mind. Other times when we had an argument, he would give me the silent treatment as if I wasn't even there. I questioned my sanity. I would talk to him and he would completely ignore me. This behavior shut down all lines of communication between us. It was so very difficult to discuss any issue that brought the slightest bit of controversy, as it would always end in an argument, volcanic eruptions, or the silent treatment. I kept reminding myself that he was better than my father, but it still didn't take away the sting and the hurt that I endured. I had a strong belief that when one married, they married for life until death. That belief held me in this marriage believing that if I just tried hard enough that things would get better.

CHAPTER 105

T he thing that made all of this so difficult to explain to others was the fact that in public Richard seemed to be the best husband and father. So I didn't even try. He took his family to church week in and week out. He was a part of men's groups at church. We were both part of a community group through church as well. He served at church as an usher. I served in the children's department, teaching Sunday school to toddlers. I would lead the Bible story part of vacation Bible school each year. How would anyone understand the things that were taking place in our home? I didn't know what to call it, but I knew that it was not normal. I didn't care what my mom said, this was not how a marriage was supposed to be. Or was it? I didn't know. *Maybe I'm just imaging things.*

One Sunday morning we were sitting in church and the kids were in Sunday school class. Worship was just about to begin and Richard leaned over to tell me that sometimes he would try to picture what the women on the worship team would look like naked. I was appalled! *Why was he telling me this? Why would he try to picture such disgusting things? Was I really that horrible of a wife? Was it my fault that he would do this? Why did he tell me this right here and at this particular moment in time?* Self-hatred and unworthiness arose in my heart and mind. If he would do this during worship in the middle of church, then how could he truly be seeking the Lord? I was so angry at him that I actually left him sitting in the pew and went to the back of the church as tears began to fall.

The reality of what my life had become began to sink in. I didn't have a choice but to put up with his addiction. How I wished for things to change! Tears fell down my checks, and I didn't bother trying to hold them back. I was utterly ashamed to call him my husband at this point in time. This was the man that I had chosen to marry and spend the rest of my life with? How could I continue to live with this addiction? It was now spreading to other areas of my life and it was getting harder and harder to pretend that nothing was wrong. People saw the tears and asked me if I was okay. I lied and told them that I was okay. How could I ever tell anyone what he had just said? My entire family would be banned from church and considered outcasts. Yet another secret that would need to be kept. The pain went deep. My heart hurt for the women who were being violated and had no clue about it. My heart hurt that my husband was the one doing that! He was so much like my dad, that it hurt even more. However, time had told me over and over again, that the issues with Richard were all my fault and that I could never talk about them with others. Therefore, I didn't have a choice other than to accept it as my lot in life.

CHAPTER 106

At one-point things got so bad at home that I took a huge risk and scheduled an appointment to meet with the head pastor of my church. I had been told by multiple people that I was undermining my husband's authority as a father when I would step in to protect my children. I wanted to know if I was "Biblically" wrong to step in when my husband lost his temper and started to get physical with the kids. I was so scared that I would be told that I was a horrible mom because my children would never see their father as one who could discipline them. My stomach was in knots, and I could barely speak when I sat in my pastor's office. The pastor's response shocked me. He basically told me that when he behaved like that, that he was stepping outside his God-given authority and that me stepping in when he blew his top was not undermining his authority, but that it was my duty as a mother to protect my children. He told me to keep on protecting my kids. He also reassured me that I was doing the Biblical thing. He told me that he would have one of the deacons reach out to him and see if they could get some type of help for him. Unfortunately, Richard fell through the cracks and nothing was ever done--and nothing changed. I had made my choice, and now I would be forced to live with that decision until the day that one of us died.

There were times he forced me to have sex even though I didn't want to then. Sometimes I was struggling with a memory or having a difficult time keeping him separate from my dad, or times when I wasn't feeling very well, or when I was simply too tired after a long day with the kids. It was such a double standard: when he wanted to have sex I had no choice but to comply. Yet, there were times when I wanted to, and he just said no, rolled over and went to sleep. Other times, I would be sound asleep and I would be abruptly awakened by my husband assaulting me and forcing himself on me. When he had been satisfied, he would simply go to sleep as I laid there trying to stay in the present. I tried to remind myself that I was married and that it was my responsibility to please my husband. *But what about my needs? Did I have the right to say no? Did I have the right to agree to sexual encounters BEFORE they took place? What about the triggering of memories: how do I to separate what Richard was doing from what my daddy did? It must just be me.* I needed to learn to distinguish the difference from the responsibilities of a married woman and the abuse of my childhood.

Many times throughout my marriage I told Richard that when he grew a beard it was an extreme trigger for me. I would explain that when my father would abuse me, most of the time he always had a beard. Thus, when I would have a sexual encounter with him and he had a beard growing, that it would automatically send me back to my youth when my dad was hurting me. It was extremely difficult to separate my dad from Richard at those moments. The first time this happened, his response was "I'm sorry," and he went to shave it off. Yet, there would be so many times in which he would grow it back out and ignore how I felt. I'd politely ask him to shave, and his response was "I'm a grown adult and if I want a beard, then I can have a beard." It was all about him and what he wanted. He had absolutely no concern for his wife who was constantly being traumatized over and over, simply because he was selfish and only thinking about his own desires and wants.

The things that he would say to me were so mean at times. He would say that I was fat and needed to lose weight. If I was skinner than he wouldn't need to look at other women. Basically, I was the reason that he had the desire to look at others. I didn't understand how being fat or skinny would have any effect on his actions. The manner in which he spoke to me at times simply broke my heart. All I could hear in the back of my mind were the words of my father, "Someday you will make your husband really happy." I was just a tool for Richard's enjoyment and since I wasn't skinny enough for him, my usefulness was over. The words stung my heart, but I tried to allow them to simply roll off of me the best that I could.

Whenever we went places together as a family, I drove because Richard was a horrible driver and literally scared all of us. He would drive at unsafe speeds, swerving in and out of traffic, or suddenly break. The fact that he did these things intentionally was the worst part. He also received quite a few tickets that we couldn't afford, so it was simply easier to drive instead of him.

CHAPTER 107

To help supplement our income, and to use the gifts that God gave me, I began to teach high school mathematics to homeschool students in the area. It was really a great deal for me. I would teach one day each week and then provide them with homework to work on for the rest of the week. This group of homeschoolers would gather at a local church every Monday. I loved teaching, and this allowed me to continue doing what I loved while still being home to raise my family. I enrolled my kids in fun classes so they would have some place to go while I was teaching. This was an excellent source of income for my family, and something that I was very good at. I ended up teaching within the homeschool community for nine years. During those years, I would go to Julie's house on Sunday afternoon to spend time with her but also to have some quiet time to grade papers. It worked out great for both of us. My presence helped her focus on her lesson plans and gave her motivation to get things done. It was a win-win for both of us.

CHAPTER 108

I became pregnant twice more but lost both babies around twelve weeks into the pregnancies. When I questioned the doctor why I had two miscarriages following two perfectly normal pregnancies, he actually told me that my husband and I were genetically incompatible for having a girl. He believed that the two miscarriages were both girls. When we got pregnant for the fifth time, the doctors gave me medication in order to sustain the pregnancy. The medication made me so sick that I had people come to help clean my house, care for the boys, and bring my family food. The sickness that had me bedridden lasted for the entire first trimester.

The baby made it full term, and we proudly gave birth to a beautiful healthy baby girl we named Elizabeth, which means "My God is abundance." It was the name that I had always wanted to name my baby girl, and now I had finally been able to do that. Giving her the same name as Beth, who had literally saved my life, was one way that I could give honor to the amazing friend that God used to save my life so many years ago. Her middle name, Marie, was the same as my adoptive mom's middle name. She was our little princess! It was clear from the beginning that Richard favored his daughter over the boys. That made me very nervous for her as she would grow into a beautiful young lady. My mind tried to go back to when I was born and how my daddy felt about me. However, I couldn't allow myself to go there for any reason at this point in time. I wanted to enjoy each and every minute of her life. Yet, I looked over my shoulder and hers all the time. The protective mode was greatly magnified with each passing season. I struggled to leave my princess in the care of her own father out of fear of what might happen. I had no way of knowing whether or not the images he had been looking at had changed to young children or if they ever would. All I knew was that my daughter would NOT suffer the way I had suffered. For the sake of her safety, I became hypervigilant and couldn't afford to ever let my guard down.

Things didn't get easier in the marriage with the birth of our daughter, but I knew that I was done having children. Richard decided to "undergo the knife" so that I wouldn't have to. The vasectomy was one of the rare times in which he was truly kind. I didn't know how to respond, as I kept waiting for the axe to fall. Thankfully, it never did.

School started a few shorts week after Beth was born and I needed to teach one day a week, so I made a special arrangement with one of the parents. In exchange for tuition for their daughter, she would watch my newborn on Mondays while at "school." In between classes, I would nurse Beth and get in some cuddles. Then this mom would care for her all day. She loved the attention, and Beth affectionally became her "baby." Beth grew up surrounded by my students and the learning environment. They all showered her with attention and affection. She was loved by many!

As my daughter grew older, my memories became more and more intense. Beth was the very image of me as a child. When I looked at her, it was as if I had looked into a mirror and saw my own reflection staring back at me. The pain, hurt, and memories tried to bubble up, but I simply continued to shove them down as far as I possibly could. I didn't want to deal with the memories, I simply wanted to enjoy my baby girl!

CHAPTER 109

As the kids grew older, I continued to homeschool them. The younger two both suffered from a speech impediment and had speech therapists come to the house for weekly sessions to help them improve. I thoroughly enjoyed teaching the kids, though it was tough teaching Joe. I realized that he had some learning difficulties and needed extra attention. The speech therapist recommended that we send him to a preschool program that would give him the special attention that he needed. The program did exactly that and provided him with all the special teachers and therapists that he would need right there at school. I decided that it would be better for him to have all that attention he needed in one place, so he began attending the program at the local elementary school. That first day was tough on Mom! To have my little boy strapped into a five-point harness on a school bus and then have it drive away was not something that any mother is prepared to do very readily. He was only three years old. Zach enjoyed waiting for the "cheese wagon" as our neighbor called it, so he could play with his little brother. We played many games of ice hockey in the winter months while we waited for the bus.

I continued to visit Julie's house on a weekly basis. It was my one time to get away from Richard and kids for a mini-break. We would do lesson plans together, plan field trips for our kids, grade papers, play Scrabble, and have heart-to-heart conversations. We both needed each other as we navigated motherhood together. There were many times that I would try to discuss what was happening at home, but I couldn't bring myself to talk about all the things that were going on. She had been friends with Richard before our wedding, and I didn't want to offend or hurt her.

CHAPTER 110

One night I showed up and we decided to start with Scrabble. I pushed up my sleeves and Julie stopped dead in her tracks. She reached across the table and grabbed my arm. "What is that? What happened?" she asked. Immediately tears began to fall as my secret was finally out in the open. Are you cutting? Yes. I had to try to explain, but I was unsure of how much to share. There were times that she just couldn't handle the full truth of my past, because it broke her heart knowing the abuse that I had to endure as a child. I simply explained that at times the emotional pain and hurt were so overwhelming and I didn't know how to get it to stop. At those times, I would cut slices into my forearms to cause physical pain for a short period of time. That burst of physical pain would stop the emotional pain, even if it was only temporary. I would then "nurse" myself back to health in a way that I knew how to do. I assured her that the cuts were never life-threatening but just surface cuts. Tears fell down her cheeks as she realized the amount of pain that I must be enduring in order to cause me to cut myself. She made me promise to call or text her the next time that desire came. I promised to try. This was a habit that started in high school. I wasn't sure if I could break it with just a simple promise to a friend, but I would try. That was the best that I could offer.

Throughout the years of our friendship, she would often inquire about the cutting and if I was overcoming it. Sometimes, I could honestly say, "Yes." Other times, I had to say, "No, I gave in because I was too overwhelmed." She was the only person who knew of this coping mechanism. Julie was the first person I had been completely honest with. It was a very special friendship that I treasured deeply. Unknowingly, she had saved my life in more ways than she would ever know or understand.

CHAPTER 111

Late one afternoon, my brother called to tell me that Dad was in the hospital on life support and that we (implying just he and I) were leaving in the morning to go visit him. I was so shocked that I simply agreed to go. I didn't sleep well that night as the thought of seeing my dad again was not in my plans. I left with my brother, and when we arrived at the hospital I was confronted with the family that had not seen me since I was eight years old. It was very awkward to say the least. Then came the moment that I was dreading. my brother and I went in to see our dad. As we walked in, the nurse informed us that most of his vital organs were shutting down. As the surviving children, we needed to decide whether we wanted to continue life support or take him off of it. I couldn't understand why his brothers and sisters didn't make that decision but had left it for us to make. We decided that since his major organs had already shut down, that there was no point in continuing life support. So, they discontinued it.

In my spirit, I heard the still small voice of the Lord telling me that I needed to take my dad's hand, tell him that I forgave him, and then share the Gospel with him. I sat there fighting with the Lord in my heart. There was no way that He could possibly expect me to do that. *He wanted me to touch him? He must be joking with me.* I sat there debating with God in my head, *After all that he did to me, you want me to forgive him? I understand that forgiveness is more for me than it is for him, but still! That is asking a lot of me.* At least the fact that forgiving is more for me than him, I could understand. To share the Gospel with him? I don't want him in heaven, he should burn in the pit of hell for the things that he did! *I understand, God! I know that you died for him too, but me? Why me? You are asking a lot of me!* Yet the voice would not stop with its gentle nudging. Therefore, I sat in his room waiting for a time in which I could do what I had been asked to do.

My aunt never seemed to leave the room. Then, she started telling me that my dad was so heartbroken when they took me away from him and, to this day, he never understood why they took me away. I was shell-shocked. Listening to my aunt go on and on about how heartbroken my father was.

Seriously? What about me? With burning anger rising up on the inside of me, I looked right at her and asked if she wanted to know why I was taken away. She nodded, so I told her that my dad had sexually and physically abused me and that was why they took me away. *Maybe I had been too blunt, but I was done with the lies.* She didn't know what to say. She got up and left the room.

I was finally alone with my dad. I ever so slowly got up and picked up my dad's hand, fighting bile in my mouth at the sheer touch of him. I did what God asked me to do. I told him that I forgave him and asked him if he wanted to accept Jesus. I then spoke a prayer and said that if he wanted to, he could agree with asking Jesus into his heart. Once I was finished, I left the room to join my family in the waiting room. *Did he accept my forgiveness? Was he sorry for the torture that I endured under his care? Did my words affect him?* There had been no response, but whether he heard me or agreed in prayer with me or not, I had been set free. I realized that God was his judge and jury, not me. I had given him my forgiveness. God had given him one final chance to change his heart and accept His forgiveness. Whether he did or not, was not my concern. Did forgiving him suddenly change the evil events of my childhood into acceptable things? Did it somehow make it easier to deal with those events? The answer to both of those questions was a resounding NO! Yet, as I walked away, I discovered that I had been a prisoner in a cage of bitterness and unforgiveness. When I forgave my father, the door to my cage was flung wide open and I flew out of that cage. By forgiving my father for the evil things that he had done to me, I had opened the doorway to allow God to forgive ME for the things that I had done wrong. In Matthew 6:14-15 (TPT) it says, "And when you pray, make sure you forgive the faults of others so that your Father in heaven will also forgive you. But if you withhold forgiveness from others, your Father withholds forgiveness from you." I had forgiven my father only to find the Father had forgiven me; I had been set free! My father's future was in God's hands now. For his sake, I prayed that he accepted God's forgiveness; though in the depths of my heart were hopes that he didn't. Parts of me wanted to see him suffer just as much as I had suffered. But the Lord clearly reminded me of His words in Romans 12:19 (TPT), "Beloved, don't be obsessed with taking revenge, but leave that to God's righteous justice. For the Scriptures say: 'Vengeance is mine, and I will repay,' says the Lord." God's vengeance would be so much greater than anything that I could've dished out. For in Mark 9:42 (TPT) it says, "But if anyone abuses one of these little ones who believe in me, it would be better for him to have a heavy boulder tied around his neck and be thrown into the sea than to face the punishment he deserves!" Those promises in God's Word had successfully reminded me that God is the only Judge of my father, and that

He is a Righteous Judge at that. Dad lasted a few more hours and then passed away.

The next couple of days were a blur. My brother told me that since I went to church that I could work with the pastor to plan his funeral. Was he kidding me? *You want ME to plan the funeral and eulogy of the man who tortured, beat, and raped me? You expect ME to find KIND things to say?* I was blown away. I decided to compile information and memories of my family members to put together the things that would be said, as the things that I wanted to say about him I knew would not be shared. I learned about a different side of my dad through the things that my extended family remembered about him. Overall, it was a good service and things went well. The biggest struggle was how we were going to pay for his funeral. My brother thought that there was life insurance, but it turned out that his company had swindled it away from him. He had nothing, so we chose the least expensive option: cremation. My brother borrowed money from a cousin that he would have to pay back. Even though I had absolutely nothing to do with my dad for the past thirty years, I put up some money as well, simply because I couldn't allow my brother to pay for the whole thing himself. The money I put forth was actually our mortgage payment money for the next month, but I hoped that Richard and I could make it work.

The next couple of months were hard as I struggled with my dad's death. I still don't know how I felt about what God had asked me to do. *Did it make a difference? Did he actually pray that prayer? Did God ask me to do that, not so much for his sake, but for mine? Will my dad be in heaven when I get there? Honestly, that one is so hard for me to picture and accept. Yet, I know that if he is, when I get there, I will be so glad to see my Jesus, that I won't care anymore.* Life slowly returned to our usual version of normal. About six months later, we were in serious trouble with the mortgage company. We had asked for help from them two months after my dad's funeral, and they told us what to do. We followed their advice and now a couple of months later, they denied ever telling us what they told us, and the damage was irreversible. We were going to be foreclosed on, though it would take about six months to complete the process. It was so hard to not become bitter and angry at my dad. I took a risk to help family, and unfortunately it didn't work out for us. We were told that the process would take about six months and that during that time we would be able to stay in the house rent-free. The searching for a new place to live began along with the packing and the thinning out of our belongings.

CHAPTER 112

After attending a local youth group's worship night, we began to make connections with the members of another church. It was amazing to see my kids actively pursuing the love of God and seek after Him with their whole hearts. I, too, started to seek God with everything that was in me. I attended youth group with my kids on Thursday evenings, church on Sundays, and prayer meetings three times a week. The prayer meetings were really early in the morning. I wanted to go so badly that I would place my sleeping children in the car and drive twenty minutes to get there. Once I arrived, I would carry my kids inside and set them on the floor with their blankets, then I would join the adults as we prayed. God began to transform my heart and soul during this time. Sometimes when my oldest couldn't get back to sleep, he would actually join the adults in prayer. This momma's heart was full! Priscilla was one of the people who came to morning prayer. I enjoyed listening to her pray and secretly desired to pray as she did. It was like God was her best friend, and she was simply talking to her friend. Yet, she prayed with an authority that I had never heard before. I wanted to have that kind of relationship with God, so I pressed in with all that I had. I wanted to be friends with God.

I wanted to learn all that God had in store for me, and I knew that in order to do that, I needed to read the Bible more. A friend and I began to study the Word together to hold each other accountable. We would read a couple of chapters each day and then get together to discuss the things that God had showed us. It was really fascinating to see the different things that we each pulled from the same passage. We both learned so much during this time.

God began to show me so many things and to heal so many wounds of my past. One of those areas that He brought healing to was the need to self-harm. Since I was studying, praying, and worshipping more, I discovered that I no longer had the desire to cut. Instead of cutting to release the emotional pain, I would turn to God and He would help me through it. The relief that I received from not self-harming was beyond description. God had taken an old coping mechanism and showed me that it was no longer needed. He became the supplier of all that I needed. The difficulty in my marriage was still there. The painful memories were still there. God didn't take the pain away, He simply helped me find a better way of dealing with that pain. Pretty soon one week free turned into two weeks, which turned into a month, which turned into three months; eventually I had gone so long that the idea of breaking that clean cycle was a motivation in itself. I didn't want to start all over, so I would turn to God and He would help me through any rough patch. God became my true friend!

CHAPTER 113

On New Year's Eve, my family went to a friend's house for a party. I was swamped with grading papers for the homeschool students since packing and going through the contents of an entire house had put me really behind. So, I brought my papers along with me to grade while I socialized with my friends. I was sitting in a chair trying to get some work done while listening to a conversation that was happening around the island in the kitchen. One of my friends, Priscilla, was talking about a program called In the Wildflowers[1]. I was intrigued and decided to put down my grading and move closer so I could hear the entire conversation instead of just bits and pieces. Priscilla was describing a program for those who had been through physical, sexual, emotional and spiritual abuse. A small group of women would gather together for a weekend to walk through this program. It was designed to bring healing and restoration to the abusive wounds of the past so that they could move into the freedom that God had for them.

I was so confused. I asked Priscilla, why would anyone voluntarily choose to talk about the abuse from their past? If it was in the past, then doesn't it just need to stay in the past? It made no sense to me why someone would volunteer to revisit the pain. Priscilla then said the following, "It's like having the courage to take the lid off of a garbage can so God can clean it out to prevent the rats from being attracted to the trash." I literally had no words. What she said intrigued me yet truly frightened me. *Was there rotten trash in my life that was still attracting the rats? Would I have the courage to face the abuse for an entire weekend? Was I willing to finally stop running? Was I willing to drop the walls and the open all the doors to allow the things buried deep, deep down, to finally have a voice? Must secure those doors! I don't have time to deal with these things.* Yet, the idea of not having to hide these things away all the time was quite intriguing. It was so scary to contemplate all that had happened, but the message had been received in my spirit and God would not leave me alone about this program. I went online and inquired about it. A woman by the name of Valerie responded to my request for more information. She told me if I was interested that I would need to pay the fee as soon as possible as it was first come, first served.

After praying about it, and with Priscilla's words resounding in my head, I made the decision to attend. It was scary, but I was choosing freedom over fear. *I was done hiding.*

In a couple of days, I received the registration paperwork. I had to fill out a very long questionnaire, which was even longer for me as I had to answer questions about my biological family as well as my adoptive family. Then I had a phone interview with a counselor to make sure that this program would be a good fit for me. This questionnaire really forced me to take a deep and honest look at my life. In order to get the most out of my weekend, I chose to be completely honest with myself and with others when answering each question. It took me quite some time to fill out that form, but since I was being honest it would be worth it in the end. I didn't want superficial healing, I wanted deep healing that would last. By the time I was finished, the document was eight typed pages! It was scary but freeing to finally have a voice.

It was strange, the freedom that I felt by simply sending that information to Val. Then I started overthinking everything and began to freak out. *Someone knew a lot of my secrets, what if that information was made public? What if Richard found out what I shared? What would people think?* Fear and panic began to creep into my thoughts. Then I forced my mind to stop racing. *I trusted Priscilla. Priscilla trusted Val. Therefore, I had to trust Val. She was a safe person or Priscilla wouldn't be a part of this program.* Peace began to settle once again in my heart. My phone interview went very well. Now to just pray for God to prepare me and my heart for whatever He wanted to do that weekend.

About two weeks later, I was attending a worship event when Priscilla approached me with a woman I didn't know. She introduced me to Val. Panic overtook me and, unfortunately, my face didn't hide it. This was the one whom I had just shared some of the most personal information of my life story with and now she was standing in MY space, not a neutral space, but *my* space. The program was a separate world apart from my daily world and the two had collided in a very unexpected way. I had to work so hard to remember my manners. Though I did find an excuse to move away from them quickly. I had lost control of my environment and this introduction threw me into a tailspin. I needed to regain control of my mind and heart. *What did Val think of me? The woman that was introduced to Val was not me! Ugh. How will I ever recover from this? Will she kick me out of the program? Lord, you need to help me, as I have messed things up really good this time.* The worship music had started. *Yes, I needed to worship!*

CHAPTER 114

During the months before the program began, God was already working on my heart. He started pointing out specific things and leading me to discoveries that surprised even me. The major surprise that God showed me was my ability to write. I began to write "poetry," though some question if it could be called poetry. Below are the two major pieces that God led me to write before In the Wildflowers[1] began.

Cocoon

In a cocoon all tightly wrapped
Safe and secure with every surrounding known
Knowing that something's changing
Knowing that I'm changing
Fearful of the process
Fearful of what I'm going to look like
Wanting to stay where I'm at
Only because it is comfortable
Like a newborn being swaddled
Safety
Yet something is pulling me
Tugging at my heart to break out
Asking me to trust
Whose voice is that that I hear?
Why do they insist that I leave?
Don't they know it's safe and warm here?
Trust is what they keep saying
Trust
I stir a little trying to see whose talking to me
Oh no, part of my cocoon broke off!
Light shines in the tiny hole
My eyes are stinging!
What is happening?

Wait, that light is showing me that something is changing
No, I'm changing!
As I move to try to see the changes, more of the cocoon breaks off
If I keep moving, my safety will be gone
So I freeze
Trust me still echoing in my ears
How can I trust the unknown?
What is going to happen to my safety?
I somehow know that I can never go back
I have been changed forever
So I am left with a choice
Do I stay changed, but bound by my cocoon?
Or, do I fight to get out of the cocoon and see how I've changed?
Trust me
That voice is still echoing in my mind
I guess it's time to fight my way out!
It is a slow process
It hurts as I squirm to try to break more of the cocoon
I realize that major changes have occurred
I'm too big for this cramped cocoon
I have a desire to soar
Wonder where that came from?
Trust me
Okay. More wiggling
Why does that part hurt?
It feels like it is trapped or bound by something
Must focus my attention on setting that part free
Ouch! That hurts!
Must persevere!
Wow! That part's finally free!
Now I realize that there are other parts that are bound as well
Want to stop because the pain is so intense
Yet the voice has changed
It's no longer telling me to trust
The voice somehow knows that I now do
So it is telling me of the freedom that waits for me
That ultimate freedom is stirring something inside of me
Hope.
Hope that things will be different
Hope that I can be completely free
Hope that I'll never be the same
Fear of the unknown tries to creep in
NO! Hope is overtaking fear!

I want to listen to that voice!
Complete freedom
I start to imagine what that's going to look like
The voice interjects, you've stopped.
You must keep going!
So back to working on those bonds I go
Freedom lurking in my mind
No it's made its way to my heart
I want to be free!
So now I press on with great furor
The work is still hard, but the bonds are slowly falling off
I will be free of this cocoon
Realizing how limited I was within what I thought was safety
Now I'm almost there!
Just one more to go!
Freedom!
Free at last!!
Now I sit among the broken parts of my old cocoon
Knowing I am forever changed
Confused for a while as I look upon the transformations
Unsure what to do now
I've been striving to be free for so long
The voice prompts me to lift my wings
I quietly point out, I have no wings
The voice patiently repeats lift your wings
As I take some time to examine the new transformations
I realize I do indeed have wings
So with slight trepidation
I lift my wings
Then the voice tells me to relax
Relax in His presence
So I obey the voice that I've come to trust
The next thing I know, I'm soaring!
Soaring above all the things around me
Looking with a completely new perspective
I see the old broken cocoon
That I thought was my safety
Now I see that it was my prison!
True freedom to soar
Soaring
At that point I discovered whose voice it was that kept telling me to trust
It was the very voice of my Creator!
The one who designed me to soar with Him!

Wow, such freedom!
Ultimate freedom, not just to be free
But to be free and to soar with Him!

~Jen Koning (4-17-12)

Walls

I sit inside a small circle
Shivering and alone
Waiting for someone to come and sit with me
Surrounding me are many walls
They are in layers you see
Each one like a moat around a castle
Designed to keep out intruders
Ultimately for my protection
Longing for love I venture outside my walls
I can go in and out with ease
Yet when one becomes special then I retreat
Thereby forcing them to pursue me
I sit inside my circle waiting to see
Will they pass the test?
Will they find a way to scale the walls?
Only those who can are permitted inside
Yet there are so many walls separating us
Most get past the first couple with ease
The walls become even tougher the closer you get to me
Remember they were designed for my protection
Then I watch as those whom I wanted to come sit with me
They slowly get discouraged
They give up and retreat
Changing their minds
Yet they don't realize that yet another wall was just erected
Must protect
Must not get hurt
Will anyone make it through all of my defenses?
I occasionally come out and fellowship
Especially with those who make it to a certain point
Eventually I return to my circle
There I sit longing for an embrace from one who can make it to me
Yet my defenses are too strong for most
Some have come pretty close
But no one has made it in all the way

I wish I knew how to tear down the walls
I wish I knew how to stop creating the walls
I wish I knew how to stay on the outside of my walls
I wish someone could penetrate all my defenses
I so long for an embrace of love
So in the mean time I sit waiting
Shivering and alone

Then I hear a soft and gentle voice speaking to me
"You are not alone
Why do you think that you are as you continually try to hide behind these walls?
You can't hide in secret places, for I can see you
You can't flee from my spirit or my presence
For you are not alone"
But my walls are for my protection
They keep me safe
"You may have needed them in the past, but not anymore
I am with you always
I am your strength, whom shall you fear?
I am a shield around you
I am the lifter of your head
When others forsake you, I will take you up
I am your refuge and your fortress
So fear not
You have been hiding behind these walls for too long
Don't you know that I have come to bind up the broken-hearted
To bring liberty to the captives (that's you)
And to open the prison of those bound?"
Looking around me I notice that my walls have been transformed
They no longer completely surround me
They no longer force others to scale them
My walls are now a labyrinth of hedges and bushes
I can see that some of my friends are within the labyrinth
Others are in it but they have brought hedge trimmers with them
They are taking the time to trim as they go
Making the way to me easier for those that follow
I then see that I am not alone in my circle
I am in the presence of God himself
As I look around at my circle
It is bigger than I remember
And He has made it into a beautiful garden
A special haven of sorts

There were beautiful flowers beds with water flowing around them
Patches of green grass
Benches to talk and rest on
There were even fruit trees with ripe fruit ready to be eaten
"This place is for you
A place to rejuvenate and refresh
A place to fellowship with Me
A place to fellowship with your friends"
Yet looking around, it looked impossible for others to get here
He then handed me a pair of loppers
"You asked Me, how do you tear down the walls?
My answer, One at a time
Take these and start helping your friends find the path to you
The area around this garden is really overgrown
It will take time to trim it all
But I will help you
Your true friends will also help from the other side
If you get tired, then come and rest in me and with me
Eventually your friends will be able to join you here in this garden
You will also have to continue to prune your hedges
Or they may become overgrown again
Remember that Through Me you can do all things
I gave you power, love, and a sound mind
So fear not, just believe in me
I love you with an unfailing love
A love that is higher than the heavens
Remember that even if it looks daunting right now
That nothing is impossible with me"

~Jen Koning (4-27-12)

These writings gave me hope to continue pursuing my healing and my freedom. They put into words the very things that I was experiencing. In a cocoon, I was trying to find the courage to break out and be the beautiful butterfly that I was designed to be! To literally soar with the Father. Butterflies have always been special to me. You see a butterfly can go where it wants. If it finds itself in a place where it's not wanted, it can just fly away. Yet, no one turns away from a butterfly. They are beautiful creatures that everyone wants to look at and behold. I wanted to be like the butterfly and just be accepted for who I am, not what has happened to me. I wanted others to look at me and smile as they think that I am beautiful and desire to spend time with me. The other writing brought to my focus the walls that I erect to protect myself from being hurt over and over again. As I was keeping out the hurt and the pain, I was also keeping out the love of friends and family. I had to learn to let down the walls. I had to stay outside my barriers and stop retreating behind them every time someone got too close to my heart--to the real me.

So many times I would scream on the inside and wonder if anyone could hear me. I never understood why no one seemed to care. Or why no one noticed the amount of pain and hurt that I was going through, which is why I would turn to cutting, to momentarily cause physical pain to take my mind off of the emotional pain. Whether that be one of the foster homes, shelter homes, adoptive placements, or my friends: *Why couldn't they see? Why couldn't they hear?*

Screaming

Trapped.
Scared.
Feeling completely alone.
Wanting so desperately for someone to notice.
So much pain.
Need to talk.
Pressure building inside.
Reaching out failed.
Again and again.
Must not scream. Must try again.
Return to regular activities.
Pretending that everything's fine.
As people scurry about completing their tasks, no one sees.
Hiding has worked so well.
Pressure building inside.
It's getting too high.
Need to release the pressure.
Try talking with this person, door shut.
Try a different one, door shut.
Door after door, they shut.
Not high enough of a priority.
Too busy to notice.
Too busy to pause.
Pressure building.
If I scream, will they hear me?
It starts real soft and sporadic.
Like a tea kettle.
Building in intensity.
Now a loud and high pitched noise.

Screaming at the top of my lungs.
Why doesn't anyone hear?
So I scream louder.
No one hears.
My throat hurts from screaming.
My ears hurt from all the echoing.
I collapse.
Alone.
Trapped.
Why can't anyone hear me?
Am I really not that important?
Everyone thinks I'm tough and strong.
Little do they know that I'm falling apart on the inside.
As I sit completely worn out, I look around me.
I'm trapped within a glass house.
Sounds bouncing off the glass walls.
There appears to be no way out.
Confusion sets in.
How did I get here?
How do I get out?
How will others ever hear me?

These words echoed in my heart and mind as it described me so accurately for so much of my life; but God was showing me another way. He was showing me the way out. I had to have courage and find the right people to talk to. He showed me that Priscilla and Val were those people, and that this program would be the place to start giving voice to the hurt and pain that I had trapped inside of me. I had so many different voices trapped inside glass houses that I needed to learn how to set them free. I had to begin to trust again. He told me that both these women loved Him deeply and they could be trusted with the deepest of secrets. So, I listened to God, trusted His Voice, and continued to prepare my heart for all that He was going to do.

PART V – THE TRANSFORMATION

CHAPTER 115

T he weekend finally arrived, and I was as ready as I could be. My heart was open and ready to receive all that God wanted to accomplish. The other participants were complete strangers to me, and I was very shy at first. *He told me that I could trust Priscilla and Val, but what about these other women? Could they be trusted as well?* Then God gently nudged me. *They are in the exact same boat as you are in. Are you going to allow fear to keep you from all that I have for you? Or are you going to step out of the boat and out onto the water?* I decided to step out of the boat. I wanted all the freedom that God had in store for me, and I would do the hard work and trust the process. There were privacy agreements that we all agreed to, so I can't go into any specifics of that weekend. I don't ever want my new friends to question me or be fearful that I would share information about their stories. What I can tell you is that God showed up in a huge way for all of us. For me, it was a chance to actually connect with the little girl that was trapped inside of me-- the one who was so scared and lonely and didn't understand that it wasn't her fault.

We had the opportunity to sign up to receive a prophetic word from the leaders. I had never had a prophetic word given to me and, to be honest, I didn't even know what that meant. But it sounded intriguing and I was open for all that God wanted, so I signed up and was the second one. I still remember those prophetic words that were spoken that night. They have been confirmed many times by friends and complete strangers since that first telling. My initial reaction to this word was disbelief. I couldn't see it happening, but I told God, "In your timing, Lord. In your timing." Are you curious as to what that prophetic word was? Well, you are reading it right now! The word that I received was that I would be writing a book. There were other parts to my prophetic word, but those are still between God and me as I wait for His perfect timing.

Val played many songs that weekend, but one really spoke to me. This song felt as if it was coming from my own life, and I could hardly believe it. Tears fell down my face as she played "The Real Me" by Natalie Grant and my walls began to crumble. The song spoke about the games we play when we put on different types of masks instead of being "the real me." How many times had I been screaming on the inside and wished that people could see the REAL ME, not the one that I pretended to be? How many times have I put on that "plastic" smile? How many times have I pushed others away simply because they were getting too close? How many times have I been hiding in my own mind? Then to hear in the song that God sees me! He sees the REAL me. He thinks that I'm beautiful. He loves me just the way I am. I don't have to change in order for him to love me. I don't have to have it all together first. He loves me just as I am. I could be the Real Me in front of Him. I don't have to mask my weaknesses from Him. I can put all of the masks down. The walls fell and God began to work in ways that I may never truly understand.

CHAPTER 116

I found so much healing as more writings poured forth that weekend. Priscilla convinced me to read them to everyone throughout the retreat. There were many tears shed and memories that were finally given a voice for the first time. It was a life-changing weekend. I had found the courage to remove the lid, and God had begun taking out the trash and cleaning my heart. There were lies that were revealed and replaced with the truth. New friendships formed as we shared things that couldn't normally be shared. There was freedom. When it was over, I felt like a completely different person from the one who began the program. It seems so strange to think that one weekend could bring about so much change, but it did. Now, that being said, did everything get all sunny and rosy-side up? That would be a resounding NO!

One of the biggest revelations that I had that weekend was that the things that were happening in my marriage were the very definition of abuse. I could no longer pretend that it wasn't. I was a child of God, and I deserved to be treated as such, not as a discarded toy or play thing. My kids and I all deserved to be treated differently. Now, was I guilty as well? In some ways, yes. I didn't give Richard some of the respect that he deserved. I was controlling at times and, when I got frustrated, I could yell with the best of them; but the way he spoke to us or blew up at us or grabbed us, leaving bruises in the wake, were all forms of abuse. Those things needed to stop! I now understood that I had the power to politely demand that they change, as God began changing me as well.

CHAPTER 117

One thing that really impressed me was that among all the evil that truly existed in this world and that was done to children, God was always present. He was crying and holding these precious children as mankind chose to side with evil and hurt these innocent ones. Some of the things that were done to these precious children were unfathomable, and my heart ached hearing some of the stories. Despite the evil, God showed up and helped protect these kids in a way that the world doesn't always understand. The level of evil was so intense that a child would be incapable of understanding the depths of torture and would die if they couldn't find a way to deal with that trauma. God gave these children a way to "spilt" their minds into different parts in order to keep on living. Some of those parts would hold the memories of the abuse tucked away so they could deal with it at a later time. Some would hold all of the anger. Others would stand up as protectors making sure that no one would hurt them again. To see the adults who had spilt as children was pretty amazing. It was like they had a small community inside their heads: each part had its own role and each one performed that role so that the individual could survive and thrive. In the psychology world it's known as Dissociative Identity Disorder (DID) or Multiple Personality Disorder.

After seeing quite a few abuse survivors who had DID, I wanted to see what the Word of God might say about this topic. In Psalm 34:18 (NLT) it states, "The Lord is close to the brokenhearted: he rescues those whose spirits are crushed." Now the Hebrew word for "brokenhearted" is *shabar* (shaw-bar')². *Shabar* means: 1) to be broken, maimed, crippled, wrecked, and 2) to shatter or break. So that verse actually reads: The Lord is close to those who have shattered; He rescues those whose spirits are crushed. The Lord knows that the evil is too much for some, especially little children, so He gave them ways to cope that the world might not always understand. Here are a couple of other passages that I had found:

> Because of the privilege and authority God has given me, I give each of you this warning: Don't think you are better than you really are. Be honest in your evaluation of yourselves, measuring yourselves by the

faith God has given us. Just as our bodies have many parts and each part has a special function, so it is with Christ's body. We are many parts of one body, and we all belong to each other. In his grace, God has given us different gifts for doing certain things well. So if God has given you the ability to prophesy, speak out with as much faith as God has given you. If your gift is serving others, serve them well. If you are a teacher, teach well. If your gift is to encourage others, be encouraging. If it is giving, give generously. If God has given you leadership ability, take the responsibility seriously. And if you have a gift for showing kindness to others, do it gladly.

Romans 12: 3-8 (NLT)

The human body has many parts, but the many parts make up one whole body. So it is with the body of Christ. Some of us are Jews, some are Gentiles, some are slaves, and some are free. But we have all been baptized into one body by one Spirit, and we all share the same Spirit. Yes, the body has many different parts, not just one part. If the foot says, "I am not a part of the body because I am not a hand," that does not make it any less a part of the body. And if the ear says, "I am not part of the body because I am not an eye," would that make it any less a part of the body? If the whole body were an eye, how would you hear? Or if your whole body were an ear, how would you smell anything? But our bodies have many parts, and God has put each part just where he wants it. How strange a body would be if it had only one part! Yes, there are many parts, but only one body. The eye can never say to the hand, "I don't need you." The head can't say to the feet, "I don't need you." In fact, some parts of the body that seem weakest and least important are actually the most necessary. And the parts we regard as less honorable are those we clothe with the greatest care. So we carefully protect those parts that should not be seen, while the more honorable parts do not require this special care. So God has put the body together such that extra honor and care are given to those parts that have less dignity. This makes for harmony among the members, so that all the members care for each other. If one part suffers, all the parts suffer with it, and if one part is honored, all the parts are glad.

1 Corinthians 12: 12-26 (NLT)

In these passages, God is describing the Church as a whole. Within the Church are many members and each one has been giving a particular gift, role, or job. With that gift or job, they are to function as one body. No member or part is more or less important than the others; each one is important and has a special function, even if we think that it isn't. This was the same principle in which God gave some children the ability to create this same spiritual concept within their own mind, so they could survive the horrendous abuse that they were forced to endure. God also tells us in 1 Corinthians, that the "same Spirit" is the source of all the gifts that are given to the members of the body and that He (the Holy Spirit) alone decides which gifts each one will receive. So, if God, through the Holy Spirit, decides that a child should have multiple gifts in order to survive, then who are we to question that? Who made us the judge or jury of the acts of God? He alone knows what His plans are and how that will ultimately play into His master plan. This amazing process is not something to fear. We as a culture tend to fear what we don't understand. I choose to celebrate with these women for being brave and courageous enough to acknowledge their brokenness and accept the different gifts of God. To use those gifts is to survive and, ultimately, to give hope to others. These women were hurt on so many different levels that my heart broke at the extent of evil but rejoiced that they had survived, and that God was going to use them and their stories to further the Kingdom by bringing healing to other individuals similar to them.

CHAPTER 118

When I returned home, I began to pray more frequently like I've never prayed before. I began to write more and more poetry as the Lord directed me to do. I remember being so excited that I would call Val on the phone just to read to her the new poem that God had inspired me to write. I was just filled with life, and it overflowed to every corner of my existence. I was so impacted by this one weekend that I asked if I could assist her and Priscilla with for the remaining three In the Wildflowers[1] sessions that summer. She said, yes.

I ended up helping to prepare the materials that would be handed out to each participant, as well as actually attending each session to help with different aspects of the program. I attended each one ready to see the healing and freedom that would occur in the lives of the attendees. However, with each session, I was transformed a little bit more with each one myself. I thought that God was pretty amazing! I went just to serve the ladies who would be coming and to assist Val and Priscilla only to have God show up and teach me something new each time. Every time I went through the program, I healed a little more and had even more freedom.

At one point, I decided to send my mom an email with some of the things that I had written. She wrote back and asked who wrote it because it was really good. I told her that *I* had written those pieces. She could hardly believe that I was the author because I was a horrible writer in high school and my grammar left something to be desired. Yet, God had grabbed a hold of my heart and nothing was too difficult for Him, even turning a mathematician into a writer! One of the other major changes was how I carried myself. I was beginning to understand my worth, and I wouldn't allow others to trample on me any longer. I carried myself with my head lifted instead of hanging it in shame.

CHAPTER 119

The kids were enrolled in public schools for the first time in five years, as I had considered going back to school to obtain a better paying job to help with finances. Richard and I were unsure at this point but felt that our homeschooling days were over. It was a struggle for me, but the kids adapted well. Zach would be in sixth grade, Joseph would be in fourth grade, and Beth would be in second grade. Zach and Beth seemed to do very well with the transition, but Joseph struggled a bit. He had the beginning signs of ADHD and struggled academically. The school wanted to give him time to adjust before testing him to see if there were any learning deficiencies that would need special attention. It was a bit strange for me to have so much free time on my hands during the day!

The bank had given us a move out date for our home and, after much searching, we had finally found a house to rent about twenty minutes from where we currently were living. The house that we were going to be renting was much smaller than our current one, and we couldn't possibly take all of our things with us. We moved into our new place the weekend before Christmas. We had help lined up for Saturday, but on the Friday before moving day we ended up spontaneously moving all of our furniture along with some boxes to fill in the gaps on the trailer. Since it was just three of us doing this, we simply placed the furniture into the new house and thought that when we had more people on the next day that we could arrange it where we needed them to go.

Moving day arrived, December twenty-second, and we loaded the trailer in sunshine and thought we were blessed. After we finished, we started driving to our new house and drove right into the middle of a snowstorm. When we arrived, it was a race trying to get the boxes into the house before the heavy and wet snow soaked everything beyond their limits; I wasn't sure if the boxes would hold up. We were forced to simply put things wherever we could find room instead of placing them in the correct rooms, just so we could get them in out of the snow and so that they wouldn't fall apart. We finally brought in the last box and thankfully none of them collapsed on us. Now began the process of unpacking. The majority of our help left since the boxes were inside, but some stayed and helped. It was so difficult to move the furniture where we wanted it, as boxes were in the way everywhere we turned. We ended up handling those boxes SO many times before they were finally unpacked. It took a bit of work, but we made it.

CHAPTER 120

When I tucked the kids into bed on Monday night, Christmas Eve, they asked if we were going to have a tree for the presents to be under when they woke up. I told them, "We'll just have to see. I'm not sure I even know where the tree is right now." When I saw the disappointed look in their eyes, I determined in my heart, that this move would not hinder their Christmas. I would find our tree, no matter what! After searching for quite some time, I found the mini-Christmas tree to put up along with a few decorations. We actually set up the tree on top of a few boxes and placed the tree skirt for our large tree underneath it. It covered the top of the box and made it more festive. Then I found the boxes labeled "Christmas Presents" and unpacked the wrapped gifts to place under the newly decorated tree.

I decided to leave the tree lights on all night so the kids would be surprised when they woke up. Richard and I awakened to excited voices and came out of our room to see our happy children. I'm so thankful that God had helped me find that tree and the move wouldn't be ruining our Christmas tradition. We started the celebration by reading the Christmas story together and opening presents, all among the boxes.

CHAPTER 121

Things had gotten a little bit better with my marriage and, for the first time, I had hope that we were going to make it. I had a flutter in my heart when he wasn't around, and my heart jumped with joy when he came home. We still had some issues to work out, but at least we were communicating with each other for the first time in twelve years. I continued to assist Val as her assistant for a non-profit ministry. Each week I would go to her house and help her with whatever needed to be done. Most of the time I formatted or edited documents and occasionally traveled with this ministry to assist with concerts that ultimately led kids to Christ. It was awesome to see the kids that were ultimately impacted by this ministry. I treasured the times that I had with Val. She had become a very important person in my life and a friend in whom I could confide about all things both past and present. Val became a sounding board for my ideas and thoughts. Most of the time, I figured out my own answers simply by talking about them out loud. It was a fantastic gift that I had been granted.

CHAPTER 122

The following fall, when my kids were eight, eleven, and twelve, I left for a week to help Val and the non-profit ministry at an event in Ohio. I hadn't left my kids very often as I was unsure of what would happen if I wasn't there to intervene on their behalf, but as things were better between Richard and me, I chose to step out in faith. It was a great week. Then, upon my return, I saw the computer sitting in the middle of the living room and Richard was in the bathroom. I went over to put the computer away and the images that I saw made me want to throw up! My children had actually looked at it and wanted to know why daddy was looking at those things. That was the final straw. I couldn't take any more.

For the sake of our children, I told Richard that he needed to get some help. I had pleaded with him to stop for himself and the sake of our family. I had pleaded with him to stop for the sake of our marriage. I had pleaded with him to stop for me. I had pleaded with him to stop so he wouldn't pass this addiction on to his children. He ignored all of those pleas over the years, and now that trash had fallen on the eyes of our children! I was furious. I told him that he needed to leave and find a place to live while he sought help. He agreed to go. He went to stay with his sister, but he told her that I kicked him out for no reason. Eventually he ended up at his mom's house. He did finally tell his sister and mom why he moved out.

Richard did start counseling but didn't dive very deeply into the reasoning behind his actions. He told me that the reason why he looked at that stuff was because he was lonely due to the time that I spent with the ministry and my new friends. I looked right at him and said, "Try again! You need to dig deeper! I only started working with this organization about nine months ago and you have been looking at that stuff since our first year of marriage twelve years ago, if not before!" Once again, he tried to put the blame for his addiction onto someone else so he wouldn't have to truly face the real reason that he was addicted.

CHAPTER 123

After Richard had moved out, there was such a noticeable difference in my children and myself. It made me think of all the safety questions that the doctors ask when you go for a visit. I had been hearing those questions at the doctor's office over and over. I had always responded out of instinct and rout memory. "Do you feel safe at home? Do you have a safe place to go home to?" I had always answered those questions with a resounding *yes*. However, with Richard out of the house, I had a peace that I had never known. I actually felt safe for the first time in over twelve years. My house had finally become a safe place. I no longer lived in constant fear day in and day out. The really sad thing was that I wasn't the only one who was experiencing that peace. I noticed changes in all three of my kids. They were much more at peace and relaxed, and it was evident that they were feeling relief even if they couldn't express that in words.

I attempted to set boundaries during this time of separation in order to give Richard the space he needed to seek help, but also so the kids and I could heal as well. After attending a couple of counseling sessions with Richard, it was clear that he wasn't going to abide by any boundaries that I set. Richard and I agreed that the kids would stay with me for Thanksgiving. I invited a friend, Jessica, to celebrate with us. The kids really wanted their dad home for Thanksgiving dinner. I told Richard that he could come over for dinner, but that after the meal was finished he needed to leave. Richard agreed to these boundaries. However, when dinner was over, he didn't leave. I was so wound up and full of anxiety. I announced to the kids that I was going to take Jessica home, and when I returned Daddy would be leaving. He didn't leave until three to four hours AFTER dinner was over.

When we discussed Thanksgiving Day at his next counseling appointment, his counselor asked him how he thought it went. He replied that it went great. Then the counselor asked me the same question. My reply was that Richard did not abide by the boundaries that we agreed upon. His counselor asked Richard if he agreed to the terms of him coming over for dinner, and he said that he did. The counselor asked him why he didn't leave after dinner was over. He said that he didn't leave because he didn't want to leave. He was having too good of a time and chose to stay even though the boundaries we had agreed upon were being violated. Even the counselor was a bit taken aback by his response. Richard wanted what he wanted and didn't care what anyone else wanted. I left that session realizing that he didn't even see that anything was wrong with what he was doing. I told myself that, at this point, it was not worth my time to attend his sessions, and that I wouldn't come back until he became more serious about his issues.

CHAPTER 124

T he following summer, I allowed Richard to stay with the kids at our house while I assisted with three more In the Wildflowers[1] weekends. God was moving powerfully, and I loved being a part of it. Since I had been through the program four times already, I thought that there wasn't much more I could get out of it. But was I wrong! God was probably laughing at me in heaven as He lovingly looked down thinking, "Just wait, my daughter, just wait. I have more freedom than you can imagine, just for you!"

During these sessions and throughout the summer, I began to have new memories slowly surface into my conscious awareness. They would start in my dreams. I would wake up from what I thought was a nightmare. I couldn't figure out why I would dream about such horrible things, only to later understand that it was my mind's way of helping me accept those events as things that I had actually endured. I had simply repressed them due to the severity of the abuses that were done to me. However, because I was finally in a safe place with a good support system, in the depths of my mind I knew that now I could face those memories. It was a real struggle to accept those things as real events in my life.

However, God showed me that it was part of my story. It was like a puzzle was being put together and I would receive one piece at a time. Once I figured out how each piece fit, then I would get another piece. I am still getting new pieces, but I trust the process and understand that over time the puzzle will be complete and whole. Another thing that God revealed to me was how much He loved me and the different gifts that He gave me to help me survive. He was weeping along with me when I was being raped while speaking into the ear of my father trying to get him to stop what he was doing. That image will never disappear for me. It truly showed me how much God loved me--even before I knew Him! It was one powerful gift that He gave me that summer.

Another gift from God that summer was to recognize that the ability to split into different parts in order to survive the horrific abuse had saved not only some of the attendees, but me as a child. You may ask how that could possibly be a gift. Wouldn't that be considered a curse? To be honest, sometimes it does feel like a curse, but most of the time I view it as a gift for a season of my life. I have had compartmentalized parts of my psyche that held memories of horrific abuse that I went through at such a young age. Those parts would hold on to those specific memories in my subconscious until I was able to deal with them. I have had parts that held on to all of the anger for the things that I had to endure. If not for this ability to separate these thoughts, I would have been overcome with rage that would have destroyed my life. I have had parts that were super protective of me and protective of the potential that others might hurt me. No one can sit here and tell me that it's not real. I have conversations and debates in my head at times, which I know is not typical of the thoughts people often bounce back and forth in their heads. These particular thoughts are from the child's viewpoint, the angry parts, the protective parts. It gave me a very rounded perspective to realize that my thoughts were both those of myself as a child and as an adult.

Maybe you still can't see how this could be a gift. You tell me how a small child of four or five years of age could possibly survive being raped by two men at the same time; being locked in a cage naked; having that cage lifted into the air and then jabbed at with stakes and spears just because I wouldn't voluntarily do what my father wanted me to do; being tied up with my legs and arms spread eagle style while being raped and tortured; being urinated on; being sprayed with ejaculation while being laughed at; being forced to perform oral sex; having a man ejaculate in your mouth; to look at a gift of a brand new nightgown and begin to dread what would happen next, for a new nightgown always meant that I would be taken to a building in which strange men would get to play round robin with all the little girls that were brought that night; to have your own father sex traffic you; to be forced to participate in bestiality; being locked in a room tied up for hours on end trying to break your spirit; being raped by cousins simply because you didn't hide well enough and were found in a twisted game of hide-and-seek in the woods. You see, NO child could ever endure the things that I have without losing their mind and just giving up on life. It was like my heart had shattered into many pieces during those tortuous and traumatic events. The individual pieces were locked securely away in the recesses of my mind until the day that I decided I wanted to put the puzzle together. Each memory, each part, is a piece of that puzzle. Only God knows how many pieces my puzzle contains and He is so faithful. "But even if we are faithless, he will still be full of faith, for he never wavers in his faithfulness to us!" 2 Timothy 2:13 (TPT) He has promised to complete what He began.

"Being confident of this very thing, that He who has begun a good work in you will complete it until the day of Jesus Christ," Philippians 1:6 (NKJV).

I knew that despite the gift that I had received, it was a gift for a season of my life. It was never meant to be a place to stay! Psalm 147:3-5 (TPT) says, "He heals the wounds of every shattered heart. He sets his stars in place, calling them all by their names. How great is our God! There's absolutely nothing his power cannot accomplish, and he has infinite understanding of everything." God placed EVERY star into the sky and NAMED each one. That demonstrates his infinite power. God also said that he "heals the wounds of every shattered heart." To me, this meant that God would indeed heal my shattered self. I would be whole. This shattered heart and mind were simply for a season of life, and God had other plans for my next season. I strived to reach for that healing, while trying desperately to believe that amongst the new memories it was indeed possible.

CHAPTER 125

I will not tell you that it has been easy recovering these memories. I will not tell you that it has been easy accepting these events as real. But as my good friend Val said to me, "What reason would you have to make this all up? How could you possibly recall these memories in such vivid detail if it didn't really happen? How could your body physically react as if it's undergoing the abuse all over again if it didn't experience it in the first place?" These questions were repeated to me over and over as I processed the events of my childhood and began to accept them as the truth. Sometimes I still need to ask myself those questions to reaffirm that this is real and not made up or a figment of a demented imagination. If you know me, you probably would never have guessed that I was fragmented. There are lots of people that I meet who are "fragmented" and don't know it. I see the signs, and some day they will understand that it's nothing to be ashamed of. It was a gift from a loving and caring Father trying in the best way possible to help these hurting children survive the atrocities that they had to endure.

When I find myself struggling with a new memory, God will speak to me often through the lyrics of a song. I could add probably five chapters on all the different songs that He used, but I will limit myself to just one for now. The song is entitled: *Another in The Fire* by Hillsong UNITED.

This song serves as a reminder that no matter what happened to me or what might happen in the future, that there is always someone in the fire with me. This song is a culmination of many Bible stories wrapped up into one song: Daniel and his friends being thrown into the fiery furnace and there being another figure in the fire, and all of them came out of the fire without even smelling of smoke or having a single burnt fiber (Daniel 3:19-27); the parting of Red Sea, where all the Israelites passed through on dry ground (Exodus 14:21-31); the Jordan River during harvest season when the waters were at their highest levels and stopped flowing when the priests, carrying the Ark, stepped out in faith into the water (Joshua 3:13-17); Jesus being flogged and hung on a cross to save everyone from the consequences of their sins (John 19:1-37); how three days after Jesus was buried in a tomb, it was found empty (John 20:1-9); Paul and Silas were in stocks in prison when there was an earthquake and the prison walls began to shake and the prison doors flew open (Acts 16:24-26); Peter in prison bound between two guards and suddenly there was a great light in the darkness and his chains fell off (Acts 12:6-9); God promises to never leave or forsake us (Deut. 31:6, 8; Joshua 1:5). For me this song reminds me of all the stories in which God never left or forsook His people. He has never left me either. He has always been by my side, whether I knew it or not. He was always in the "fire" with me and he always "held" back the seas so I wouldn't drown. This knowledge was extremely important to me as I encountered new memories: I KNEW that I was not alone. He was--and is--with me always, for He is a good, good Father, so unlike my earthly father.

God showed up many times throughout that summer and during those In the Wildflowers[1] sessions. I received even more healing that I could never explain no matter how many words I used. God began to take that orphan child and transform her into His child--every part of me. Nothing was beyond His ability to transform.

Despite the changes in my relationship with God and the new memories that arose, my marriage was still on the rocks. It appeared to be at a stalemate. Richard was content where he was. I was not content, and I wanted a closure for my children and myself one way or another. We deserved at least that much.

CHAPTER 126

During one conversation with Richard about his progress, he said the following: "When I told you that I was sorry and that I promised to try to stop looking, I actually had no intention of ever stopping." His words were yet another onslaught in the abuse that he so freely dished out. He went on to explain that he didn't feel that I had a right to tell him what to do and only said what he knew I wanted to hear to get me off his back. My heart sank inside. *Would he ever change? Would I ever be able to trust this man again?*

After almost two years of no change on his part, and with him still living at his mom's house, I thought that I might offer a bit of incentive to compel him to make some changes. I filed for a divorce thinking that it might give him a kick in the butt and a desire to change. I went out to my car for some privacy and called him and had a very calm and peaceful conversation with him. I asked him if over the last two years he had made any changes to show that an effort was being made on his part. His reply was, no. I then told him that since he wasn't making an effort to change, and the kids and I deserved some kind of resolution to this situation, that I would be filing for a divorce. I was personally tired of answering the questions from my children that were on repeat: "Where is daddy?" "When is daddy coming home?" My responses were getting old, and I disliked the taste of them rolling off my tongue: "Daddy is getting help." "I don't know when Daddy is coming back home." Instead of pleading with me to not file for a divorce, he totally agreed and said that he understood.

Tears began to fall down as I ended the phone call. Here was my husband willingly giving up his family so he could continue with his addiction. I was devastated and had no words for the ache in my heart but also for the ache and hurt that would be in my children's hearts once they fully understood the truth. My husband who spoke vows to be by my side till death do us part was not willing to fight to keep us together. My heart was breaking. I was once again alone, but this time I was bringing three young kids along with me. We were finally safe and I needed to keep that in the forefront my mind.

Yet, I struggled with the fact that I would soon be a divorced woman. I was willingly breaking my covenant with God, and that was so difficult to accept and process, though many friends told me that he broke that covenant first. However, I was the one who would be beginning this process, so wasn't I the one at fault? Despite the fact that I would soon be divorced, I couldn't believe in the depths of my heart that I wasn't justified in my actions. Richard had been committing adultery in his heart for almost fifteen years. He broke his wedding vows every time that he looked at those images. He was also abusive to his family, and I knew that God would not expect me to stay in a marriage like that. I kept trying to make myself accept that I didn't do anything wrong, but it was a daily battle. I had just accepted the responsibility of raising three kids as a single mom who wouldn't get any breaks except for two to three hours once a week. I had given up my full-time job to raise and educate my children, and now I had to find a job in order to support them. However hard this season would be, I knew in the depths of my heart that the decision was the best one for both my children and me.

CHAPTER 127

Grandpa Arno was an amazing grandparent. There were so many times that our inside joke of "brain damage!" kept us laughing many, many years after the original memory. This man played such a huge role in my life that is hard to explain. Yet, to honor him, I will try. My biological dad's parents had left a horrible impression in my heart and mind of what grandparents were supposed to be like. So, when I met Grandpa Arno and Grandma Margie, I had expected them to be the same as my previous grandparents. Yet, at every turn, they continued to prove that wrong! Grandpa Arno was a very honorable man. He served his country in World War II. He loved his family, but he loved his Lord and Savior more. I remember going to his house on Sunday afternoons and holidays. I could sit with him for hours chatting away about life and God. He would occasionally pull out his Bible. One could see that it was well used.

One year he had the opportunity to participate in a program called Talons Out Honor Flight. He and a group of others were flown to Washington, D.C. to see their memorials and to be honored as true heroes. I remember being told that there was a parade upon their return at Wings Stadium, and I was invited to be there with the kids to welcome him home from his flight. I had planned on going, but my kids were just recovering from being sick, and the arrival time was delayed. Honestly, I didn't understand what the flight was all about until afterwards, so I made the decision to not attend and allow my kids to get some much-needed rest. That has come to be one of my biggest regrets! I wasn't able to properly honor a man who deserved so much respect, and I wasn't there to show that to him. You see, not only did he serve his country, but he also served his church, his family, and as a model of redemption for me. He showed me how grandparents are supposed to love their grandkids; how they are supposed to treat their grandkids; how they are supposed to teach and instruct them; how they are supposed to guide them; how they are supposed to pass on values; how they are supposed to pass on a Godly heritage. He had given me the biggest gift one could give me, and he didn't even know it. This man was a living testament of what love, strength, courage, and honor really meant. I was grateful for the opportunity to call him my grandpa and for my kids to know him as Great Grandpa.

My heart broke when I was informed that he had passed away. I knew that he was now pain-free and in heaven with his Lord and Savior, but my heart still ached. I experienced so much loss with his passing. There would be no more family gatherings on Christmas Eve. There would be no more Sunday afternoon visits. There would be no more memories and values passed on to my kids from their amazing great grandfather. The tears wouldn't stop and neither did the tears from my children. When he was buried at Fort Custer with full military honors, my heart exploded in pride and admiration but also with a deep sense of loss. I had lost my last grandparent, and I wished with all my heart that my kids had had more time with him.

CHAPTER 128

At one point, I was overwhelmed with new memories surfacing one after another and, with the pending divorce, I needed to seek out some counseling of my own. I found a place that offered free therapy and decided to give it a try once again. My counselor was Amy, a name I've changed for privacy purposes. We talked about the new memories that were surfacing, but mostly we talked about my separation from Richard and the pending divorce. Amy helped me process the many raging emotions of him not being there. We discussed how I felt relief but guilt at the same time. This counseling office also happened to provide free food to families once a month. So, I began to take home a couple bags to help reduce the food bill.

At this time, I was working three different jobs while attempting to find a full-time job to bring more stability for us during this time. I was substituting at my kids' schools, but it was only about eight months of the year. I had no income for the summer months, so I had to have something else in place. I was also working as a caretaker for a few elderly people. I would shop for groceries, prepare food, give baths, help them to the bathroom, and occasionally clean. My other job was cashiering at a local grocery store. I was always home for dinner each night and never gone for long when my children were home from school. When I would be gone, I would have my oldest who was thirteen look out for his siblings, and he could always call me or ask his friend's mom who lived nearby if help was needed.

Surprisingly, Amy became concerned about my children. She called Child Protective Services. I actually had a police officer show up at my door. He told me that there were allegations of neglect, not enough food, lack of proper clothing for my kids, and that my kids were left unsupervised for long periods of time. He stepped into my house and could see cupboards full of food. He could see my kids were healthy, and that they had taken showers. I told him that my oldest would occasionally watch his siblings for a couple of hours after school until I got home from work, but it was never for long periods of time. He simply dismissed the case and apologized for bothering me.

I was furious! How could my counselor call CPS on me? I was a single mom trying to provide for my kids. I may have taken free food, but that did not mean that my kids EVER went without a meal! I have skipped a meal or two, but I made sure that my kids always had food three times each day. As a former foster child who was in the system, there would be NO WAY that I would ever put my kids in jeopardy of being placed into that situation! I loved my kids and made sacrifices that they probably will never understand. I couldn't understand how a counselor could make such wild accusations with no proof whatsoever. It boggled my mind! Needless to say, I never returned to see Amy. I was done with counselors! I would simply continue to deal with things as they came up with God and the friends that he had provided.

CHAPTER 129

God began to show me that I was worthy of being loved, and that I was indeed blessed with the very thing that I had dreamt of--a forever family. When I was a pre-teen, I had in my head what I desired in my adoptive parents. Like any child, dreams are often lofty and unattainable. Then I had been adopted into an amazing family. They loved me and supported my dreams and aspirations just as they did those of my siblings. I was given opportunities that I wouldn't have had otherwise, such as going to college. Over the years, I had been extremely hard on them as they failed to be the ideal parents of my dreams. However, in reality, I couldn't have asked for a better set of parents. Simply because they didn't express love to me the way that I expected it did NOT mean they didn't love me. I was treated the same as my siblings: I was allowed to play sports; I was taught how to do things; I was given privileges and responsibilities; I was disciplined (not beaten) when I did something wrong; I was given birthday and Christmas gifts; I was clothed and fed; I was praised and encouraged to follow my dreams; I was never left out or abandoned; I was told that I was loved. They traveled all the way from California to meet their grandkids and to spend time with me. I was always included in family gatherings. You see, I wasn't an orphan: I WAS FAMILY!

However, I didn't always treat them like family. As a result of my wounds, I pushed away the very thing that I longed for. I didn't understand how to truly accept the love of others, though it was the one thing that I craved the most! My heart had been so damaged that it had a bazillion holes in it. Every act of love and kindness plugged a hole and allowed me to grasp a tiny bit more of their love. I was so hungry for the love and attention of my parents. It may have appeared as if I was ungrateful, but I didn't know how to tell them that they had just plugged another hole. Inside I screamed for them to keep going, as their love was felt even if they couldn't see the manifestation of it on the outside. My parents and their family have redeemed so many relationships for me. My prayer over the years was that they would truly understand that I loved them the best way that I knew how, and that I knew beyond a shadow of a doubt that they loved me as their daughter--not as an adopted daughter--but as their *daughter*.

CHAPTER 130

I had many friends that God placed in my life as support throughout this whole process, and I wouldn't be where I am without their love and encouragement. Val continued to be a huge support in ways that no one else had ever been to me. While we worked together on different projects for the ministries, our days were filled with laughter and deep discussions about God, life, and whatever things I struggled with. She loved me in ways that at times I simply couldn't comprehend or understand. In one of our conversations, she told me, "If I had known you when you were younger, I would have adopted you!" The idea that someone else would have made the sacrifice to adopt me was mind-boggling. I had so many people and families tell me that I was unworthy and unwanted; thus, her words echoed in my heart for months to come as I contemplated my worth and value.

Sometimes our work days were interrupted when new memories would surface. We would spend the day talking about them, and Val had a way of giving me the freedom to speak about events and abuse that no human ear had ever heard. During those times, she helped me to bring the memories out of the darkness of secrecy into the light and truth. She helped me find the lies that I had believed and to replace them with the truth of God's Word. There were many times in which she would use my daughter to minister to me. When I would tell her something that had happened to me and how I was filled with self-blame and disgust at my younger self, she would ask me, "If the same thing had happened to Beth, would you blame her?" My reply was always a resounding NO! She would then turn the tables and ask, "Then why do you blame yourself?" I greatly disliked it when she compared me to my daughter, but it was exactly what I needed to hear in order to stop blaming myself for things that I had zero control over. This process helped me to gain perspective and to stop blaming my younger self for not having the power or knowledge of my adult self. Val never held the abuse and rapes that I endured against me. She never thought that I was inferior or any less deserving of being loved. Val loved me with a love that was unconditional, and that love filled many of the holes within my heart and soul. She taught me that I was worthy of being loved and worthy of being protected. The assistance she gave me in processing memories, the knowledge that she gave freely, and the gift of friendship all made Val an invaluable asset and irreplaceable in my life. She was--and is--a treasured gift that I hold close to my heart.

Val and I had many conversations about my marriage and the upcoming divorce. She was a sounding board and refused to allow me to beat myself up for choosing to take that action. One of the major revelations that God gave me as I struggled through accepting the divorce was the following: out of my wounds and selfish desires to have a family as soon as possible, I made the hasty choice to marry Richard. Therefore, "I have to take responsibility for lowering the standard of purpose on my life by settling for potential."[3]. When I got married, I settled for less than God's best choice simply so I could fulfill my own dreams. I wanted a family so badly that it hurt sometimes. I wanted to have children so I could love them the way that I never was loved. I broke off my engagement to Richard the first time because I knew that it wasn't right. Then for five years I waited and waited. I prayed for God to bring someone else across my path, but there were no other possibilities on the horizon. It had appeared that Richard had changed, at least on the outside. He seemed to love the Lord, he went to church, and he wanted me back. It felt good in my brokenness to have someone desire me. However, I knew deep down that I shouldn't marry him, but I chose to ignore that feeling. The mistake was mine. I made the choice, and I had to live with it. It was a poor choice, but God blessed me with three amazing children that I wouldn't wish away for the world! In taking ownership of my decision to get married, it set me free from the shame and guilt of filing for a divorce. Currently, I am waiting for the man that God has reserved for me. I know he's out there and, in time, God will have our paths cross. This time around, I will wait for him.

CHAPTER 131

O ne day Val and I took a day and dedicated it to an inner healing session. It was a very difficult day speaking about memories that had never been given a voice. Nobody had ever heard the details that had been protected by the deep secrecy code of my daddy and hidden behind so many layers of protection within my mind. After the session was over, I lay on her couch and told God out loud that I forgave my dad and my mom for all that they had done and failed to do. Tears of release fell down my cheeks as I soaked in the peace and love of God. God had taken all the parts and integrated them into one. I was free! I slept so well that night. The next day, I went to church and had a very special encounter with the Lord's presence. I actually wrote about the experience in my journal, because I didn't want to forget the things that God had done in my heart during that encounter. The following was my journal entry:

It was amazing to worship this morning at church! I never thought that worshipping could be so touching. As the words and music flowed, it impacted my heart and soul in a way I can't explain. It was so hard to stay standing as God touched my new whole heart in a special deep way. It was a communion with him that I've never experienced. Tears flowed as his touch continued. Then the worship team played a song that made me want to dance down the aisles yet fall flat on my face at the same time, *Your Love Is Strong* by Cory Asbury. The lyrics were resounding within, and I wanted to scream them from the mountaintops! It was like hearing my story broadcasted for all to hear! His love had conquered ALL my enemies. It broke the cage that I had been trapped in and that had silenced me! Which ultimately, set me free!! I sang and rejoiced for all the love and acceptance He so freely gives me. Another line in that song seriously undid me. I've had this thought that I was always an orphan since I was a small child. People kept telling me that I'm not anymore because I was adopted both in the natural world and spiritually. I knew that but couldn't shake the orphan feelings that I was experiencing. I even felt led to title my book: *Orphan No More*. Until today, I couldn't explain why I had chosen that title, except the generic reply of being in and out of foster homes/adoptive homes; there was no emotional and/or spiritual understanding for my decision at all. UNTIL TODAY!! When I was abused as a small child, it caused me to split into dozens of parts. Each one of those parts were, in essence, orphans. No mother. No father. No family. They were alone, trapped in time within my brain. Yet since those parts were me, in essence I *was* an orphan. Abandoned. Alone. Without family. Yes, I was adopted and given a physical family, but they didn't know about my parts, so they weren't adopted when I was physically adopted. I gave my heart to the Lord and became His daughter. But I wasn't aware of my parts, and therefore they didn't make that choice as I had. So, I remained an orphan at heart. This morning it hit me. When Val and I worked through the new memories, there was a tremendous amount of inner healing that took place. During the inner healing, Jesus called each and every part home! Some, one at a time, while others went in handfuls. Each one had to experience the Love that could conquer all their enemies. Now I understood why I was told to title my book, *Orphan No More*. There was now a very special meaning behind the title of my book because it is a representation of the fact that I am NO longer an orphan now that I am of one mind. Orphan No More!! His love really is strong! I feel such rejoicing inside as I celebrate just how strong His love really is! Then I had the privilege to partake in Holy Communion. Such, such sweet love! Afterwards, we sang *Amazing Grace My Chains Are Gone* by Chris Tomlin. I sang my heart out as tears fell silently down my face from unending gratitude of my savior's love for me. Such sweet, sweet worship from a new perspective of being completely whole for the first time. Oh, my sweet Jesus, oh, how I love thee! I even had moments of spontaneous worship during musical interludes. I've never done that before. I was basking in His unending love and amazing grace!

That encounter with the Lord was so powerful. The effects of that service were held deep in my heart. It was the beginning of an even deeper and more intimate relationship with my Lord and Savior. For the first time in my life, I truly felt loved and accepted. I began to dig even further into the Word of God and found more truths to grab onto. Things were finally beginning to look up for a change.

CHAPTER 132

About a week later, the ringing in my ears returned. New memories were surfacing once again. After speaking with Val, we came to the conclusion that all the parts in the first level were integrated, but that I had created another layer of parts that were secured behind even deeper security protocols. They were buried so deeply that not even I was aware they were there. My heart was crushed. Here I had experienced freedom only to have it snatched away. *Am I on the receiving end of a horrible practical joke? God what are you doing? Why didn't you take them all with you? Why do I have to continue to suffer? It's just not fair! I don't understand why this has to be like this!* I fell into a deep depression as I struggled and wrestled with unwanted thoughts and feelings. *I am still an orphan. I will always be an orphan. Am I really doomed to live the rest of my life like this? God, you gave me a taste of freedom and now you just rip it away? How could you do that to me? I really am unwanted and unworthy. I'm simply too broken for even You to handle. I'm too damaged to be fixed. Healing is for other people but not for this orphan child. I am alone. I will always be alone.*

I fell deeper and deeper into a horrible depression. The suicidal thoughts came rushing back along with every unhealthy coping habit. I was tempted to begin cutting again. I drank more and more soda pop and gobbled up every bit of sugar I could find. I even played more and more games on my phone while I disassociated from the world. I put on the masks of survival in order to hide the hurt and pain. *No one must see how deeply I'm hurting.* My children became the only reason why I kept pushing through, even though deep down I knew that I was a horrible mother. I may have been physically present, but I was emotionally withdrawn in a world of hurt and pain so deep that I didn't know if I would ever find my way out. *Even God has abandoned me. I was an orphan. I would always be an orphan. My hope is lost. I am beyond God's reach.*

CHAPTER 133

When it came to Richard, I didn't think very highly of him. I refused to harm my children by trash-talking about their dad in their presence. I didn't want to ever put my children in the middle between their parents or make them hate their father. There were times when I wanted to explain why we had gotten a divorce or why he was acting the way that he was, but I knew that when they got older, they would figure it out for themselves. I determined in my heart to hold my tongue and to take the high road. Despite this determination, my thoughts towards Richard were not good, and it was affecting my relationships with God and with others. God began to speak to me regarding how I thought about Richard. I was angry with him, and that anger was beginning to spill out into other areas of my life. It was like a cancer that was spreading fast throughout my body, and God wanted me to address it before it destroyed me. Just as I had forgiven my biological parents, I knew that God was asking me to forgive him. I didn't know if I could forgive him for everything that he had done, but I decided that the best thing I could do was to write him a letter, so that is what I did.

Richard,

I am so angry right now that I could fill an entire letter with my angry rants, but after thinking about it, I have decided against it. It might make me feel better for a few moments, but ultimately, you'd just ignore my words or throw it away. So instead, I've chosen the route of honesty and praying that God would open your heart to see the truth behind my words.

In my observations over the years, you have been very selfish. Why you may ask? Throughout our marriage, you have only thought of you and your wants or desires for so long. You looked at porn whenever you pleased, even sneaking around to view it. Over the years, I tried to explain to you what it did to me to discover that you were looking once again, but it seemed to always fall on deaf ears. A couple of years before you moved out, I remember asking you a question: do you want this to pass down to your boys? For the door to be opened for Satan to torture our boys with it? You quite venomously replied, "NO!" I then said that would mean *that you'd have to find a way to quit if not for yourself then at least for your children. You didn't.*

Shortly thereafter, the stuff you were looking at fell on our children's eyes and I had enough at that point. I asked you to leave until you could get some help. You have admitted since then, that throughout our marriage that you had never intended to stop, but just to temporarily appease me. That broke my heart! I never wanted to police you and constantly worry or wonder what you were looking at when I was gone or when you had your electronics alone by yourself. I tried to let go and trust you, as you were my husband. I felt guilty for questioning you, yet you continued to lie to me. You made it very difficult to trust you as you kept lying to me over and over again.

You told me after you left that you hadn't looked at any porn since you moved out, I'm praying that it's still true for your sake and our kids. I guess I still don't understand that if you had truly stopped, then why didn't you try to come home? What kept you away? Your addiction was only part of the issue for me. When you were watching that stuff, it changed you. You became withdrawn from your family and especially me. You treated me like I was an object instead of your partner and wife. Whether you realize it or not you were teaching our children the same thing as they watched everything you did and spoke.

When I asked you to think about why you even started to look at porn in the first place, you told me it was because you were jealous of my friendships that I had developed in the last four years. That showed me that you were still unwilling to own up to the addiction and that you were not ready to face the consequences of your choices. You were still trying to blame someone else for your choices. I needed to see visible changes. Since I was lied to for over 13 years, I could no longer just trust you at your word. I needed proof that I could see. The kids and I deserved to see positive changes. After two years of waiting, I got tired of waiting for something that appeared like you were unwilling to show me. So, I took the next step and decided to file for a divorce. You just rolled over and gave up, no effort to try to change my mind or to try to convince me to try again. That hurt me a lot, but for the sake of our kids, I chose to move on and make the best of things. I put the boys in counseling to help them cope as not having their father in their lives is painful. They are slowly working through things and with enough time they should come to terms with the lack of involvement.

Now you may be asking yourself why am I telling you all of this? My reasons are quite simple. I felt that you deserved to know of yet another consequence for your actions that you refused to change. You will stand before God and have to account for your actions and/or your lack of actions. The other reason was because I wanted you to have some tangible reasons to change. Your children need their father in their lives. Not an empty shell. Please take this information to heart, ask God to truly forgive you, and to help you to change for the better. I warned you of what could happen if you didn't change. You chose to ignore me. You have refused to get help and/or make the hard choices to beat this addiction. My prayers are that this news will give you the motivation necessary to truly repent (not just lip service like the last 15 years) and become the man of God that your children so desperately need. It may be too late for us, but don't walk away from your children! Don't let those relationships fail!! Be a man of courage.

Jen

Writing that letter gave me such freedom within my heart. I didn't tell him that I forgave him, but I did release a lot of pent-up emotions and God used that to help me to look at him in a different light. I didn't actually send it to him or allow him to read it (because I knew deep down that it would do no good), but it had served its purpose for me. I needed to get those thoughts out of my heart and my mind so I could live and not allow those feelings to eat me alive.

CHAPTER 134

Another person that God used to speak to my hurting heart was Priscilla. Priscilla had become another mom to me, but this time it was more of a spiritual mom. It is really hard to believe that almost nine years ago I was scared to have her pray for me at church! She had such a close relationship to God that, when she would pray for people, she would receive a word in season for that person. It was very unnerving to have someone that you didn't know very well begin to tell you your personal secrets that only God knew. Eventually, I came to love those words. I found it to be a special touch from God, letting me know that He had heard my prayers.

Today, this woman is very dear to my heart and the hearts of my children. They look up to her as a grandma, and I value her opinion and look forward to simply being in her company. She encourages me in the Lord every time we get together, and I adore her. Priscilla is always telling me that "her ceiling had better be my floor." That phrase confused me for the longest time, and now it's deeply engrained in my personal walk with the Lord. The basis for this phrase is found in John 14:12 (TPT), "I tell you this timeless truth: The person who follows me in faith, believing in me, will do the same mighty miracles that I do – even greater miracles than these because I go to be with my Father!" Jesus told his disciples that he had performed miracles, but they would do even greater miracles. Priscilla didn't want me to settle for the same heights that she had attained in the span of her life. Instead, I should be using what she learned and what she had attained as the starting point in my walk with the Lord, and then reach for even greater things.

Another one of her phrases, "you can go as deep and as fast with the Lord as you desire," became a repeating phrase in my struggles and encouraged me to dive deeper into the Lord on many different occasions. Nothing was impossible or unattainable with Him! Priscilla had become one of my heroes, as the depth of her spiritual knowledge was seemingly endless. I look up to her in so many ways and, because of our relationship and the encouraging words that she so freely gives, I strive to deepen my faith walk with the Lord.

CHAPTER 135

God gave me another friend, Jodi, as a support for me during my most intense struggles. When the memories had come so fast, and I no longer wanted to deal with them, Jodi was right there praying for me. It was during those times of complete agony and hopelessness, that out of a desperation for things to be different, I would reach out to her via text and sometimes by phone. We would chat for hours, and her words were like a light that would pierce the deepest darkness of my soul. It would start so dimly, but after our conversation was over it had turned into the brightest of lights; I found myself no longer standing in the darkness. There were many times that Jodi and I would find ourselves encouraging each other as we walked down the paths in front of each of us.

Jodi would tell me that she was on my wall, interceding for me and protecting my heart from the enemy attacks. In my life there haven't been very many safe people who were willing to stand on my wall. Jodi was safe, and she voluntarily stood on that wall. When she would pray, the heavens parted, and Jesus arrived on the scene! Her prayers were full of authority because she knew who she was, and that Jesus had given her authority over the enemy. In Luke 10:18-20 (TPT) it explains the authority that Jodi had and that we all have: "Jesus replied, 'While you were ministering, I watched Satan topple until he fell suddenly from heaven like lightning to the ground. Now you understand that I have imparted to you all my authority to trample over his kingdom. You will trample upon every demon before you and overcome every power Satan possesses. Absolutely nothing will be able to harm you as you walk in this authority. However, your real source of joy isn't merely that these spirits submit to your authority, but that your names are written in the journals of heaven and that you belong to God's kingdom. This is the true source of your authority.'" Jodi was a prayer warrior, and she was relentless as she stood on my wall.

I knew that she would always be there to listen, to provide a hug that engulfed you in the love of the Father, to encourage my aching heart, and to pray for me. She would tell me, "I have enough faith for the both of us." When I was at my lowest, she believed without a doubt that God would rescue me and that I would get up on my feet once again. I relied on her strength and her unwavering faith more times than I could count. Jodi taught me that even amongst the extreme hardships of life, God was always there. She would often remind me of who I am and *who's* I am! She was one of the greatest gifts that I have received, and I was beyond grateful for a friend who truly understood my struggles and would walk beside me as I traversed life.

CHAPTER 136

During the intense struggles a couple of friends started a ministry called Stirred Up that really touched my heart. I attended my first event with them to help encourage Anna and Janice as they stepped into what God had called them to do. I had been completely swept away by the power of the evening! That one event led to another and another. I knew that those events would be filled with the presence of God, the Holy Spirit, and the Word of God. The Word that Anna would bring at these events had me returning to the Scripture to study more. God had taken the words that Anna spoke and used them to show me that He still loved me and that I was not alone. I discovered that my heart and soul were so dry and thirsty, and God started to use these events to speak to me and draw me back to Him. I experienced God so intensely at those meetings, and I just wanted more and more.

At one of the first conferences that Stirred Up held, I attended and brought my daughter and her friend along with me so they could dive deeper in their own walk with the Lord. The worship and the teachings on that day began to tear down the walls that I had erected around my heart once again. The memories that I had been recalling were very intense, and I felt so alone in dealing with them. One of the speakers that God used in a very powerful way that day was Janice. She used humor and laughter to help drop the walls, and then she dropped the Word! She read a poem entitled "My Mat for His Mercy" that she wrote, and it radically changed me.

My mat for His mercy, I'll trade it today
Because down on this mat I refuse to stay
His forgiveness and healing I will receive
All that He speaks I will believe
I'll pick up my mat, and tell the story
Of when my mess met with His glory
Jesus is the One who set me free
The lover of my soul, He is everything to me
My healer, sustainer, forever faithful friend
My rock and redeemer, Beginning and End

Down on this mat I refuse to stay
My mat for His mercy, I'll trade it today

The tears silently fell down my checks as God spoke ever so gently to my hurting heart. That poem, along with her teaching, helped me determine that I was done allowing the enemy to have his way within my mind. I would stand up and allow God to use my story to help others overcome their hardships. My mess would be used for His Glory! Every speaker that followed only took me deeper and deeper into His presence, and I knew that things had to change. *I needed to change.* These women had gently put my crown back on my head and reminded me who I was and *who's* I was. I was a child of God. I was His princess. I left that conference completely fired up and ready to walk with Jesus and dive back into the Word, knowing that God was there waiting for me with each step. I was ready to fulfill the calling that God had placed on my heart, and to write my story to help other hurting women find a voice.

One of the biggest gifts that God gave me through that ministry was the deep friendships with other women who loved the Lord. Throughout my life I have always wanted close friends that I could "do life with" --friends who loved the Lord and followed passionately after Him. These friends would be the "iron sharpens iron" type of friends. "As iron sharpens iron, so a man sharpens the countenance of his friend." Proverbs 27:17 (NKJV). When I went to these events, I would always meet women who were running after God. God began to cultivate my friendships with a lot of these women. These friendships would hold together even over the miles that separated us. We have attended concerts, weekend retreats, conferences, and other Stirred Up events together. We have prayed for each other and have prayed together as a group. We have encouraged one another via texts and social media. Each one of them is a lifeline that God had graciously extended to me, and I couldn't thank Him enough for all those blessings. He had finally answered my prayers and provided the lifelong friends that I had only dreamed of for years.

CHAPTER 137

Another great support in my life was my friend Julie. She was always there through thick and thin. She still came to visit me at my new house, which was further away, even if it was not as frequently as we used to get together. Despite that, I knew that if I needed her, she would drop everything to be at my side; she was that type of friend and still is to this day. One time she received a prophetic word/vision that she knew was specifically for me. This prophetic vision was so healing to my heart and spirit; it gave me hope that Jesus knew of my fragmentation and that He was rooting for me to be whole again. He was encouraging me to keep going. Here is that prophetic vision as Julie sent it me:

> Don't fight the transformation. God's best is so worth it, beyond anything you can imagine as you walk through it... But walk on honey cuz the devil's army (pain, hurt, despair, etc.) is behind you and He has rolled back the waters, laid a path blatantly before you to follow to His promise on the other side.

> I see you on the verge of walking along a path between two towering walls of water, within those walls are all the incidents of abuse and hurt in freeze frame of action with a particular part standing there trapped. Behind you stands Satan on the shore beckoning you, on the other shore sits Jesus in a big comfy chair. Hope, peace, love, forgiveness, radiate from His presence, His hand is outstretched awaiting your grasp... "Come to me, there will be no more *owies*, come to me that I may restore your sight, that the beauty which I behold in you, you may see in yourself. No more *owies*, I love you, let me hold you, care for you, let me carry your tears." As you walk toward Him past each scene, the part is released through the shimmering wall and their tears begin to roll down your cheeks and a small beautiful delicately carved alabaster jar catches each tear... As you pass on, each part purposefully steps in and joins you until you reach the end of the path. When you reach him, He takes the jar of salty tears and pours them over the wounds on His back. Then He reaches out and gathers all the parts of you and as you move onto

His lap the parts fuse into one being - almost like a mosaic as each reflects a color of you and He holds you. And you know beyond a shadow of a doubt you are whole, you are loved and there will be no more owies, no more tears for the things are now past - gone as the waves of water crash together and the flow is restored. You are stronger for it because of His strength at your weakest point. You are His treasure, a priceless jewel, the apple of Your Daddy's eye.

This vision reminded me of the parting of the Red Sea, when the Israelites passed through on dry land while the Egyptians followed close behind. When the Israelites made it safely to the other side, the waters fell back in place and the enemy was destroyed. I pictured the same thing with Julie's vision: the devil's army of pain, hurt, and despair was destroyed in the waters. As I've traveled that path, I have had many parts that were stuck in that freeze frame share their memories with me. Afterwards, with their job now complete, they were integrated into my mind as part of the whole, no longer a separate voice. The very things that she described in that vision were actually coming true! It was really powerful, and I longed for the day that all the memories were finished, and I no longer heard those voices. I longed to reach the Promised Land!

CHAPTER 138

God still used song lyrics to speak to me. One of the songs that God used in a very powerful way was *Clean* by Natalie Grant. God knows that I love waterfalls. When I heard this song, He gave me a vision. I'd like you to picture the following in your mind's eye. Imagine a clear sky with a few fluffy clouds scattered across it. Below that blue sky is a waterfall that runs ever so gently over rocks. The water is so clear that you can see to the bottom of the pool of water around the base of the waterfall. Trees are all around the waterfall providing just the right amount of shade. Flowers surrounding the area bring a beautiful fragrance that fills the air with a pleasant scent. Birds are softly singing and you can't help but smile. Then your gaze finds Jesus standing in the water at the base of the waterfall and He's beckoning you to come to Him. Once you step into the water, you discover that it's so, so warm. As you take another couple of steps, you begin to notice that the water has instantly become dirty and you can no longer see the bottom. Yet you hear His voice as He softly calls your name and beckons you to keep your eyes on Him as you take each step. You lift your eyes and keep stepping toward Jesus. When you get to Him, He takes your hand and you step underneath the waterfall. You close your eyes as the warm water begins to cascade down on you. Jesus then begins to ever so gently and lovingly wash you underneath the waterfall. All the failures, the fears, the mistakes, the dirtiness of what was done to you--they all wash away. When you open your eyes, you realize that He has completely washed you clean. You're no longer covered in grime or dirt. Then you look at the water flowing downstream and it's the color of blood. He took all your dirtiness and cleansed it with His precious blood that He shed on the cross. Clean. Restored piece by piece. Spotless. When I hear that song, I can't help but picture myself under the waterfall with Jesus. He cleans each part of me making them pure and spotless. There's no more shame or dirtiness, for Jesus took all of that. He restores me piece by piece under that waterfall.

Jesus wants to do the same for you. He wants to wash you clean and make you whole. All you have to do is accept His gift. He freely gives it to all who wish to accept it. Think about a present that someone gives to you. What do you do with it? Do you say thank you and then set it on a shelf somewhere? I know I don't! If someone gives me a gift, I take it and say thank you, but then I open it. Jesus died on a cross for the sins of every man, woman, and child that ever lived and would ever live. All we have to do is accept it and open it. In Romans 10:9-10 (TPT) it says, "…For if you publicly declare with your mouth that Jesus is Lord and believe in your heart that God raised him from the dead, you will experience salvation. The heart that believes in him receives the gift of the righteousness of God — and then the mouth confesses, resulting in salvation." If you would like to receive the gift of forgiveness and invite Him into your heart, then pray the following prayer with me: "Dear Jesus, I know that I do things wrong and that makes me a sinner. I give you permission to cleanse me and my heart. I ask for Your forgiveness. I believe that You died on a cross for my mistakes (sins) and You rose from the dead. I turn from my sins and invite You to come into my heart and live. I want to trust and follow You as my Lord and Savior. Amen." If you prayed that prayer, then you are now a child of God. Forgiven. Made whole. You will never be alone again, for He is with you always.

CHAPTER 139

Tere are still times when the lies of who I am start to creep in again, and I need to return to the waterfall to have Him wash away the effects of that lie and accept His forgiveness as He replaces that lie with the Truth. There are still memories that I have stuffed down so deep that when they begin to surface, it requires me to make a choice of facing those memories and surrendering them to God or living with nightmares and the lies that are associated with those memories. I am still actively walking down that path in Julie's vision. I know that someday soon I will be of one mind and no longer fragmented. How do I know that? "Now may the God of patience and comfort grant you to be like-minded toward one another, according to Christ Jesus, that you may with one mind *and* one mouth glorify the God and Father of our Lord Jesus Christ," Romans 15: 5-6 (NKJV) and "Then make me truly happy by agreeing wholeheartedly with each other, loving one another, and working together with one mind and purpose." Philippians 2:2 (NLT) These verses offered me hope that God's desire was for me to have ONE mind. No matter how hard it was, I kept on walking down that path. I knew that the shock of the memories and the intensity of them occasionally make me want to stop and catch my breath, but I must keep walking or I will risk being overtaken by the enemy.

Most people take showers daily in order to get the dirt and stink off of our bodies so we can feel and smell clean. God showed me that just as I take showers to wash my body, I also need to wash myself with the Word of God in order to clean my mind and my spirit. I must train myself to look through the eyes of my Heavenly Father and not my tinted glasses. The way that He looks at me is SO very different than how I look at myself. He said that I am clean. He said I'm not shattered but that I'm whole. I've been washed clean by his blood. He says that I'm a precious treasure. He says that I'm His child.

I must make my self-talk align with what God says about me. As part of my healing journey, God had me research in the Bible who He says I am. I then put all of those verses into a book called my *I Am Book*. I've actually handwritten over one hundred and fifty of them over the past seven years to give out to In the Wildflowers[1] participants, my Bible study members, and my friends as a reminder of who they are and *who's* they are. Yet every time that I've created one, I've implanted those Scriptures into my mind once again. It's a way for me to counter the lies of the enemy that unfortunately run deep due to the severe trauma that I've experienced in my life. I need the constant reminder of who I truly am, and not who my abusers have told me that I am.

We need to proclaim out loud who we are. In Deut. 30:19 (NKJV) it says, "…I have set before you life and death, blessing and cursing; therefore, choose life, that both you and your descendants may live." Then in Prov. 18:21 (NKJV) it says, "Death and life are in the power of the tongue, and those who love it will eat its fruit." So let us continually choose life and speak LIFE over ourselves by declaring out loud how God's Word defines us. Here are just a few of the ways that Scripture describes us:

I am God's masterpiece. (Eph. 2:10)

I am God's friend. (John 15:15; James 2:23)

I am God's chosen. (Eph. 1:4; Deut. 7:6)

I am God's beloved. (Eph. 1:6; 2 Thes. 2:13)

I am God's precious jewel. (Mal. 3:17)

I have been redeemed by the blood. (Col. 1:14)

I have been set free from sin and condemnation. (Rom. 8:1-2)

I have been washed in the blood of the Lamb. (Rev. 1:5)

I have been given a sound mind. (2 Tim. 1:7)

I have been given the Holy Spirit. (2 Cor. 1:22)

I have been adopted into God's family. (Rom. 8:15; Eph. 1:5)

I have been given authority over the power of enemy. (Luke 10:19)

I have been fearfully and wonderfully made. (Ps. 139:14)

I am meet for the Master's use. (2 Tim. 2:21)

I am loved eternally. (Jer. 31:3)

I am eternally kept in the palm of His hand. (John 10:28-29)

I am kept from falling. (Jude 1:24)

I am not condemned. (Rom. 8:1-2)

I am a new creature. (2 Cor. 5:17; Gal. 6:15)

I am His sheep. (Ps. 100:3; John 10:14)

I am protected from the evil one. (1 John 5:18)

I am more than a conqueror. (Rom. 8:37)

I am sheltered under His wing. (Ps. 91:4)

I am a Royal Priesthood. (1 Pet. 2:9)

I am Blessed. (Deut. 28:2; Gal. 3:9)

I am sealed with the Holy Spirit of promise. (Eph. 1:13)

I am one in Christ. (John 17:21)

I am the apple of my Father's eye. (Ps. 17:8)

I have an anchor to my soul. (Heb. 6:19)

I have the mind of Christ. (1 Cor. 2:16)

I have the love of God poured out in my heart. (Rom. 5:5)

I can quench all the fiery darts. (Eph. 6:16)

I can declare liberty to captives. (Is. 61:1)

I cannot be separated from God's love. (Rom. 8:35-39)

I will continue to declare and decree who I am until the day comes in which it's so ingrained in me that I can't possibly forget. You see, I'm no longer an orphan, I am a child of God. God specifically told me to call this book, *Orphan No More*. You see, as a child I created parts within my mind to help me survive. Those parts had no mom or dad. They were "orphans" by definition. All throughout my life, the feeling of being an orphan ran deep, and I never understood why I felt that way--but now I do. I was adopted by the Rosenbooms. I was adopted by God. Yet, my parts hadn't been; they were tucked away in the depths of my mind hidden from the world. That is why I've felt like an orphan for all these years. However, as I reach each part along that path that was frozen in the wall of water, they became a part of me. As each part learned how much they were loved by God and choose to go be with Jesus, then I receive a deeper love and appreciation of exactly who I am in Christ. They are no longer orphans; I am no longer an orphan. They have been adopted by God. They are now His children and are no longer orphans. You see, *I* am no longer an orphan: I am a child of God. I possess all the rights and privileges of being a child of God and nothing, or anyone, can change that. If you have accepted Jesus as your Lord and Savior, then you are His child! You possess all the rights and privileges of being a child of God and nothing, or anyone, can change that.

CHAPTER 140

Over the years, I've wondered what total integration would look like. I've read stories that one "needs" the parts in order to function. That I wouldn't be the same person if I didn't have those parts inside directing certain sides of my personality. That no one had a right to expect total integration from anyone with Dissociative Identity Disorder (DID). That they didn't want their parts to disappear forever. That one could live with many parts each functioning together as a corporate whole. I've dreamt for years of being fully integrated but wondering if I'd be recognizable if I had complete integration. Would my family and friends still love me? Would they still accept me? Would they accept me if they knew? What if total integration wasn't possible? Would they still love me, even the unacceptable parts of me? That has been the fear that has held me in bondage for years. Yet, I was tired of the constant ringing in my ear; the nonstop dialogue in my head; the debates in my head before doing anything; not knowing when a part had had enough and wanted to download the memories of the pain and torture they held onto so I could continue to live; the struggle to hold back the angry replies that snapped so quickly; the nights I'd cry myself to sleep because the loneliness was unbearable; not being able to completely share with others because the secrets had to be maintained; fearful that people would not believe me; fearful that my kids would be taken away though I had never hurt them; the levels of secrets that no one knew; trying to keep myself together on the outside when inside I was falling apart; trying to pretend that I was normal while inside I was shattered into an unknown number of parts; wanting to know if there would ever be an end. I was tired of it all! I just wanted to be real for the first time in my life. I was so tired of the secrets. God began to speak to me. He kept nudging me to keep dreaming. I dreamt of being whole, all the while chaos was running rampant within my head. I couldn't explain to anyone what it was like inside my head, not even the small number of people who knew. No one truly understood. It was a very difficult and lonely place to be!

CHAPTER 141

I attended a Stirred Up retreat to simply get away from all the demands on my time and attention in order to focus on God with zero responsibilities. It was an amazing weekend! At one point I was challenged to dream with God and to ask the question: "What if....?" For the first time in a long time, I began to dream. *What if I could finally understand what being loved is truly like? What if I was completely whole in the depths of my heart and mind? What if my idea of a good Father was completely revitalized?* My soul was beginning to come alive to the purpose and calling that God had placed on my life. During a time of prayer, I was given a word that began to change my life forever. "Father God wants me to play with him like a little girl. When I go into my secret place, I simply need to play like a little girl. The more I play with Him, the more healing I will receive. The physical hurts and the memories will go away as I simply play with my Daddy." Those words transformed me as I saw Father God holding me as an infant and a small child. Towards the end of the weekend, God gave me a verse that spoke hope to my hurting heart: "Therefore if the Son makes you free, you shall be free indeed." John 8:36 (NKJV) I left that weekend ready to see what God would do during my secret times with Him.

The weeks zoomed by as I gave all I had to God in those quiet times. I saw my parts playing with Jesus and simply having fun for the first time in a long time. They played on the swings, the jungle gym, the teeter-totter. They played soccer, baseball, and basketball with Him. I would leave my prayer closet with a smile on my face and find myself yawning as God's peace settled into my heart and soul. Those times with the Lord were irreplaceable to me. I told no one about my encounters with Jesus during those weeks.

CHAPTER 142

I accepted an invitation to a night of worship and testimonies at a friend's house. I went by myself, and it was great to be able to focus on no one but me. A friend shared her testimony of how God healed her of stage four inoperable lung cancer. He gave her a brand-new set of lungs, and she is living her life sharing the miracle that God performed in her life. She asked a question that made me contemplate deeply. That question was, "Why not you?" *Why not me? Could he really make me whole? Could he integrate all my parts at once with no psychological effects? Could he remove every lie that I believed as truth without knowing each individual lie? Could he take the unrecovered memories and not allow me to relive each and every one of them? Could he do it in an instant without years and years of counseling or inner healing sessions? Why not me? He gave her a new set of lungs. He did for her, what the doctors said was impossible. My heart desires what the world would say is impossible. According to the world, what I want is not possible: no one suddenly integrates all their parts--let alone integrates even one part. It could be so overwhelming that the person could experience a kind of "implosion" that would be difficult to control or recover from, as an avalanche of memories come flooding into the conscious mind. The entire process would be extremely overwhelming and traumatic. Yet, it is God's desire to heal and set people free. I know the scriptures are full of promises of healing and it is also full of the miracles that Jesus himself performed and those that the early Church performed. Would it really be too much to ask for a miracle for myself? Would He do the impossible for me? Why not me? I am tired of the chains that continually bind me and keep me locked in the dark prison of my own mind as I wonder what torturous thing I will remember next. I want to be set free. I want total and complete healing. I want every lie to vanish and be replaced with the truth. I want to have clarity of thought with a single-minded focus. Why not me?* The thought-provoking questions were on repeat the entire trip home and even into the next week.

CHAPTER 143

I spent my quiet times talking to Jesus about the new desire in my heart. I studied Scripture to see what it had to say regarding healing. I began to believe beyond a doubt that God could do all that I desired. His words showed that to me:

The Lord is close to the brokenhearted;
he rescues those whose spirits are crushed.
Psalm 34:18 (NLT)

He heals the brokenhearted and binds up their wounds.
Psalm 147:3 (NKJV)

He will not crush the weakest reed or put out a flickering candle.
He will bring justice to all who have been wronged.
Isaiah 42:3 (NLT)

Surely He has borne our griefs and carried our sorrows; yet
we esteemed Him stricken, smitten by God, and afflicted.
But He was wounded for our transgressions,
He was bruised for our iniquities;
the chastisement for our peace was upon Him,
and by His strips we are healed.
Isaiah 53: 4-5 (NKJV)

Then they cried out to the Lord in their trouble, and He saved them
out of their distresses. He sent His word and healed them, and
delivered them from their destructions.
Psalm 107:19-20 (NKJV)

Some of us once wandered in the wilderness like desert nomads, with no true direction or dwelling place. Starving, thirsting, staggering, we became desperate and filled with despair. Then we cried out, "Lord, help us! Rescue us!" And he did! He led us out by the right way until we reached a suitable city to dwell in. So lift your hands and thank God for his marvelous kindness and for all his miracles of mercy for those he loves. How he satisfies the souls of thirsty ones and fills the hungry with goodness! Some of us once sat in darkness, living in the dark shadows of death. We were prisoners to our pain, chained to our regrets. For we rebelled against God's Word and rejected the wise counsel of God Most High. So he humbled us through our circumstances, watching us as we stumbled, with no one there to pick us back up. Our own pain became our punishment. Then we cried out, "Lord, help us! Rescue us!" And he did! His light broke through the darkness and he led us out in freedom from death's dark shadow and snapped every one of our chains. So lift your hands and give thanks to God for his marvelous kindness and for his miracles of mercy for those he loves! For he smashed through heavy prison doors and shattered the steel bars that held us back, just to set us free! Some of us were such fools, bringing on ourselves sorrow and suffering all because of our sins. Sick and feeble, unable to stand the sight of food, we drew near to the gates of death. Then we cried out, "Lord, help us! Rescue us!" And he did! God spoke the words "Be healed," and we were healed, delivered from death's door! So lift your hands and give thanks to God for his marvelous kindness and for his miracles of mercy for those he loves! Bring your praise as an offering and your thanks as a sacrifice as you sing your story of miracles with a joyful song.

Psalm 107:4-22 (TPT)

Do not remember the former things, nor consider the things of old. Behold, I will do a new thing, now it shall spring forth; shall you not know it?
I will even make a road in the wilderness and rivers in the desert.

Isaiah 43:18-19 (NKJV)

Everything that I read said that God's desire was to heal people. *God, if your desire is in healing your people, then why can't it be me? I love you and have given my heart to you. Your word is full of promises for me. I KNOW that you can do these things for me. I give you my heart, my mind, all the lies, all the memories (those recovered and those still buried deep within my mind), and all my parts to you. I will allow you to do what you do best. I surrender it all to you, all the pieces, all the brokenness. God, please take it all and put me back together the way that I was made to be.*

CHAPTER 144

Over the next day or two, God performed a miracle! He healed my heart and mind. He took all the broken pieces that I finally had the courage to release to Him, and He made me whole and new.

Now that I'm on the other side, things are amazing. Even though I don't have the individual parts ringing in my ears, their characteristics are still there. I still sleep with a stuffed animal. I still love to color to relax. I still get mad when I get cut off in traffic. My friends still accept me for me (most of them have no clue that I was different). I still cry when I watch Hallmark movies. I still get extremely protective of children who are taken advantage of. I still love those whom the world has labeled "unwanted." I'm still me! For years I believed the lie that I couldn't let go of these parts simply because I thought it would change me and that I would no longer be the same person. What I've come to discover is that God is the greatest artist of all time. He took all the different parts of me--the child, the protector, the angry parts, the problem solver, the peace keeper, the faithful one, the Godly one, the one who held onto all the pain-- and merged the best qualities of each part into a beautiful mosaic. That mosaic is a masterpiece! Nothing is missing and each quality or part that is in the final mosaic is in the perfect proportion. I'm not exactly sure why I waited all these years to ask God to heal my shattered heart and mind, but I'm grateful it finally arrived. I have no desire to go back to the way I was--for I'm even better than I was before!

CHAPTER 145

Throughout the years, I have been broken into many pieces by the very people who should have protected and cherished me. I've spent my life trying desperately to hide the brokenness and to appear "perfect" and undamaged so others would love and accept me. I have tried desperately to hide the broken places of my heart and mind, thinking that if others saw the brokenness, then they would reject me because I was too damaged. However, the Japanese think much differently about things that are broken. They developed an ancient art called *kintsugi* that uses gold (which is prized for its beauty and value) to repair pottery that had been broken. The places where the pottery was repaired with gold ended up stronger and more beautiful than before, as the golden "veins" in the pottery reflect the light and draw in the gaze of observers. "Kintsugi reminds us that something can break and yet still be beautiful, and that, once repaired, it is stronger at the broken places."[4] I have been broken so many times and my heart and mind were in pieces. I learned that I don't need to hide the brokenness. "My scars show pain and suffering, but they also show my will to survive. They're part of my history that'll always be there." ~ Cheryl Rainfield"[4]

Now I've discovered that God is so creative! He has taken all the broken pieces of my life and put me back together with pure gold. The places where I was broken are now places that shine with the glory of God. God crafted my repair so that I could be used to help other people see the beauty that exists in the ones that the world has labeled "broken," "unwanted," "damaged," "forsaken," "abused," and "worthless." You see, now I'm truly a child of God, and I now have a new purpose in life. It's no longer hiding the wounds of my past and the broken pieces, but my purpose is to help others understand that their brokenness does NOT disqualify them from being a child of God or from being used by God to help others. My purpose is to help set captives free! I want the entire world to know what the blood of Jesus has done for me. What He did for me, He will do for you!

And they overcame him by the blood of the Lamb and
by the word of their testimony, and they did
not love their lives to the death.
Revelations 12:11 (NKJV)

ABOUT
KHARIS PUBLISHING

KHARIS PUBLISHING is an independent, traditional publishing house with a core mission to publish impactful books, and channel proceeds into establishing mini-libraries or resource centers for orphanages in developing countries, so these kids will learn to read, dream, and grow. Every time you purchase a book from Kharis Publishing or partner as an author, you are helping give these kids an amazing opportunity to read, dream, and grow. Kharis Publishing is an imprint of Kharis Media LLC. Learn more at https://www.kharispublishing.com.

BIBLIOGRAPHY

The sources for Bible quotes are noted by appropriate abbreviations throughout the book.

Verses marked NKJV are taken from the *Holy Bible: The New King James Version*. Nashville: Thomas Nelson, Inc., 1982. Print.

Verses marked NLT are taken from the *Holy Bible: New Living Translation*. Wheaton, Ill: Tyndale House Publishers, 2004. Print.

Verses marked TPT are taken from *Holy Bible: The Passion Translation*. Passion & Fire Ministries, Inc., 2020. Print.

1 Woodley, Julie. *In the Wildflowers*. North America, Julie Woodley, 2008.

2 Green, Jay P. *The Interlinear Bible: Hebrew-Greek-English: with Strong's Concordance Numbers Above Each Word*. Peabody, Mass: Hendrickson Publishers, 1986. Print.

3 Holt, Alissa. *#Unfiltered*. United States, Alissa Holt, April 2019, P. 98.

4 Johnson, Emma. "Kintsugi: The Art of Being Broken." *WellBeing Magazine*, 5 Aug. 2020, www.wellbeing.com.au/mind-spirit/mind/kintsugi-the-art-of-being-broken.html.